HELL

A Detailed History of an Idea

Gustav Doré, *The Vision of the Valley of Dry Bones*, 1866, engraving.

HELL
A Detailed History of an Idea

Stephen J. Vicchio, Ph.D.

Minneapolis

Minneapolis

FIRST EDITION JUNE 2024

Hell: A Detailed History of an Idea

10 9 8 7 6 5 4 3 2 1

Cover image: John Martin, *Pandemonium*, 1841.
Oil on canvas, 48.4 x 72.8 in. Louvre, Paris, France.

Cover and interior design: Gary Lindberg

ISBN: 978-1-962834-16-2

This book is dedicated to my many intellectual mentors over the years, including William F. Albright, Kingsley Price, Thomas Benson, John Sexton, Marvin Pope at Yale, John Barton at Oxford, and Bill Shaw at St. Andrews. Much of the content of this book I have learned from these men.

Table of Contents

Part I: Hell in the Ancient World

Part II: Hell in the Medieval World

Part III: Hell in the Modern World

Part IV: Appendices

Part I
Hell in the Ancient World

A mural from a temple in northern Thailand. The unclothed spirits of the dead are brought before Yama for judgment. Phra Malaya watches from above as beings are fried in a large oil cauldron.

Chapter One
Hell in Comparative Religions

If I had my choice, I would kill every reporter in
the world, but then I am sure we would be
getting reports from hell before breakfast.
—General William T. Sherman

Hell hath no limits, nor is it circumscribed in one self place,
for where we are is hell, and where hell is must we ever be.
—Christopher Marlowe

If you are going to go through hell, keep going.
—Winston Churchill

Introduction

The main goal of this first chapter is to describe and discuss many of the views of the religions of the world on the idea of hell. More specifically, we will introduce and discuss the perspectives on ancient China, India's early Hinduism and Buddhism, and views on hell in Africa, among Native Americans, in early Europe, as well as Oceania.

We will open this chapter with some observations on what the religions of ancient China have had to say about the notions of hell and of punishment in the afterlife, particularly the idea of what the Chinese call *Diyu*, a traditional word that means "Earth Prison."

This first section of Chapter One will be followed by a discussion of the places in traditional Indian religions where the idea of hell and after death may be found, particularly in Hinduism, Jainism, and among the Sikhs in the Punjab region of the Indian subcontinent.

These two sections will be followed by introducing and then discussing the ideas of hell and after death to be found in African religions, among the Native American faiths, and in places in Oceania, such as Fiji and the Philippines, for example, where these ideas may be found, as well.

In the fourth and final section of Chapter One, we shall explore the ideas of hell and after death found in some of the contemporary world's other faiths. Among these, we shall make references to beliefs and practices among the Seventh-day Adventist, the practitioners of the Bahá'í faith, the Meivazhi, among the Jehovah's Witnesses, and The Church of Jesus Christ of Latter-day Saints or the Mormons. We will begin, then, to hell in the Chinese religions, section one of this first chapter.

The Idea of Hell in Chinese Religions

Traditionally, the classical Chinese word *Diyu* has been employed to describe the realm of the dead or even "hell" in the history of Chinese mythology and folk religion. *Diyu* is related to a second Chinese term, *Naraka*, a word used to designate traditional Chinese beliefs about the afterlife. Over the centuries, these two Chinese terms have had many popular interpretations and reformulations.

For most of Chinese history, *Diyu* has been seen as a subterranean maze with various levels or chambers to which the souls of the dead have been assigned after their deaths. The purpose of this activity is to get these souls to atone for the sins they have committed on Earth. The exact number of these levels of *Diyu* differs from age to age, but the idea of levels of hell is found in Taoism, as well as Hinayana and Mahayana Buddhism.

In traditional Chinese, the word for these levels of *Diyu* is the same word for a "court." Some Chinese traditions say there are three or four of these courts, while others say there are ten courts or even as many as eighteen. Each of these courts is ruled by a judge or a *Yama*.

Each of these courts deals with a different aspect of atonement and punishment. Most Chinese legends about them say that sinners are subject to gruesome torture until their deaths, after which they are restored to their original state so the torture can be repeated.

Another early Chinese tradition speaks of people going to Mount Taj, Jiuyuan, or even Feng Du after death. In fact, in China today, temples have been built on Mount Taj as tourist attractions. The art in these temples includes depictions of *Diyu.*[1]

The souls of the dead may pass from one court to another, depending on the decisions of the *Yama.* After much atoning, a soul may be sent for reincarnation. In the meantime, souls pass from one court to another.

In most contemporary views of the afterlife in China, there are believed to be ten courts, each overseen by a *Yama* king. These may be summarized this way:

Court Name	**Judge**
Jiang	Qin'guang
Li	Chujiang
Yu	Songdi
Lü	Wuguan
Bao	Yanluo
Bi	Biancheng
Dong	Taishan
Huang	Dushi
Lu	Pingdeng
Xue	Zhuanlun[2]

Each of these ten courts is ruled by a different *Yama* or judge. They are divided according to when a person has died in the Chinese year. They are also divided according to the sins for which they are being atoned.

In a text called *Questions about Diyu,* there is a tradition in China about the levels of *Diyu* that began during the Tang Dynasty. It suggests that there are 134 courts of hell. These courts were later simplified to eighteen. Sinners feel pain and agony just like living humans. The sinners in the Tang Dynasty document cannot die, but in the end, their bodies will be restored to their original condition.

The tortures in the *Questions about Diyu* are explicitly sketched out. They include being steamed, fried in an oil cauldron, sawed in half, struck by vehicles, pounded with a mortar and pestle, ground in a mill, crushed by boulders, having sharp instruments driven into their bodies, and many other punishments.[3]

In the traditional Buddhist tradition, eighteen courts are related to eighteen types of offenses. These can be summarized this way:

Court One: Those Who Gossip
Court Two: Adultery
Court Three: Discord in the Family
Court Four: Crimes of Retribution
Court Five: Hypocrisy
Court Six: Arsonists
Court Seven: Blood Shedders
Court Eight: Schemers
Court Nine: Rapists and Thieves
Court Ten: Abuse of Animals
Court Eleven: Kill or Abandoned Babies
Court Twelve: Waste Food
Court Thirteen: Lack of Respect
Court Fourteen: Suicide
Court Fifteen: Tomb Raiders
Court Sixteen: Thieves and Robbers
Court Seventeen: Abuse Power
Court Eighteen: Those Who Skirt the Law[4]

While Buddhist heaven is designed for holy beings and prepared for the virtuous who will live pure and happy lives, there is, upon their deaths, a painful underground hell for those who did not behave well morally in this life. In addition to being a place of punishment in Buddhism, it is also one of six different states of existence—gods, men, monsters, hell, hungry ghosts, and animals. These six states of being are interchangeable through the process of reincarnation, with no state being a permanent one.

These six states of being are also described in Buddhist art as visually represented by a wheel divided into radiating panels. The eighteen judges specify the crimes of specific evil deeds and decide the level of punishment. The most evil sinners in Chinese Buddhism are sent to Court 18. They must work their way up the ladder until they are finally worthy of rebirth.[5]

The ancient Chinese Taoists often adopted tenets of other religions. Thus, we find a belief in the notion of the *Naraka*, as well as a doctrine of a Taoist hell with many deities and spirits who punish sin in a variety of horrible ways. In Taoism, the *Naraka* is ruled by Yanluo Wang, the king of hell or *Diyu*. For the Chinese Taoists, *Diyu* is a maze of underground levels and chambers where the souls are taken to atone for their earthly sins.[6]

As in other Chinese traditions, the number of these *Naraka* is a matter of some dispute among traditional Chinese folk religion, Buddhism, and Chinese Taoism. Some traditions speak of three or four courts, while others maintain as many as ten, or in Buddhism, eighteen as we have suggested earlier.[7]

Nevertheless, in most Chinese traditions, the soul is referred to as a "Ghost." After these ghosts have atoned for their sins and have repented, they are given what in Taoism is called the "Drink of Forgetfulness" and sent back into the world to be reborn or reincarnated, possibly as an animal or a poor or sick person, for even more punishment.[8]

This brings us to the notion of hell in Indian religions—Hinduism, Jainism, and the Sikh faith—the topic of the second section of this first chapter.

Hell in Indian Religions

There is no notion of hell in the religion of the Vedas, the oldest of Indian religious traditions. The Rig Veda does mention three different realms of existence: the *Bhur* or the "Earth," the *Svar* or the "Sky," and the *Bhuvas* or "Middle Region," but says nothing of hell.

In later Hindu literature, especially in the Upanishads and the law books of the Puranas, more realms of existence are mentioned, including the use of the Sanskrit noun *Naraka*, which is equivalent to the English "hell." The god *Yama* is the ruler of *Naraka*. It is a place of punishment, a place for the expiation of sins in early Hinduism.[9]

People who have committed grave sins go to *Naraka*, where they go through punishment in accordance with the sins they have committed.[10] The god *Yamarajah*, who is also the god of Death, presides over the realm of *Naraka*. Details of the sins committed by individuals are recorded by a figure known as *Chitragupta*, the record keeper in *Yama*'s court. Chitragupta points out an individual's sins, and *Yama* orders the appropriate punishment.[11]

Originally a Sanskrit term, the word *Naraka* is employed in some schools of Hinduism, in Buddhism, as we have seen earlier in this chapter, as well as in Sikhism and Jainism. A modification of *Naraka*, that is, *Neraka*, is used in Indonesia and Malaysia.[12]

In many legal texts of the Puranas, sixteen different realms, or courts of *Narakas*, are described—eight cold and eight hot realms. The cold realms in the Puranas have the following names:

1. *Arbuda*. This is a Sanskrit word that means "blister." Arbuda is a dark and frozen place full of blizzards, where residents are naked and alone.
2. *Nirarbuda*. This place is even colder than Arbuda. The residents' bodies are covered with frozen blood and pus.
3. *Atata*. This is the "shivering" *Naraka*. The only sound made there is the chattering of teeth.
4. *Hahava*. This is the "lamentation" *Naraka*, where the residents only make laments.
5. *Huhuva*. This is another realm of teeth chattering.
6. *Utpala*. The "blue lotus" *Naraka*. The cold makes the skin turn blue.
7. *Padma*. Blizzards crack open frozen skin.
8. *Mahapadma*. The entire body cracks into pieces, and the internal organs are exposed to the cold.[13]

In the Puranas, each of these *Narakas* is twenty times longer than the one before it, and thus also twenty times colder. The Puranas also speak of eight "hot" realms, or *Narakas*, or Indian hells. These may be summarized in this way:

1. *Sanjiva*. The ground is made of hot iron.
2. *Kalasutra*. Saws and sharp axes cut souls into pieces.
3. *Samghata*. Souls are smashed between giant boulders.
4. *Raurava*. The "screaming" *Naraka*, where fiery blazes away burn.
5. *Maharaurava*. Reserved for people who have hurt others.
6. *Tapana*. Souls are impaled with fiery swords.
7. *Pratapana*. The "great heating" *Naraka*, where the temperature is always increasing.
8. *Avici*. The "uninterrupted" *Naraka*. Souls are roasted in a giant, blazing oven with terrible suffering.[14]

Like the cold *Narakas*, the hot *Narakas* are progressively hotter, twenty times hotter than the one before it. In Hinduism, there is no external hell, nor is there a figure like Satan. There are, however, hellish states of mind for those who think and act wrongly. These states consist of fear, hate, jealousy, bigotry, and anger, and they are brought about by one's own thoughts and deeds. These states, however, are not eternal. They can be changed by positive karma.[15]

According to Hindu history, the world in which we live is a moral world, or *Mrtyulokam* in Sanskrit. It is ruled by Death, or *Kali*, who is a manifestation of *Brahman*, or Ultimate Reality itself.

Upon death in the Hindu faith, the *Atman*, or Self/Soul, proceeds along one of three paths. Some of the *Atman* are liberated and experience what is called *moksha*, the release from the wheel of rebirth; some are reincarnated, and the Atman moves on to a new body. There is also a third path, the path to hell in the subterranean worlds, or *Adhogati* in Sanskrit. These are the sixteen places, both hot and cold, that are reserved for those who have committed grave sins.[16]

In the Hindu faith, there is no particular judgment day. Every day is judgment day, where one's actions and thoughts are weighed, and karma keeps accumulating according to the karmic principle that "You get what you have earned."

Along with Hinduism and Buddhism, Jainism is one of the three ancient Indian religions still in existence. The name "Jainism" is derived from the Sanskrit verb *ji*, which means "to conquer." It refers to the ascetic battle to fight against one's human passions so that one might gain enlightenment.

Jainism is an ancient Indian religion that teaches that the way to spiritual liberation and bliss is to live a life of harmlessness and renunciation. The Jains believe all living things possess living *Jiva*, or "Souls." Each of these souls is considered of equal value in Jainism, and the overall moral principle is something called *Ahimsa*, or the belief in non-violence.[17]

Early on, the Jain tradition incorporated the idea of *Naraka* into its cosmology. Among the Jains, the word *Naraka* is employed to speak of what is called the "lower realms," or seven levels of hell. In Jain cosmology, these seven levels of the underworld have the following names:

Name	Meaning	Depth
Ratna Prabha	Jewels	180,000 yojanas
Sharkara Prabha	Gravel	132,000 ys
Valuka Prabha	Sand	128,000 ys
Panka Prabha	Mud	120,000 ys
Dhuma Prabha	Smoke	118,999 ys
Tamaha	Darkness	116,000 ys
Mahatamaha	Extreme Darkness	108,000 ys[18]

The lower a hell is, the wider its base, but the thickness of the hells decreases the lower it is situated in the Jain scheme. Thus, for example, the seventh hell has only a single layer, whereas the third hell has nine layers. In Jainism, the three highest levels of hell are where the semi-divine beings dwell.

In Jainism, the length of stay in a *Naraka* is not eternal, but it is usually very long, often billions of years. Some souls or *Jivas* are born into these levels of hells as a direct result of that Jiva's karma. One may move up or down this ladder depending on one's karma. Thus,

Jainism, like Hinduism and Chinese forms of Buddhism, employs the ideas of *Narakas*, karma, and subterranean punishment in their cosmologies.[19]

We may make the following conclusions about the use of the idea of *Naraka* in the Jainist religious tradition. First, the Jainist idea of the *Naraka* is different from the Abrahamic religions on hell because one's place in a *Naraka* is not based on the result of a decision made by a Divine judgment. Secondly, the length of time in a *Naraka* in Jainism is finite, not eternal. Thirdly, the time spent in each *Naraka* is usually very long, measuring billions of years. And, finally, the *Jiva*, or "soul" in Jainism, may be punished in the *Narakas* and may also be reborn or reincarnated in them.[20]

One of the founders of Jainism, a man known as the *Mahavira*, in a dialogue with Sudharma Swami, a follower of *Mahavira*, the student asks the master what the punishments in the hells of Jainism are like and what the great sinners in the *Narakas* are like. The *Mahavira* responded this way:

> **The impudent sinner, who injures many beings without relenting, will go to hell. At the end of his life, he will sink to a place of darkness and great suffering. Head downwards, he comes to the place of torture. The prisoners in hell lose their senses from fright and for not knowing which direction to run. Going to a place like a burning heap of coals on fire and being burnt, they cry horribly. They remain there alone, shrieking aloud.**

Jain scripture also sketches out the three most common conditions that are the causes for being reincarnated in hell. These are "Killing or causing pain with intense passion." Secondly, excessive attachment to things or worldly pleasures while constantly indulging in cruel and violent acts. And finally, a vowless and unrestrained life.

A final Indian faith is known as Sikhism, a monotheistic faith that arose in the Punjab region of the Indian sub-continent around the fifteenth century CE. This makes the religion of the Sikhs one of the most recent world faiths. Sikhism developed from the spiritual teachings of Guru Nanak (1469–1539), the first of the great Sikh teachers. There are nine other Gurus who succeeded him.

The Sikh scriptures open with a text called the *Mul Mantar* in which there is a fundamental prayer about what is called in Punjabi the *Ik Onkar*, or "One God." The Sikhs emphasize *Simran*, a word that means "the remembrance and the meditation on the words of God," which can be expressed through *kirtan*, or prayer, and internally through *naam japna*, or a "meditation on His name."

Followers of the Sikh faith also believe that what keeps people from this meditation and remembrance of God are what are called the "Five Thieves." These are lust, rage, greed, attachment to things or people, and ego.

For the Sikh, Heaven and Hell are not places for living in the hereafter. They are part of the spiritual topography of the present life. They refer to good and evil stages of life, respectively, and can be lived now during our earthly existence. Noted scholar Guru Arjan explains that those who become entangled in emotions, detachment, and doubt are already living in a state of hell.

This brings us to the idea of hell to be found in African and Native American traditions, the topic of the third section of this first chapter on hell in comparative religions of this study of the history on the idea of hell.

Hell in African, Native American, and Oceania Religious Traditions

Among the many African religious traditions, there is no standard point of view about the nature of the self, death, survival after death, as well as the idea of hell and/or a place of punishment after death.

There are several places in the history of African religions where belief in hell can be seen. In East Africa, for example, among the Swahili, hell has been given the name *Kuzimu.* This idea of people being punished in a realm known as *Kuzimu* was first developed in the seventh and eighth centuries under the influence of Arab merchants coming to the East African coast. The Arabic word *Jahannam*, or "hell," quickly became the Swahili term, *Kuzimu*—a word that means "to cut off," presumably to be cut off from life.[21]

The influences of Arab culture on East Africa and places where Swahili is spoken can be seen in a number of ways. First, the word *Swahil*, from which the name comes, is an Arabic word that means "coast." Secondly, numbers in Swahili have either a Bantu origin, like one, two, three, four, and eight, or from the Arabic *sita*, or "six;" *saba*, or "seven;" and *tisa*, or "nine." Finally, another way that the influence of Arab culture can be seen in East Africa is how many Eastern African nations are now considered Islamic states, such as Somalia, Djibouti, Sudan, and Mauritania, for example.[22]

Among the Swahili people, *Kuzimu* was a cold and desolate place. It is the opposite of the warmer *Jaaniw*, the sacred dwelling place of the ancestors. This is most likely a cognate of the Arabic word *Jahanah*, or "Heaven."

After death, the spirit of the person makes its way to *Jaaniw*, where it will be greeted by the ancestors, where it experiences eternal bliss, or it will be turned back and forced to reside in *Kuzimu*, but only on a temporary basis and not eternally, unlike the Muslim tradition where one's residence in hell is an eternal one.

Among the Tutsi tribes of Rwanda, there is a belief that might be called "Paradise Lost," by which Imana, the creator God, created two separate worlds, one above the Earth and one below the Earth. Those above the Earth receive the benefits from living a life of virtue in this life, a kind of heavenly state.[23]

The world below is the opposite of the world above. It is for people whose lives on Earth were not of a stellar, moral character. Thus, these people will reside in a subterranean, murky existence in the afterlife. According to Tutsi mythology, humans continue to suffer hardships in this world until one day, when the length of their expiation is over, they move to the land of the Sky. For the Tutsi people, they understand happiness and immortality to be dependent on how well they maintain the link between themselves and God.[24]

Among the Muslim peoples of Senegal and Gambia in Northwest Africa, we also see a decided influence from the Muslim idea of *Jahannam*, or "hell," on their beliefs, where in both countries, more than 95 percent of the population are Muslim.[25]

Finally, the Yoruba tribe of West Africa believed that the human person consists of an outer self—the body, and an inner self—the soul. At the end of one's life, he or she will give an account of one's earthly life to *Olodumare*, a god who will determine one's afterlife. The soul of the dead will either travel; to *Orun rere*, or Paradise, or *Orun apadi*, or "the hell of Potshards," where one suffers a wretched afterlife. In all of Africa, the views of the Yoruba tribe are more like Christianity and Islam than any other tradition.[26]

Many religious traditions of Native Americans—but not all—have put forth explanations for what happens after death. Many claim there is an afterlife of some type, that death is not the end of life but a continuation or transition of life. In some Native American cultures, life in the afterlife is quite like life on Earth, while in others, there are several afterlife possibilities, often based on a person's actions in this life.

Thus, there is no such thing as an organized Native American set of religious beliefs about the afterlife. There is no central set of rules or beliefs about the matter, and traditionally, rules about religions were often not written down among Native Americans, only passed from generation to generation.

Each tribe had its own specific traditions regarding death rituals. Myths, and symbols, as well as how to prepare the dead for burial, cremation, or other means of disposal. One common theme in Native American tribes was/is the belief in the soul and its journey into the afterlife, although this usually does not involve the ideas of Heaven and Hell.

Many Central and South American Indian tribes professed beliefs in hell in their earliest recorded histories, including the Aztecs and Mayan, for example. The Aztec hell was known as *Mictlan*. They believed that souls of the dead travel there, a neutral place far to the north. The journey to *Mictlan* takes four years after death, and travelers go through difficult tests along the way. Among these tests was passing a mountain range and passing a river of blood that contains fearsome jaguars. It is this period of testing that the Aztecs see as a kind of hell-like existence.[27]

In the Mayan religion, there is a place known as *Xibalba*, or *Metnal*. It is a dangerous underworld that consists of nine separate levels. The road out of *Xibalba* is said to be very steep, thorny, and forbidding. Among the Mayans, ritual healers would recite healing prayers that banished certain diseases to *Xibalba*.[28]

Among the Pueblo Indians of North America, there are explicit prohibitions against the idea that tribe members may be punished after death. For the Pueblo, the idea of life after death is simply a continuation of life on Earth. In this life, the spirits do not reward or punish. Why would they, then, do it in the next life?[29]

The Cheyenne of the great northern plains in North America believe that the souls of the dead travel to the Milky Way, also called "The Way of the Departed," to the place of the dead. On arriving at the Milky Way, the spirit of the dead is reunited with family and friends. But there are no corresponding beliefs about the dead being punished after their Earthly existence.[30]

Among the Caddo tribe of the Southern Plains, it was believed that the living could send messages to their deceased relatives and friends by passing their hands over the body of a dead person and then over their own body in a similar fashion.

In many Native American cultures throughout North America, the names of the deceased are not in many cases of whom words are spoken. The deceased may be spoken about, but only in an indirect way that does not use the name. Among the Navajo, for example, the name of a dead person was not spoken for a year following the death. And after this year was over, the name was rarely mentioned afterward, as well.[31]

Among many of the Indian nations in Massachusetts, there was the idea that after death, the deceased would go on a journey to the Southwest, eventually arriving at a village where it would be welcomed by its ancestors. In a similar way, the Narragansett in Rhode Island viewed death as a transition between two worlds at the time of death. In her 1911 ethnographic study of the Omaha tribe, Alice Fletcher tells us, "There does not seem to be any conceptions of the ideas of rewards and punishment after death."[32]

In many Native American tribes, the death of a child has different rituals than those for an adult. Among the Ojibwa or Chippewa tribes, a doll would be made from the hair of the dead child. The mother would carry it around with her for a year, symbolizing the grief she is carrying. Other death rituals in many North American tribes include painting the dead person's face red, the color of life, or washing the body with yucca before burial. Sometimes, feathers are tied around the head of the dead tribe member as a communal form of prayer.

Other common death rituals in some tribes include "smudging." This involves the burning of special herbs such as sage, for example, and smoking it with a ceremonial pipe that also may be incorporated into the funeral ritual, which was usually led by the tribe's medicine man or spiritual leader.[33]

The Seminole tribe would place the body of the deceased in a small open-sided building called a "Chickee." Then, the entire tribe moves away from the spot, fearing contamination from the deceased. Before moving, the deceased's possessions were thrown into a lake or a swamp.[34]

In some rare instances, tribes would construct special totem poles, which were vertical wooden structures with symbolic figures or carvings on them. This mortuary pole is not a very common practice, but it is believed that the spirit of the dead person was placed into the totem and left as a permanent memorial to the person.

Finally, one common theme of many Native American peoples is a belief in the transmigration of the soul or reincarnation. This belief was found among the Sioux people, as well as the Gitxsan in the Northwest and the Lenni Lenape. In most of these, not only are humans reincarnated but animals as well. For example, this view can be found in the Northwest coastal area of the Gitxsan.

Among many North American native peoples, reincarnation or transmigration of souls is not something that just happens to humans but to animals, as well. Thus, in the Northwest of America, a hunter would thank the spirit of an animal that has just been killed so that that spirit could be reincarnated into another animal of its kind. It was also believed that the new animal would have good feelings toward the hunter and would allow its physical form to be harvested again.[35]

Among the peoples of Oceania, in pre-Christian Fijian mythology, there was a belief in an underworld called *Murimuria.* According to Fijian mythology, after a person dies, his soul is brought over a stretch of water by a ferryman, and on the other side, the soul has to fight many dangers through what is called the "Path of the Souls," or *Sala Ni Yalo* in the Fijian language.

There is no chance of survival for unmarried men. Those who survive the path are judged by the god *Degei.* The rest try to cross the lake by boat, but the boat always capsizes. Eventually, the souls sink to the bottom of the lake, where *Murimuria* is. There, the souls of the dead are punished or rewarded accordingly.[36]

Murimuria is considered neither a place of happiness nor of unhappiness. The residents there are characterized by both punishment and peace. Some of the souls there are punished for sins committed while on Earth, but the offenses do not always correspond to Christian understandings of sin. Those who have killed in this life are forced to pound muck with clubs, which is considered the gravest punishment.[37]

Those women who have not had their ears pierced are forced to carry great blocks of wood on their shoulders. Women who have not been tattooed are chased by ghosts in *Murimuria*. These ghosts carry sharp shells to tear at the skin. Those who have performed an act that displeases the gods are laid in rows on their faces and turned into taro beds.

In some Melanesian islands, paradise is known as *Burotu*, where Deg, the god of the dead, judges the newly dead ghosts. Those who do not attain *Burotu* are consigned to *Murimuria*, which serves the same function as in Fiji.[38]

In the Philippines, the underworld is known as *Kasanaan* where the souls of the dead may go to be punished. In many of the Polynesian islands, the underworld is called *Ingor* or *Inga-Atos*, another realm of the dead in the Oceania region.

In both ancient and modern times throughout Europe, several cultures have had their own destination for hell, separate from the traditional Christian view. Among these are *Uffern*, a word for hell in Celtic and Welsh mythologies; the Finnish *Tuonela*, the realm of the dead or the underworld in Finland; and *Manala*, a synonym for the same word. In Estonia, the underworld is known as *Toonela*, or *Manala*; and in Breton's mythology, a place called *Anaon* was a word to designate hell.[39]

Many other European cultures in their histories have specific names for the underworld, whose technical scholarly name is "Chthonic," a classical Greek term that means "under the Earth." It may also refer to the deities and spiritual beings found there, especially in ancient Greece. The Classical Greek *Khthon* means "Earth," so Chthonic implies "under the Earth."

Among these European cultures who believed in an underworld were the following:

Ferri, Albania
Avilag, Hungary
Aizshule, Latvia
Anipilis, Lithuania
Gimle, Hel, Vingorf, Norse mythology
Nak and *Peklo*, Slavic mythology
Xalja-witjan, Proto-German
Helle-rune, Old English
Helli-witi, Old Saxon[40]

This brings us to the fourth section of this first chapter on the notion of hell in the world's contemporary comparative religions, particularly views of hell among the followers of the Bahá'í faith, the Seventh-day Adventists, the Meivazhi, as well as several other religious traditions.[41]

The Views on Hell in Other World Faiths

The Bahá'í faith was a new religion established in Persia in the nineteenth century. Initially, it spread from Persia throughout the rest of the Middle East. Today, there are over five million members of the faith. The Bahá'í movement was started by a central figure named the Bāb (1819–1850), who taught that God would soon send a prophet of the stature of Jesus or Muhammad. Another figure called the *Bahá'u'lláh* (1817–1892) claimed to be that foretold prophet.[42]

Among the followers of the Bahá'í faith, the traditional descriptions of Heaven and Hell are considered to be representations of spiritual conditions. Closeness to God is considered to be in a heavenly state, while remoteness from God is thought of as a hellish experience. The followers of the Bahá'í faith believe that the soul is immortal and after death, it will continue to progress until it finally attains being in the "presence of God."

The Seventh-day Adventists believe that death is an unconscious state of sleep until the resurrection of the dead at the end of time. They base this belief on Biblical texts such as the Book of Daniel 12:1–3 and Ecclesiastes 9:5, as well as several passages in the Book of Revelation like 20:4–6 and 12–15.[43]

The Jehovah's Witnesses, on the other hand, hold that the soul ceases to exist when a person dies, and therefore hell is a state of nonexistence. In their view, Gehenna is distinct from Sheol or Hades in that it holds the possibility of resurrection. For the Witnesses, Tartarus is thought to be a metaphorical state of debasement, beginning with the fallen angels in Genesis 6.[44]

In The Church of Jesus Christ of Latter-day Saints, or the Mormon Church, followers are taught that hell is a state between death and resurrection in which spirits who did not repent while on Earth must suffer for their sins in the afterlife, at least according to the Doctrines and Covenants 19:15–17.[45]

The *Meivazhi*, a word in Tamil that means "the True Path," is a syncretic, monotheistic faith in the Tamil Nadu region of India. The *Meivazhi* have their own scriptures in the Tamil language that consist of four volumes. They believe that after death, certain people have incorruptible bodies, and these are people who are immortal and reach salvation.[46] In fact, the Meivazhi look for ten "signs" after death that indicate one is immortal. These are:

1. No stench.
2. No stiffening.
3. The body will be light in weight.
4. The body sweats as time passes.
5. The body exhibits warmth.
6. The natural condition of the throat is maintained.
7. The knuckles crack.
8. The disappearance of deformities.
9. A look of youthfulness and cheeriness.
10. The body does not decay.[47]

This brings us to the major conclusions we have made in this first chapter. In the second chapter to follow, we will introduce and discuss the places in the religions of the ancient Near East where beliefs about hell and/or a place of punishment may be found.

Conclusions

We began the opening section of this chapter with an analysis of the ideas of hell and after death in traditional Chinese religions, including Chinese Buddhism and traditional Chinese Taoism.

Most of our attention in this first section has been on the idea of the *Diyu*, or the maze of underground hells in Taoism, as well as in Chinese Buddhism. We also have introduced the idea of the *Naraka* in Chinese culture, a classical Chinese word for a "court," in which the souls of the dead are judged.

In the second section of this chapter, we explored the places in Indian religions where the issues of hell and after death may be found. Among these Indian religions we have explored were Vedic Hinduism, Jainism, and the Sikh faith. Among the conclusions we have made about hell and after death in Indian religion were that the word *Naraka* was originally a Sanskrit term and that the Vedas made no comments about our questions at hand, but the legal texts of the Puranas do.

In fact, we have shown that some of these legal texts suggest there are as many as sixteen "realms" or "courts" of *Narakas*—eight hot and eight cold. We also suggested that in traditional Hinduism, there is no judgment day because every day is Judgment Day in terms of the progression of one's karma.

In this same section, we have shown that Jainism also incorporated the ideas of *Narakas* and punishment after death into their systematic theology. In fact, we outlined the seven traditional Jain *Narakas*—their names, meanings, and depth in the Jain scheme of the afterlife.

At the close of the second section of the first chapter, we introduced the Sikh religion, followed by the Sikh views about the ideas of hell and after death. As we have seen, for the most part, the Sikh faith eschews any metaphysical views of the afterlife, arguing instead that for the Sikh, Heaven and Hell are right here in this life.

In the third section of Chapter One, we explored the ideas of hell and punishment after death in Africa religions, Native American faiths, and in the Oceania region of the world.

We made comments about views of death among the Swahili peoples in Africa and their idea of Kuzimu, or hell, perhaps borrowed from Arab invaders who came to East Africa centuries ago. We also discussed the views on death and the afterlife of the Tutsi tribes, as well as the views on death and punishment among the Muslim people of Senegal and Gambia.

We also spoke of the beliefs on death, hell, and punishment among the Yoruba peoples of Nigeria and Mali, including their ideas of *Orun rere*, or Paradise, and *Orun Apadi*, the name given to the "Hell of Potshards."

Regarding the Americas, we have shown that the Aztecs and the Mayans had clear names for a hell-like state. The Aztec hell was called *Michtlan*, and the Mayans called their hell *Xibaldi*.

We also discussed the issues of hell and after death in the thought of many North American Native peoples including the Pueblo, the Cheyenne, the Caddo tribe, the Omaha, the Narragansett, the Chippewa, and the Seminoles, among many others.

In the same section of Chapter One, we also pointed out that many North American tribes were firm believers in the transmigration of the soul or reincarnation, often of human beings as well as of animals.

At the close of the second section of this first chapter, we explored several examples of the ideas of hell and after death in the cultures of Oceania, including beliefs among the Fuji and their idea of *Murimuria* and the underworld in the Philippine islands known as *Kasanaan*.

We also have shown in the third section of Chapter One that many traditional European societies have names for the underworld, including Albania, Hungary, Latvia, Lithuania, the Norse people, Slavic mythology, and many other European societies.

In the fourth and final section of Chapter One, we introduced and discussed the views on hell and after death in a host of contemporary world religions. These included what the Seventh-day Adventists, the Jehovah's Witnesses, the followers of the Bahá'í faith, the Meivazhi, and the Mormon Church followers have had to say about hell and after death.

The focus of the second chapter of this history of views about hell and after death is an exploration of what the religions of the ancient Near East have had to say about the ideas of hell and after death. Among the cultures we shall explore are the ancient Egyptians, the Sumerians and Babylonians, the Persians, the Greeks, and the Romans.

It is to the ancient Near East, then, to which we turn next.

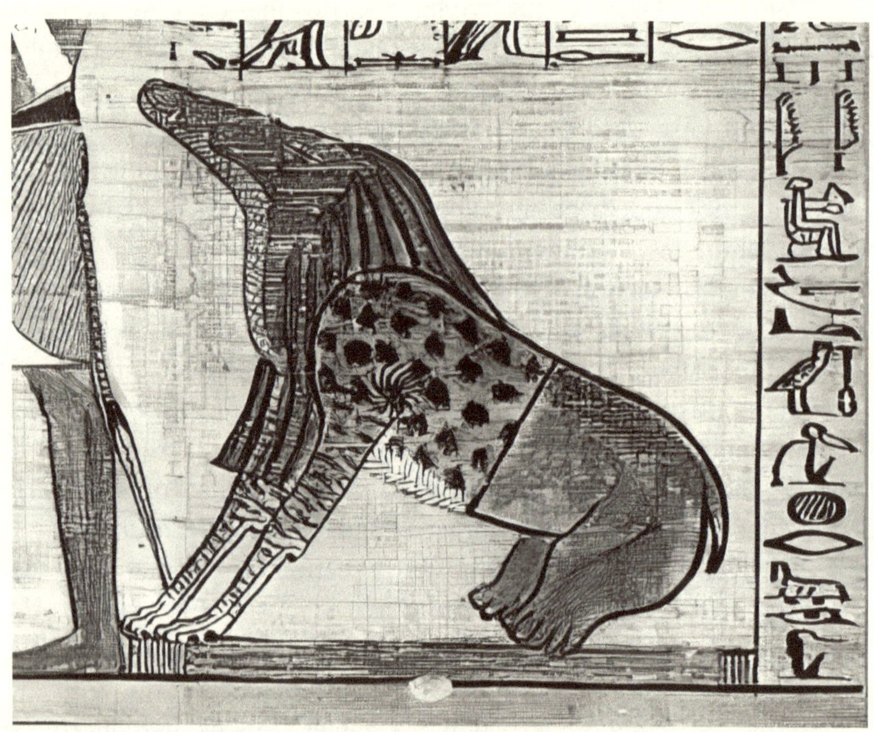

The figure of *Ammit*.

Chapter Two
Hell in the Ancient Near East

Hell has three gates: lust, anger, and greed.
—Bhagavad Gita

Maybe this world is another planet's hell.
—Aldous Huxley

What is hell? I maintain that it is the suffering of being unable to love.
—Fyodor Dostoyevsky

Introduction

The purpose of this second chapter is to explore the ideas of hell and after death in the cultures of the ancient Near East. We aim to accomplish this goal by examining and discussing the perspectives of the ancient Egyptians, the Sumerians, and Babylonians, the views of the ancient Persians, as well as those of the Greco-Roman world in ancient history.

This chapter will proceed by examining, in turn, the views of hell and after death in a section on ancient Egypt, followed by separate sections on Mesopotamia, Sumer, and Babylon, followed by a section on the views of the ancient Persians, and finishing our analysis on ideas of hell and after death in ancient Greek and then ancient Rome.

We turn first, then, to perspectives on hell and the possibility of punishment after death found among the religious beliefs of the ancient Egyptians, the subject matter of the first section of Chapter Two of the study of the history of hell and the idea of punishment after death.

The Idea of Hell in Ancient Egypt

Modern scholarly understandings of ancient Egyptian notions of hell and after death is based, for the most part, on six ancient texts. These may be summarized this way:

1. *Book of Two Ways*, also called *Book of the Ways of Rosetau*
2. *The Book of Amduat*, also known as *Book of the Hidden Room* and/or *Book of What is in the Underworld*
3. *The Book of Gates*
4. *The Egyptian Book of the Dead*, or *The Book of Going Forth by Day*
5. *The Book of Earth*
6. *The Book of Caverns*[48]

It is clear that the ancient Egyptians believed in the concept of an afterlife, but what that concept entailed is not so easy to ascertain. The Egyptian burial practices, however, are evidence enough that they took the idea of survival after death very seriously indeed. But what exactly was the ancient Egyptian notion of hell? This is the goal of this first section of Chapter Two.

The Egyptian notions about hell and after death were an elaborate system filled with souls and demons. These demons were to be "conquered," at least according to the explicit instructions of *The Egyptian Book of the Dead.*[49]

The hearts of the deceased—the part of a human being that contains the self—were weighed against a feather. If the heart was heavier than the feather, then the soul would be destroyed, and the heart would be swallowed by a demon named *Ammit*, who was known as "The Swallower of the Damned."[50]

The figure of *Ammit* was depicted in ancient Egyptian art as being composed of part crocodile, part lion, and part hippopotamus. But *Ammit* was only one of the many demons in the Egyptian underworld that also included lakes of fire, serpents guarding the gates of the underworld, and, of course, the God of Chaos, usually referred to as *Apep* in ancient Egyptian documents.[51]

Apep, also spelled *Apepi* and *Apophis*, was the ancient Egyptian deity who embodied Chaos, or *Izft*, in the ancient Egyptian language. *Apep* was the opponent of *Ma'at*, or "Light." *Apep* usually appears in ancient art as a giant serpent. The god *Apep* first appeared in the Eighth Dynasty and was honored in the names of the Fourteenth Dynasty kings. In fact, one of the Hyksos kings was named *Apophis*.[52]

The Hyksos were probably of Levantine origin and established the Fifteenth Dynasty of Egypt from 1650 to 1550 BCE. Their base was the city of Avaris in the Nile River Delta, where they ruled the northern part of Egypt. The Hyksos period was the first time that a foreign invader ruled Egypt.

The Egyptians believed that the pharaoh, who was an incarnation of the sun god *Ra,* had the ability to make sure that the world of the living was preserved and protected from the many demons of the underworld. This was accomplished by making it through the underworld. In this sense, views about heaven, hell, and survival after death were based on the soul's ability to survive the journey through the underworld, ostensibly with the god Osiris.[53]

With the rise of the Cult of Osiris during the Middle Kingdom, religion was made democratic, and salvation was now offered to even the humblest followers of the cult. Moral fitness became the dominant factor in determining a person's suitability for eternal life. At death, a person faced a judgment by forty-two divine judges. If a person led a life in consort with the precepts of the goddess *Ma'at*, who represented truth and proper living, then a person was welcomed into the heavenly "Reed Field."[54]

The purification for those considered worthy appears in inscriptions of what is called the "Flame Island," where humans experience the triumph of good over evil and the idea of rebirth akin to the rebirth of Osiris.[55]

For those who were damned among the ancient Egyptians, there was complete destruction into a state of non-being, and thus there was no eternal torture for the morally imperfect. For those who were not worthy in the weighing of the heart would lead to complete annihilation of the Self.

The "Tale of Khaemwese," also known as *Setne II*, is an Egyptian demonic tale attested to in a papyrus from Roman Egyptian times. It describes the torment of a rich man who, while on Earth, lacked charity toward others. He learns his lesson when he dies and sees the blessed state of a poor man who also has died. The poor man is judged positively, while the rich man in the tale meets the fate of complete annihilation.[56]

The idea of the "Lake of Fire" was first mentioned in the Book of Two Ways coffin text in the *Book of the Dead*, chapter 126. Like the "outer darkness," the Lake of Fire is a place of regeneration for the sun god *Ra* and his blessed human followers, to whom water and nourishment are offered. The Lake of Fire, however, is a place of destruction for the damned. Birds even fly away from it when they feel the heat of the lake.

The Lake of Fire is filled with bloody water, and the great stench of putrefaction rises from it like an evil vapor. In chapter 126 of the *Egyptian Book of the Dead*, the shores of the Lake of Fire are guarded by four baboons who sit at the bow of the barque of Ra and are connected to the rising of the sun.[57]

Those who reach salvation in the ancient Egyptian model are granted access through the "Secret portals of the West." Those who do not travel through the portal, the damned, are swallowed up by the god *Ammit* mentioned earlier. *Ammit* is responsible for devouring their corpses, or even their shades or shadows, snatching hearts and inflicting injury without being seen.

By the Eighteenth Dynasty, another demon appeared in later versions of chapter 125 of the *Egyptian Book of the Dead*, which became consistent with the activities that followed it in chapter 126. By Roman times, we begin to see evidence of *Ammit*'s wrath. In one depiction, the monster Ammit sits beside a fiery cauldron into which the puny bodies of the damned—stripped of their mummy wrappings—are thrown.

In this late period of Egyptian history, concepts began to be influenced by images from other cultures during the Hellenistic period, such as the image of the Great Sphinx as one who consumes humans who cannot answer its riddle. In turn, later representations of Christian views of hell from Coptic and early Christian sources also appear to have influenced Egyptian views at the time.

In general, however, the ancient Egyptians believed the dead had one of two fates. Either one made it through the "Portal to the West" receiving salvation in the process, or one is devoured by *Ammit* and thereby ceased to exist. This brings us to the second section of this second chapter, a discussion of hell and after death in the mythologies of Mesopotamia—the Sumerians, Babylonians, and Akkadians, among other peoples at the top of the Fertile Crescent.

Hell in Mesopotamia: Sumer, Babylon, and the Akkadians

Unlike the rich corpus of ancient Egyptian funerary texts we have seen earlier in Chapter Two, there are no comparable "guidebooks" for Mesopotamian details about survival after death, hell, and the idea of punishment. Instead, ancient Mesopotamian views must be pieced together from a variety of sources across different genres and geographical areas.

We will use the term "Mesopotamia" in this section to refer to the views of various cultures in the northern portion of the Fertile Crescent in the ancient world. These cultures include:

The Sumerians (3000 BCE)
The Akkadians (2350–2000 BCE)
The Babylonians (2000–1600 BCE)
The Hittites (1600–1180 BCE)
The Canaanites/Ugarits (1350–1200 BCE)
The Assyrians (910–609 BCE)

The most famous literary text from these cultures that speaks of the issues of hell and death is the *Epic of Gilgamesh*, which recounts the fate of the dead in the netherworld and describes grief and mourning myths, rituals, and symbols. Two other important texts from the region are *Enkidu and the Netherworld* and *Ishtar's Descent into the Netherworld.* Other sources for discerning Mesopotamian views of the afterlife include archaeological inscriptions discovered in the area, as well as economic texts that record disbursements for funeral costs or the Cult of the Dead.[58]

There are also extant many references to death and the afterlife in royal inscriptions and edicts, other chronicles, as well as royal and private letters, lexical texts, cultic commentaries, magical and medical texts, and formulations for omens and the formulae for blessings and curses.[59]

Like all cultural systems, views about heaven, hell, and punishment after death are not static. They evolve over time. Views often changed as well, depending on the socio-economic conditions. Nevertheless, the views of the Sumerians and their successors provide a wide array of perspectives on death, heaven, hell, and punishment after death, as we shall see next.

For the most part, ancient Mesopotamia conceptualized the netherworld or the underworld as the cosmic opposite of the heavens in these cultures, that is, the place where the gods reside. Life in the netherworld was thought to be a shadowy version of life on Earth. Metaphysically, the underworld and the heavens were thought of as being great distances from those living on Earth, but physically, the netherworld was underground and so was not that far away.

Any evidence for a group's beliefs about hell and a place of punishment after death is usually found within the cosmogonic beliefs of their mythology. In all the cultures listed earlier in Mesopotamia, the gods live in a place in the sky—in the heavens—while their relatives, contrary gods, reside in the underworld. Chthonic deities with names like *Death* and *Irkalla* live in a world that is permanently without joy, a world where there is only dust to eat and drink.

From surviving texts, this dark underworld was often called *Kur* or *Kurnugi*. It was principally associated with the fertility cycles of the plant kingdom, and these cycles gave rise to narratives about fertility gods and goddesses who descend into the netherworld where they may be captured or imprisoned. Their subsequent rescue and/or resurrection restores fecundity and fruitfulness to their life on Earth.

Among the Sumerians, the afterlife was a dark, dreary cavern located deep beneath the Earth where the inhabitants were believed to continue a shadowy version of life on Earth. In Sumer, this bleak place was known as *Kur* and was ruled by a goddess named *Ereshkigal*. All souls of Sumer had the same fate. A person's actions in his life on Earth had nothing to do with the world to come.[60]

The souls or shades in *Kur* had nothing to eat but dried dust. The deceased person's relatives could pour provisions through a clay pipe that was embedded into the grave, thereby allowing the shades to drink.[61]

The Sumerians believed that the entrance to *Kur* was located in the Zagros Mountains in the Far East. It had seven gates through which a soul needed to pass. A god named *Neti* was the gatekeeper. Ereshkigal's assistant, or *suktal*, was called Namtar. Another class of demons called the *Galla* were also believed to reside in the underworld. Several extant poems describe the Galla dragging human beings to the netherworld.[62]

The Zagros Mountains are a range of hills located in ancient Persia or present-day Iran. The mountain range has a total range of 1,600 km, or 900 miles. The range begins in northeastern Iran and follows Iran's western border while covering much of southeastern Turkey and northeastern Iraq. From there, the Zagros Mountains continue beneath the waters of the Persian Gulf.

The East Semitic name *Irkalla* was used to designate the name of the king of the underworld. The Akkadians called this god *Nergal*. Among the Akkadians, Ereshkigal is the wife of Nergal.[63]

In general, then, the Mesopotamian views of the Sumerians, the Akkadians, and the Babylonians all posited a cosmogony that included a heavenly realm of everlasting life for the gods, where the only mortal permitted to enter was the human figure Utnapishtim, a prototype of Noah. His distinctive privilege was connected to his role as the saving of humanity in the Great Flood, which was significant in a region where drought and flood often reigned.

The netherworld of Mesopotamia was a region of dust or clay beneath the surface of the Earth but situated above the primeval waters known as *Apsu*. Kur or Kurnugi included a seven-gate palace called the *Palace of Ganzir,* but it was not a place of purgation or damnation. Rather, it was the permanent lot of all mortals. The only activity in this life of the shades in Kur was the consuming of dust.

Indeed, it is hard to ignore the prevalence of dust in Kur and the similarities between this dusty, quiet land of the dead and the dusty climate and environs of the north Fertile Crescent. Bodies were placed underground, in dusty caves for burial, or in grave shafts left to desiccate on an open bench in a tomb before being moved to a secondary burial. They were put there without coffins or sarcophagi, which were introduced later in the ancient Near East. In Mesopotamian burials and the netherworld there was a prevalence of dust and dirt.

In Sumer, Babylon, and among the Akkadians, the netherworld did not develop into a place of purgation or punishment. The shades of the dead were simply warehoused in a state of sensual deprivation ruled over by the gods in the underworld. It was a long, grey, and overall duty existence.

The society of the Hittites was another matter entirely. First of all, they were an Indo-Aryan people, most likely from Central Anatolia around the twelfth century BCE. Secondly, the Hittites left no evidence or any surviving texts about the fate of the common person or if there was a place of the dead. Hittite kings and queens were expected to enjoy a positive existence after death, but there is no evidence that they attempted to influence their fate through prayer or offerings. Thirdly, unlike the other Mesopotamian fertility myths, in the Hittite myth of Telepinus, he does not descend into the underworld as in other cultures. Instead, Telepinus simply hides himself away.

Finally, the Canaanites inhabited a geographical area that comprised most of the area of Palestine/Israel. Their capital was the city of Ugarit, and their language was Ugaritic. Most of our knowledge of the Canaanites, other than Biblical sources, is from archaeological digs of Ugarit from the eighteenth century BCE. It is generally believed that they were an ethnic group originating in Lebanon, but their fate became entwined with the Israelites, Egyptians, Phoenicians, and other cultures of Mesopotamia.

Among the Canaanites, the god *Mot* presided over the Land of the Dead. It was a damp, dark, unpleasant place, much like a grave. Entry to this land was from death's territory—the barren, hot desert. For the Canaanites, there is no evidence that death was anything but the universal cessation of life. For the Canaanites, death was equivalent to death, and death and extinction were the fate of all.[64]

Even with that said, the Canaanites did have a fertility myth that included the descent of their chief god, the Great Baal, into the underworld, where he, in fact, confronts Mot, the ruler of the underworld.[65]

This brings us to the third section of Chapter Two, in which we will explore the views pertaining to the idea of hell and after death as these ideas appeared in ancient Persia and the main religion there, Zoroastrianism.

Hell in Ancient Persia and Zoroastrianism

The ancient Persian religion Zoroastrianism flourished on the Iranian plateau for at least 1,200 years from the sixth century BCE until the seventh century CE and the rise of Islam in the region. Zoroastrianism still survives today among about 250,000 believers, mostly in India and Eastern Iran. The religion is based on the teachings of a man named Zoroaster, also called Zarathustra, a religious Prophet from Northeastern Iran. The scholarly consensus is now that Zoroaster most likely lived around 1200 BCE, but previously, scholars argued for a date closer to 600 BCE, in the period known as the Axial Age.[66]

The actual dating of the Zoroastrian movement is important because it incorporates many elements that may have influenced religions like Judaism and Christianity, as well as faiths found in ancient Greece and Rome.[67]

We do know that Zoroastrianism went through two periods of great transformation if not more than two. The first when it incorporated elements of the Old Indo-Aryan religion, and the second when it developed the idea of *Zervan*, or "Time," into its metaphysical scheme.[68]

Very early on in Zoroastrianism, believers began to assent to an idea in which the deity *Zervan* is a First Principle, a Creator god who engendered equal but opposite twins, Ahura Mazda and Angra Mainya, one Good and one Evil. This period is sometimes called Zervanism, in which this timeless and spaceless and unique deity, which was *Aka*, or One, gave rise to two fundamental principles of the universe, one morally Good and one Evil.[69]

The earliest Persian references to Zervan appear on tablets dated in the thirteenth or twelfth centuries BCE, found at an archaeological dig of the ancient Mesopotamian city of Nuzi. Zervan was also known as the god of fecundity or plant growth, maturity, and decay. Zervan is said to be related to two separate versions of time—Limitless Time and the Time of Long Dominion.[70]

The latter version of Time emerges from Infinite Time, which lasts for twelve thousand years and then returns to it. Zervan was originally associated with three other deities: *Vaya*, or "Wind;" *Thvarshtar*, or "Space;" and *Atar*, which means "Fire." Zervan was the Chief Persian deity before the advent of Zoroastrianism and its moral dualism between Ahura Mazda, the Good principle, and Angra Mainya, the Evil principle. Zervan was associated with the *Axis Mundi*, or the "Center of the Universe." In early Persian art, Zervan was most often depicted as a winged creature with the head of a lion and a body encircled by a great serpent, representing the daily motion of the sun.[71]

The notions of ideas like heaven, hell, individual judgment, the resurrection of the dead, and a final judgment at the end of time may all have had their origins in ancient Persia and Zervanism. For the followers of this faith, the Final Judgment was known as *Frashgird*. It was employed in ancient times to indicate a final renovation of the universe at the end of time when presumably evil will be destroyed, and everything else will be in harmony and unity with Ahura Mazda, or the Good God.[72]

The Zoroastrian afterlife began with a three-day period after death when the soul sits in the head and prays about its future. Next, the soul must cross a river that grows more difficult as the soul proceeds. Weeping relatives swell the river with their tears. The ordeal of a judgment then takes place at the *Chinvat Bridge*, where the soul meets three angels of judgment. These are *Mithra*, *Srosh*, and *Rashnu*.[73]

The bridge is said to stretch from the *Alborz Peak*—probably *Mount Damavand*—to heaven, or *Daitih Peak*, near the river by the same name. Most scholars now suggest that this was most likely the *Aras River*. But since this account is partly mythological, specific geographical points are not always crystal clear.

Some early Zoroastrian texts speak of individual judgment as a balancing of good thoughts, good words, and good deeds against their opposites. Consequently, it was said that the bridge was like a wide walkway for those who were good and a narrow, razor-edge for the wicked who fall to hell.

For Zoroastrian men, after death, their souls meet young maidens who are reflections of the souls' own thoughts, words, and deeds. Very few early Persian texts describe the Old Persian hell. Only one early text describes it in any detail. It is called the *Book of Arda Viraf*. The hero of the tale is named *Arda Viraf*, but it is difficult to determine his perspective, whether he is looking down on the activities of hell or if he is simply passing through it. This makes the geography of hell for these ancient Persians difficult to comprehend.[74]

For the evil ones on the Chinvat Bridge, there are three destinations for these souls. These were called the *Dush hukjt*, or "Place of Evil Words;" the *Dush-hucarsht*, or "Place of Evil Deeds;" and the *Chakat-i-Saitih*, a desert below the Chinvat Bridge. These same early Persian texts also indicate the existence of an even deeper region, a pit of hell that was known in ancient times as *Drugaskan*, a place that is said to be so dark that all souls who go there are instantly struck blind.[75]

The *Book of Arda Viraf* describes eighty-five different punishments tied to specific sins that are the causes of those punishments. Both men and women are among those punished, with men slightly outnumbering women. Children only appear in the catalog of punishments if they have disrespected their parents.

This catalog of sins in the *Arda Viraf* includes:

Sodomy
Adultery
Theft
Lying
Perjury
Deceit
Slander
Extortion
Making false contracts or covenants
Breaking of promises
Homicide

The *Arda Viraf* also enumerates other sins, including:

Abuse of a spouse.
Abuse of children, including abortion and infanticide.
Sorcery, apostasy, and profanity.
Crimes against the social order.
Crimes against animals. (neglect, abuse, murder)
Crimes against the self. (laziness, vanity, miserliness, excessive grief)

The *Arda Viraf* also tells us that the standard punishment for the majority of these crimes is for the wicked to be fed fetid and putrid vitals while waiting thousands of years in the accompany of demons until the Final Resurrection at the end of time. These punishments are so excessive that E. W. West's translation, called the *Sacred Books of the East*, stops mid-way in the translation with a note that says:

> **From here onward, the pictures of tortured souls become so extreme and nauseous that we cannot continue this report.**

Demons are often mentioned in the *Arda Viraf*. The Old Persian word employed to designate these demons is the word *Khrafstars*. This word is used as a general term for demons, demonesses, as well as serpents, snakes, scorpions, and even hedgehogs.

The idea of the Chinvat Bridge may well be the model for other bridges to the afterlife found in medieval visionary texts like the *Vision of Tundale*, for example, a twelfth-century text of otherworldly visions. The narrative of the Chinvat Bridge may also be the progenitor of certain medieval European romances such as the *Perlesvaus,* a thirteenth-century Old French Arthurian legend also known as "The High Book of the Grail."

While many descriptions of hell that originated in Europe describe a place where punishment is inflicted on sinners by all sorts of demons, devils, and infernal creatures, in Zoroastrianism, *Duzakh*—the Old Persian word for "hell"—punishments appear to be self-imposed obligations, executed without guards watching over the sinners. They eat fetid things, masturbate, tear themselves, and perform endless and fruitless tasks of their own volition.

This brings us to an introduction and analysis of the ideas of hell and after death found in artifacts from ancient Greece, the subject matter of the fourth section of Chapter Two of this history of attitudes and views of hell.

Hell and After Death in Ancient Greece

The notions of hell and after death in the ancient Greek religion and mythology were always related to the god *Hades*, or *Haides*, who was the king of the underworld. In fact, Hades' name in Greek history became synonymous with death, or *Thanatos*, itself.

Hades was the eldest son of *Kronos* and *Rhea*. He and his brothers, *Zeus* and *Poseidon*, defeated their father's generation of gods, also known as the *Titans*, and in the process, claimed ownership of the *Kosmos*, or Universe. Zeus was given the sky, Poseidon the sea, and Hades was to be the lord of the underworld.[76]

Perhaps the most well-known story about the Greek underworld is that Hades took an unwilling young goddess named Persephone under the Earth to serve as his queen. Persephone was allowed back to the land of the living because she had eaten pomegranate seeds, while with Hades, she had to return to the underworld annually.

Other narratives about the underworld included Theseus being trapped on a throne in the underworld and various other heroic journeys made to the Land of the Dead to rescue people down below. [77]

Several myths about these journeys employ the noun *Nekuia*, a synonym for the underworld. Usually, these voyages to Nekuia involved the journey of a living human hero, most often the son of a god but, in one case, a fully mortal female, chiefly to gain information about the Land of the Dead. Even though Hades was believed to be outside the realm of time and space on Earth, we, nevertheless, know some details of the ancient Greek vision of Hades.

For one thing, access to the Greek underworld was believed to be "somewhere in the West." The underworld is not unlike Heaven and Hell in the Judeo-Christian tradition, but there are some similarities as well. Hades had an area known as the "Elysian Fields," which was very much like the Western idea of heaven.

The ancient Greek underworld also had a dark, murky, tortuous area known as *Tartarus*, a pit beneath the Earth, corresponding to the Western idea of hell. Tartarus was also the home of the Night, or *Nyx*, at least according to Hesiod's *Theogony*.[78] *Nekuia* also had a special area for different types of deaths in a place called the "Plain of *Asphodel*," which was a joyless realm inhabited by ghosts. This plain is the main place where the souls congregate in the underworld—neither torturous nor pleasant, but nevertheless in worse condition than those on Earth.

Similar to the Judeo-Christian Judgment Day, or the ancient Egyptian system that weighed the soul to determine one's fate, the Greeks employed three formerly mortal judges to determine the fates of souls.

Hades, the god of the dead, does not manage his kingdom alone. His "employees," if you will, include Persephone, his wife; *Hectate*, a mysterious nature goddess associated with sorcery and magic; and the *Erinyes*, or "Furies." These are goddesses of vengeance who pursue their victims even after death. There is also the figure of *Charon*, the Ferryman of Hades.

The job of Charon in Hades is to transport the souls of the newly dead across the River Styx, which divides the world of the living from the world of the dead. A coin was paid to Charon for the passage. It was sometimes placed in the mouth of the dead by relatives back on Earth. Some Greek sources relate that if one could not pay the fee, or those whose bodies were left unburied were destined to wander the shores of the underworld until they were allowed to pass.[79]

Other ancient Greek mythological figures associated with death and the underworld include Hermes, the three judges, and the serpent-tailed *Cerberus*. Hermes was known as the "Conductor of Dreams" and a Chthonic god. He herds the dead towards Nekuia. In Greek art, Hermes was usually shown conveying the dead to Charon.[80]

The names of the three judges of the dead were *Rhadamanthus*, *Minos*, and *Aeacus*, who were renowned for their judgment and fairness. Minos is said to have brought laws to Crete. Aeacus is said to hold the keys to Hades.[81]

The River Styx was at the entrance to the realm of Hades. Styx was also the river that flowed around the underworld. The god associated with Styx is only invoked in the most solemn of oaths.[82] In classical Greek, the word Styx meant "shuddering." And expressions of loathing related to contemplating death. In Homer's *Iliad* and *Odyssey,* the gods swear by the waters of the Styx as their most sacred oath. The historian Hesiod personified Styx as the daughter of Oceanus and the mother of emulation, Victory, Power, and Might.

Cerberus was the serpent-tailed multi-headed hellhound with three, to as many as fifty, heads. The hero Hercules was told to bring

Cerberus up to the land of the living as part of his labors. The task of Cerberus was to guard the entrance to Hades on the surface of the Earth and to make sure that no ghosts escaped. Most Greek accounts of Cerberus have the hound as possessing three heads, but Hesiod, in his *Theogony*, has the number of the hound's heads as fifty.[83] [84]

Finally, it is important to distinguish between Hades, the god, and Hades as the underworld. About the former, Hades was the only god of the ancient Greeks not to reside on Mount Olympus. Instead, he lived in a dark place beneath the Earth. The god Hades also had a helmet made by Hephaistos that rendered the wearer invisible. This is also the helmet worn by Athena when she fought Ars in Homer's account of the Trojan Wars. Perseus also wore the same helmet in his quest for the head of Medusa.

On the other hand, Hades, as the Land of the Dead, is synonymous with *Thanatos*, or Death. In this form, Hades is the final resting place for the souls of the dead. It is a foreboding place for the living on Earth. It was not necessarily a place for punishment and expiation, but in some areas of Hades, it could be.[85]

This brings us to the fifth and final section of Chapter Two, in which we will explore the perspectives of the Romans and the Etruscans on the ideas of hell and the notion of punishment after death.

Hell among the Romans and Etruscans

In this final section of this second chapter, we will explore the views of two other ancient Near-Eastern cultures on the issues of hell and after death, the Etruscans and the Romans. The former culture existed as Etruria, and its people were known as the Etruscans. The Etruscans were a race that lived near present-day Tuscany, Umbria, and Lazio. Their area of control in Italy was from the Po Valley in the north to the Campania in the south.[86]

The Etruscans established their empire beginning in the eighth century BCE. In his *Sketches of Etruscan Places*, D. H. Lawrence describes the Etruscans as, "An ancient people who settled in central Italy in the eighth century BCE. Among pre-Roman civilizations, only the Greeks compared in wealth, power, and influence."[87]

The Etruscans were the sworn enemies of the Romans, whose fledging Republic was still scrapping with its Latin neighbors, while the

Etruscans were establishing a trade empire across the Mediterranean Sea. The Etruscans were as sophisticated and cosmopolitan as the Romans were austere and insular.[88]

Recent archaeological digs have revealed a good bit more about the Etruscans than we had known previously. The Etruscans used to be referred to as "mysterious" because none of their literature had survived, other than the remnants of ritual and mythic texts. What we know of Etruscan architecture and daily life comes mostly from their incredibly ornate tombs, which appear to be replicas of their houses.[89]

Treasure was also included in their tombs, together with necessities they believed they would need in the afterlife. From the evidence of Etruscan funerary practices, it is clear that their afterlife was not so much an underworld as it was an afterword.[90]

The character of the Greek *Charon* can be seen in the Etruscan artifacts. He is known as *Charun* in their language and appears to be the Gate Keeper rather than the Ferryman among those in Etruria. For the Etruscans, the dead were met at the entrance to the Great Beyond by a winged demoness named *Vanth*. One Etruscan tomb painting shows Vanth wearing a pleated skirt, short hunting boots, and protective gear crossing her bare chest.[91]

An eye is painted on each of Vanth's wings. Two snakes twist around her lower body. Vanth is often depicted as holding a torch in one hand and a key in the other. The torch acts as a beacon for the dead souls to help them find the entrance to the afterlife. In one Etruscan tomb, Vanth is shown holding a scroll of names that may suggest that they had some sort of judgment day.

We also know that the souls of the Etruscan dead faced a perilous journey over both land and sea, where monsters and demons were believed to lurk. The fiercest of these was a winged creature named *Tuchulcha* that had donkey ears, a vulture's beak, grey-blue skin, and two coiled serpents twisting around each arm.[92]

For the Etruscans, the final destination for the souls of the dead was not an underworld but a sumptuous banquet attended by their dead ancestors, family, and friends. The future for the Etruscans, then, after death was neither an ecstatic heaven nor a fearsome hell, but rather a continuation of their sensual lives on Earth.

For the most part, the Romans came to adopt the practices of the Greeks when it came to hell and after death. They adopted a belief in Hades during the imperial times, but the early Romans did not see it as experiencing an afterlife. Instead, they believed that the souls of the dead joined an amorphous mass of spiritual beings known as the *Dii Manes*, a Latin noun that means something like the "Kindly Ones."

The name of these spirits is ironic because they were considered fearful and needed to be placated by the relatives of the dead in case the Kindly Ones rose to torment Them. Calling them by a positive name, then, appears to be another attempt at appeasement of the Kindly Ones.

In Roman mythology, *Pluto*, or *Plouton*, was the ruler of the underworld. The name Pluto is the Latinized name of the Greek Plouton. Pluto is also the name of the Ruler of the Dead throughout Latin literature. In Greek times, Plouton was one of several Greek names used as substitutes for Hades. The Greek historian Strabo, however, made a distinction between Hades and Plouton.

Often, when Pluto was depicted in Roman painting and sculpture, he was shown as a bearded figure with a long staff in his left hand and the three-headed Cerberus at his right side. The Latin name *Dis Pater* was another name for Pluto that was used widely by the Romans. The name was most likely derived from the Indo-Aryan *Pitar*, the Sanskrit word for "Father." And the underworld was the "Land of the Fathers," if you will.

This brings us to the major conclusions on the ideas of hell and after death in the cultures of the ancient Near East. The subject matter of Chapter Three, to follow, is the phenomena of hell and after death to be found in the literature of the ancient Jews.

Conclusions

The goal of this second chapter has been to explore what cultures in the ancient Near East had to say about the issues of hell and after death. We began the chapter with an analysis of the ancient Egyptian's views about death, survival after death, hell-like states in Egypt, and the notion of punishment after death.

We began the first section by enumerating six separate ancient Egyptian texts that dealt with death, hell-like states, and punishment after death. Among these texts were the *Book of Two Ways*, the *Book of Gates*, and the *Egyptian Book of the Dead* along with three other important ancient texts in the Egyptian corpus.

We also introduced a figure named *Ammit*, who was responsible for devouring corpses. We also spoke of the process of weighing the hearts of newly deceased Egyptians to see if they were heavier than a feather and worthy, or not, of salvation.

We also introduced the role of the ancient Egyptian deity *Apepi*, the god of Chaos. We indicated the place of the Osiris myth and the role that Osiris played in Egyptian mythology in the ancient world. We also have shown the basic geography of the Egyptian underworld, including the place of the Lake of Fire in their cosmology.

We showed that the ancient Egyptians believed that the Land of the Dead was to the west, and that one entered it through a portal on the Earth, and that one of two destinies awaited any soul who entered the portal—one either reached salvation or was consumed by the god Ammit.

In the second section of Chapter Two, we explored what the cultures of ancient Mesopotamia had to say about the existence of a hell-like place in the afterlife, as well as the phenomenon of punishment after death.

Among the cultures we have discussed were the Sumerians, the Akkadians, the Babylonians, the Hittites, the Canaanites, the Assyrians, the Persians, the ancient Greeks, the Etruscans, and the ancient Romans. Indeed, one after the other, we have examined the beliefs of these ancient cultures in regard to death, the existence of an underworld or hell-like place, as well as the phenomenon of punishment after death.

The ideas about Zervan, or time, and Ahura Mazda, the good god, and Angra Mainya, the evil god, were also some of the foci in our discussion of Zoroastrianism and the ancient views about death, hell, and the phenomenon of punishment after death, among these people of ancient Persia.

Regarding the ancient Greeks, in addition to Hades, we also discussed the places of the River Styx, Charon the Ferryman, Hermes, and Cerberus, the multi-headed hound of hell in ancient Greek mythology. We indicated that the ancient Greeks used the noun *Nekuia* as a synonym for Hades as the place of the underworld, not as the role of a god.

Along the way in Chapter Two, we spoke of Hades as both a god and the name of the Greek underworld. We have also spoken of the similar role of the god Pluto as the Ruler of the underworld in Roman culture.

We also pointed out that only one Zoroastrian text provided a detailed description of the ancient Persian funeral rites and practices. This text is the *Arda Viraf*, many depictions of which have been discovered in archeological digs of sites in ancient Persia.

We also spoke at some length on the role that the *Chinvat Bridge* played in the history of Zoroastrian views about death and the afterlife, as well as the role of *Dhuzan*, the old Persian word for "hell" in Zoroastrian society.

We introduced and discussed the views of the ancient Hittites regarding death and punishment after death, as well as ideas found on these issues among the people called the Hyksos.

Finally, we have spoken at some length about the death and funerary practices among the Etruscans in Northern and Central Italy beginning in the eighth century BCE and shown that the Etruscans were a sophisticated and cosmopolitan society, much more so than their neighboring Romans.

Above all, what we have seen in this second chapter is a rich and variegated collection of perspectives on death and the afterlife in the many cultures of the ancient Near East, both great and small.

In Chapter Three to follow, we shall explore the phenomena of hell and after death as they are discussed and appear in the literature and the archeology of the ancient Jews. As we shall see, the most important notion of the Jews in these regards is a place that Classical Hebrew sources refer to as *Sheol*.

Edvard Munch, *Self-Portrait in Hell*, 1903.
Oil on canvas, 32.2 x 25.9 in. Munch Museum, Oslo, Norway.

Chapter Three
Sheol and Hell in the Hebrew Bible or Old Testament

The road to hell is paved with good intentions.
—Saint Bernard of Clairvaux

For the world is hell, and men are on the one hand the tormented souls there, and on the other hand, the devils who reside there.
—Arthur Schopenhauer

There is something more terrible than
a hell of suffering. It is the hell of boredom.
—Victor Hugo

Introduction

The purpose of this third chapter is to explore the notions of the underworld and the possibility of punishment after death found in the Hebrew Bible or Old Testament. This goal will principally be fulfilled by looking at what the ancient Jews had to say and write about a murky underworld known as *Sheol* that appears some sixty-six times in the Jewish scriptures.

We will begin Chapter Three with a section on how the word *Sheol* was translated in modern renderings since the 1611 translation of the King James Version of the Bible. Additionally, we will discuss the three most common scholarly judgments about the etymology of the Classical Hebrew noun *Sheol*.

In the second section of Chapter Three, we will explore what the Hebrew Bible or the Old Testament says about what goes on in *Sheol*. As we shall see, this will be the central section of this chapter.

In the final section, we shall raise the question of what form of survival after death can be found in *Sheol*, as well as whether the ancient Jews did or did not believe that the dead are punished there. We move, then, to the translations of how the word *Sheol* has been rendered in the English translation from the seventeenth-century King James Version of the Bible.

The Idea of Sheol in English Translation

The Classical Hebrew noun *Sheol* appears sixty-six times in the Hebrew Bible or Old Testament. In the King James Version, it is generally rendered in three separate ways. Firstly, in many instances, *Sheol* is translated as a synonym for the "grave," or the word *Qeber*. The KJV translators render *Sheol* as "grave" thirty-one times. Two good examples are Genesis 37:35 and Ecclesiastes 9:10 (KJV).

In the passage from Genesis, the KJV translators gave us this:

> **And all the sons and all his daughters rose up to comfort him; but he refused to be comforted; and he said, For I will go down into the grave unto the mourning of my son; thus, his father wept for him.**[93]

At Ecclesiastes 9:10, the KJV translators render the verse this way:

> **Whatsoever thy hand findeth to do, do it with thy might;**
> **for there is no work, nor device, nor knowledge,**
> **nor wisdom, in the grave [*Sheol*], whither thou goest.**

Secondly, the Hebrew word *Sheol* is sometimes translated in the KJV as "pit," as a synonym for either the noun *bohr* or *shahat*. This can be seen at Numbers 16:30 to 33 and Proverbs 1:12, two good examples of this phenomenon in the King James Version. In the former, the passage from Numbers, we find the following translation:

> **They, and all that appertained to them, went down**
> **alive into the pit [*Sheol*], and the Earth closed**
> **upon them; and they perished from among the congregation.**

At Proverbs 1:12, the KJV translators render the verse this way:

Let us swallow them alive like *Sheol*,
Even whole as those who go down into the pit. [*bohr*]

Thirdly, in thirty-five places, we find that the KJV translates *Sheol* as "hell." It is interesting that nearly all of these are found in the Prophets, or the poetic books. Among the examples of Sheol as hell in the KJV translation are the following passages: Psalms 16:10, 55:15, 86:13 (RSV), and Isaiah 14:9, among many other passages. The first of these, in the KJV, tells us this,

For thou wilt not leave my soul in hell,
nor wilt thou suffer thine Holy One to see corruption.

At Psalm 55:15, the seventeenth-century English translators provide this translation,

Let death seize upon them, and let them go down quickly into hell; for wickedness is in their dwellings and among them.

At Psalm 86:13, we find a similar translation of *Sheol*,

For great is the mercy toward me; and
thou hast delivered my soul from the lowest hell.

Finally, in our last example, the one at the Prophet Isaiah's 14:9, The King James translators provide this rendering:

Hell [*Sheol*] from beneath is moved for thee to meet
thee at thy coming. It stirreth up the dead for thee,
even all the chief ones of the Earth; it has raised
them up from their thrones all the kings of the nations.

Another good example of where the KJV translators rendered *Sheol* as "hell," in the Book of Jonah 2:2. The 1611 English scholars gave us this for the verse:

And said, "I cried by reason of mine affliction
unto the Lord, and he heard me out of the
belly of hell cried I, and Thou heardest my voice."

Here the writer of the Book of Jonah implies a relationship of Jonah being in the belly of the whale, as well as the "belly of hell," the implication being that "belly of hell" means the "belly of Sheol."

Some more modern English translations prefer simply to leave the word *Sheol* untranslated. One example of this phenomenon is the translators of the New International Version, or the NIV. The Jerusalem Bible (JB), the Goodspeed Bible (GB), the New Revised Standard Version (NRSV), and the Revised English Bible (REB), all also leave the word Sheol untranslated.

There is also some disagreement among the Hebrew Bible or Old Testament scholars about the etymological origins of the word *Sheol*. For the most part, these scholars are divided among three separate points of view. One camp maintains that the Classical Hebrew word *Sheol* comes from the verb *sha'al*, meaning "to ask." A second view finds the origin of *Sheol* in the Hebrew verb *sha'ol*, or "to be hollow."

Finally, a third theory, the one endorsed by William F. Albright and the one the author prefers, as to the origin of the Hebrew term *Sheol* is the Old Babylonian word *Sualu* that implies "a place beneath the Earth." This third possibility appears to be the most likely answer to the origin of the Hebrew *Sheol*.

There is also some indication that the Hebrew word *Sheol* is also connected to the noun *Abaddon*. This can be seen at Psalm 88:10 and 11, Job 26:6 and 28:22, and Proverbs 15:11. In the last of these, the one from the Book of Proverbs, the Revised Standard Version translators has *Sheol* as parallel to *Abaddon*. It tells us:

Sheol and _Abaddon_ lie open before the Lord, how much more the hearts of men?

At Psalm 88:10 and 11, we see the idea of *Abaddon* again parallel to the notion of *Sheol*. These verses ask in the Revised Standard Version:

Dost thou work wonders for the dead? Do the shades rise up to praise thee? Is thy steadfast love declared in the grave, or thy faithfulness in _Abaddon_?

The writers of the Book of Job see that *Sheol* and *Abaddon* are associated at 26:6 and 28:22. The former relates,

Sheol is naked before God and Abaddon has no covering.

The latter verse from the Book of Job, the one at 28:22, the RSV gives us this:

Abaddon and _Death_ say, "We have heard a rumor of it with our ears."

The Classical Hebrew word *Abaddon* is employed seven times in the Hebrew Bible or Old Testament. These come at Proverbs 15:11 and 27:20; the Book of Job 26:6, 28:22, and 31:12; and Psalm 88:1. The word *Abaddon* is sometimes translated as "Destruction," for the root of *Abaddon* is the Hebrew verb "to destroy." In all seven examples, however, of the use of *Abaddon*, it is tied inextricably to the noun *Sheol*, such as at Proverbs 27:20:

Sheol and _Abaddon_ are never satisfied
and a man's eyes are never satisfied.

Or Proverbs 15:11 that the King James Version gives us:

Sheol and _Abaddon_ are before Yahweh—
how much more then the hearts of the children of men.

This brings us to the second and central section of Chapter Three, where we will attempt to answer the question, "What goes on in the ancient Jews' realm of the dead called *Sheol*?

What Goes on in Sheol?

Among the scripture of the ancient Jews, we may find five separate kinds of answers pertaining to the question raised at the head of this section. These may be summarized this way:

1. Comments related to *Sheol's* depth and direction.
2. Comments related to the physical conditions of *Sheol.*
3. Comments related to the knowledge of human beings in *Sheol.*
4. Places where *Sheol* is personified.
5. Other general comments about *Sheol.*

In terms of our first category, Job 7:9, Psalm 86:13, Ezekiel 31:14–18, Proverbs 9:18 and 15:24, for example, all tell us that *Sheol* is "down." In the NRSV, the first of these relates,

As the cloud fades and vanishes, so those who go down to *Sheol* do not come up.

At Psalm 86:13, we find the same judgment about the ancient Jewish Land of the Dead,

For great is your steadfast love toward me. You have delivered my soul from the depths of *Sheol*.

The same conclusion about where *Sheol* is, can be found at the Prophet Ezekiel's 31:14 to 19. Verse 14 tells us this:

For all of them are handled over to death to the world below; Along with all mortals, With those who go down into the Pit. [*Sheol*]

The final verse of Proverbs 9:18 also indicates the direction of *Sheol*. It relates,

But they do not know that the dead are there, that her guests are all in the depths of *Sheol*.

This notion of *Sheol* being "down" or "deep" can also be found at Proverbs 15:24, Ezekiel 32:21 and 27, and Ezekiel 31:15–17, among many other passages.

Our second category of comments about what goes on in *Sheol* is related to the physical conditions of the land of the dead among the ancient Jews. The Book of Job 17:16 and Isaiah 38:19 tell us that *Sheol* has "Gates." Job 24:9 indicates that there are subterranean primeval waters in *Sheol*, and Psalm 18:5 relates that Sheol has "cords" within it.

Psalm 141:7 indicates that Sheol has a "mouth," as does the Prophet Isaiah 5:14, as well as appetites. Job 3:16–19 suggests that being in *Sheol* is like the life of a "stillborn child," and there, "the wicked cease from troubling." At Job 3:19, we learn that "the small and the great" are in Sheol together, "and the slave is freed from its owner." Clearly, the state of things in *Sheol* is an egalitarian place.

This de-emphasis of social status in *Sheol* is also discussed at Isaiah 14:9 to 11. There, the prophet relates:

The realm of the dead below is all astir to meet you at your coming. It rouses the spirits of the departed to greet you—all

those who were leaders in the world. It makes them rise from their thrones, all those who were kings over the nations. They will all respond and say to you, You also have become weak, as we are; you have become like us. All of your pomp has been brought down to the grave along with the noise of your harps. Maggots and worms are spread beneath you, and you are covered with worms.

There are four conclusions that may be made about this passage in the Prophet Isaiah:

1. The word translated as "spirits" is the term *Rephaim*.
2. There is no preferred social status in *Sheol*; all are "like shades."
3. The spirits or shades in *Sheol* are "weak."
4. Maggots and worms can be found in *Sheol*.

In consort with most of the cultures of the ancient Near East, the Psalmist at 103:14 suggests that the most relevant feature of the conditions of *Sheol* is the "Dust." Two different Classical Hebrew words are employed to designate dust. The first of these is the word *aphar*. It is employed at Ezekiel 26:10, Genesis 2:7, 3:14, 16, 18:27, and 19; Numbers 19:17 and 23:10; and Joshua 7:6.

The other Classical Hebrew word for "dust" is *abaq*, which is also sometimes employed to indicate "powder." *Abaq* may be found at Exodus 9:9, Isaiah 5:24 and 29:5, as well as Nahum 1:3. Both *aphar* and *abaq* are used in connection with the conditions of *Sheol*.

Psalm 49:12–20 tells us that in *Sheol*, our form "wastes away" (verse 14), much like "beasts who perish" (verse 20). Ezekiel 32:27 indicates that *Sheol* has a "midst," and Psalm 88:5 relates that *Sheol* is "dark and deep." The Book of Job 14:7–14 tells us that "people may hide there."

The Book of Proverbs 30:16 compares life in *Sheol* to a "barren womb." The Prophet Isaiah, at 14:9 to 11, tells us that there are maggots and worms in the Jewish underworld, *Sheol*.

Finally, one way that is also employed in the Hebrew Bible or Old Testament scripture speaks of where *Sheol* is found in three places where it suggests that it is of the greatest possible distance from heaven and where the God of Israel, Yahweh, resides. This judgment and three texts may be found at the Book of Job 11:8, the Prophet Amos 9:2, and Psalm 139:8.

The first of these three texts relates,

They are higher than the Heavens above, what can you do?
They are deeper than the depths below, what can you know?

The answer to this rhetorical question should be,

Not very much in *Sheol*.

Prophet Amos' book at 9:2 tells us:

Though they dig down to the depths below from there my hand will take them. Though they climb up to the Heavens above, from thee I will bring them down.

The Psalmist, at 139:8, tells us this,

If I go up to the heavens, thou are there.
And if I make my bed in the depths, You are there.

The implication appears to be that the depths of *Sheol* are as far away in the Universe as one can be from God in His heavens.

One final point about the geography of *Sheol* is that comments about it are often made in the Hebrew Bible or Old Testament in connection to the Classical Hebrew word *Dumah*, meaning "silence." Thus, *Sheol* is called the "Land of Silence," such as at Psalm 94:17, where the psalmist relates:

Unless Yahweh has given me help, I would as soon have dwelt in the silence of death. (Author's translation)

At Isaiah 21:11, the prophet speaks of what he calls "The burden of *Dumah*," or silence, in the context of speaking of the Jewish land of the dead—*Sheol*. The word *Dumah* is to speak of a tribe or region in Arabia. It is also used as the name of one of Ishmael's sons.

Finally, in many places in the Hebrew Bible or Old Testament speak of *Sheol* as being a place of darkness and disorder. One case in particular, for example, is the Book of Job's 10:22, where the NIV gives us this translation:

To the land of the deepest night of utter darkness and disorder, where even the light is like darkness.

Our third category about what goes on in *Sheol* pertains to places where the reader is told about what the shades of the dead can know or do in the murky underworld called *Sheol*. The Book of Job's 11:8 and 9 inform us that nothing can be known there, as well as the fact that it is "long and deep."

Psalm 6:5 tells us that *Sheol* is "a land of no memory." Psalm 31:17 says it is a "silent place." Psalm 88:3–7 and 10–12 also indicate *Sheol* is a "land of forgetfulness," where there "is no memory," and at verses 5 and 6, we are told that *Sheol* is a forsaken place where no help can be given. The Prophet Ezekiel, at 9:10, suggests there is no activity in *Sheol*.

The fourth category of the uses of *Sheol* in the Hebrew Bible or Old Testament can be seen in those places where the Hebrew Land of the Dead is personified. Indeed, in many passages, the idea of *Sheol* is particularly anthropomorphic in its nature.

Psalm 6:5 mentioned above is one example of this phenomenon to personify *Sheol*. The Book of Numbers 16:30 is another good example of the personification of *Sheol*, where it speaks of "swallowing the shades with all that belongs to them, and they go alive into *Sheol*."

The Prophet Ezekiel, at chapter 32:18 to 32, one of the longest passages on *Sheol* in the Hebrew Bible or Old Testament, speaks of the *Rephaim* or "shades" in *Sheol* as "slain," "laid to rest," in "bed," and "in their graves." These are all examples of anthropomorphisms of the Hebrew Land of the Dead.

The Book of Job 26:5 and 6 offers us another personification of *Sheol*, where it relates, in the Revised Standard Version,

The shades below tremble, the waters and their inhabitants.
***Sheol* is naked before God and Abaddon has no covering.**

This suggests that the *Rephaim* may "tremble" like humans and that there are primeval, subterranean waters beneath the Hebrew Land of the Dead—*Sheol*.

The idea of subterranean waters that lie beneath *Sheol* can be seen in the account in Genesis of Noah and the flood. At Genesis 7:10 to 12, the writer relates:

And after seven days, the waters of the flood came on the Earth. In the six hundredth year of Noah's life, in the second month, on the seventeenth day of the month, on that day all the fountains of the deep burst forth, and the windows of the Heavens were opened. The rain on the Earth fell for forty days and forty nights.

The expression "and the fountains of the deep burst forth" suggests that when the rains began, they came from above and beneath the Earth. A few verses later, still in Genesis 7, at verses 19 and 20, the water "covered fifteen cubits upward did the waters prevail." This also seems to establish that the waters in Noah's flood came from above and beneath the Earth.

Finally, at *Qoheleth*, or Ecclesiastes in English, at chapter 9:5, the writer of the book also personifies the idea of *Sheol* when it relates,

For the living know that they will die, but the dead know nothing, and they have no record of reward, but the memory of them has been lost.

The inhabitants of *Sheol* are but a shadow of their former selves. In fact, they are called *Rephaim*, or "Shades."

The fifth and final category of remarks about *Sheol* are general observations that do not fit with the other four categories. These are random, general thoughts and observations that often have nothing to do with what is around them, nor are they related to other ancient Jewish remarks about *Sheol*.

For example, Job 21:13 relates that people may "suddenly go there." The same book, at 14:13, relates that people may "hide there." The Book of Proverbs 30:16 likens *Sheol* to a "barren womb," also another personification, and "a land not satisfied with water, nor a fire that never says, "Enough!"

At the Song of Songs 8:6, it suggests that *Sheol* is a place of cruelty. The psalmist, at 141:7, tells us that "bones may be strewn" in *Sheol*. Job 26:6 indicates that *Sheol* may be "naked." Psalm 139:8 indicates that even God is in *Sheol*. The text relates:

If I ascend to Heaven, Thou are there.
If I make my bed in *Sheol*, Thou are there.

In a passage in Ezekiel 31:14 to 18, the word *Sheol* is used three times—verses 15, 16 and 17. Verse 15 is associated with "mourning." Verse 16 speaks of foreign nations being "cast down into *Sheol*." And those "slain by the swords" in verse 17 tell us they will also be sent to *Sheol*.

The Prophet Isaiah at 14:9 to 11 speaks of the possibility of the "shades," or the *Rephaim* in *Sheol* can be roused. The word most likely has a Phoenician origin. King Tabnit of Sidon curses any prospective despoiler of his tomb, "That there is no resting place for you with the *Rephaim*." The noun is used at Psalm 88:10, Proverbs 2:18, 9:18 and 21:16.

The King Tabnit was a Phoenician who lived at the beginning of the fifth century BCE. His tomb is decorated with two separate and unrelated inscriptions—one of these is in Egyptian hieroglyphics, and the other is in Phoenician script. The sarcophagus was made around 490 BCE and discovered in 1887 by Osman Hamdi Bey at the acropolis near Sidon. King Tabnit's body was remarkably preserved when the lid was removed.

The same noun *Rephaim* spelled the same way in Hebrew, also sometimes refers to a race of giants in the Hebrew Bible or Old Testament. This can be seen at First Chronicles 11:15 and 20:4, for example, as well as at Joshua 15:8, Deuteronomy 2:11, Second Samuel 5:18, 22 and 23:13.

The Prophet Hosea at 13:14 suggests several other attributes of *Sheol*. This text tells us:

> **I will ransom them from the power of the grave [*Sheol*]; I will redeem them from Death. Where, oh death, are your plagues? Where, oh grave [*Sheol*] is your destruction.**

Four separate conclusions can be made about this verse from the Prophet Hosea. First, the Shades may be ransomed from *Sheol*. Second, they may also be redeemed. Third, there is no disease to be found in *Sheol*. Finally, *Sheol* appears to be a "place of destruction."

One final attribute of the ancient Hebrews' *Sheol* is that it is said to be a place where the *Rephaim*, or Shades, are "gathered to their people." At Genesis 15:15, for example, Yahweh says to Abraham, "Thou shall go to your fathers in peace." When Abraham died, it was said of him that "He was gathered to his people," at Genesis 25:8.

The same judgment is made of Jacob at Genesis 49:33, as well as of Ishmael at Genesis 25:17. Aaron is gathered to his fathers at Numbers 20:26, 27:13 and 32:50. Moses goes to his fathers at Genesis 27:13, 31:2 and 32:50; and King Josiah after his death was also "gathered to his fathers," at Second Kings 22:20 and Second Chronicles 34:28 both indicate.

The Classical Hebrew verb employed in many of these passages about going to one's fathers is the word, *acaph*, or "to gather." In general, it is only employed in one of two different ways. Either the "gathering" of a harvest, or "gathering to one's fathers."

This brings us to the final section of Chapter Three: the ideas of *Sheol* and the possibility of punishment after death in the Hebrew Bible or Old Testament, in which we will attempt to answer another question about *Sheol*. That is, is there any evidence that the ancient Jews believed in any sort of survival after death?

The Ancient Jews, Sheol and Survival after Death

Our final task and section of Chapter Three is to answer the following questions. What views of survival after death are implied in the sixty-six references to *Sheol* among the ancient Jews? Did they, for example, believe that it may be a hell-like place or that the *Rephaim* may be punished there after death?

To answer these questions, we must examine the many uses of the words *Nefesh* and *Ruah* in the scriptures of the ancient Jews. The former word comes from the Semitic root NFSH, that is the origins of the Hebrew verb "to breathe." It also sometimes means "will" and even "life" and some emotions such as "anger." The classical Arabic word *Nafs* is the Islamic term for "Soul."

The word *Nefesh* is used many times throughout the Hebrew Bible or Old Testament. We will point to three examples to determine how the noun *Nefesh* is used. They come at Genesis 2:7, Psalm 23:3 and 103:1. The passage from Genesis speaks of God breathing the "breathe of life" into Adam's nostrils. Here *Nefesh* means "breathe."

At Psalm 23:3, the psalmist tells us speaking of God:

> **He refreshes my soul [*Nefesh*]. He guides me along the right paths for His name's sake.**

At Psalm 103:1, we find the same use of the noun *Nefesh* of which the text tells us,

> **Praise the Lord my soul [*Nefesh*], all my inmost being, praise his Holy Name.**

Nefesh is also used for "wind" at Job 1:19; anger at Job 4:9b; "life" at Job 9:21; "soul" at Job 21:25; "wind" at Job 13:15, and "soul" at Job 30:16.

A Hebrew cognate of *Nefesh* is the word *Neshamah*, which comes from the same Semitic root NSH. It is used five times in the Book of Job, each to designate "breath." In the Hebrew Bible or Old Testament, *Neshamah* is also employed thirty-two times—two times as "Spirit," eighteen as "breath," and twenty-two other times.

The bottom line on *Nefesh* is that it usually means "Soul," but not a soul that can disconnect from the human body at death. Rather, the ancient Jews held a view of the Self as a kind of psycho-physical entity, where the Soul only exists where there is a human body that is working.

Similarly, the Hebrew noun *Ruah* means "spirit" as well as "wind." At Jeremiah 15:1, it appears to mean "will." At Jeremiah 13:16, "Soul." At Ecclesiastes 12:7, *Ruah* means "Spirit," which is its general meaning in the Hebrew scriptures. But nowhere in the Hebrew Bible or Old Testament does *Ruah* mean a spirit that disconnects from a human body at death. In this sense, *Ruah* means a psycho-physical unity, just as the word *Nefesh* often does.

The point of all this is that generally speaking, in the Hebrew Bible or Old Testament, when you are dead, you are dead, and you stay that way. Death, for the most part, means extinction of the Self. There are a few possible exceptions to this rule, and we will examine some of them now.

At the Book of Job 19:25–26, in the NIV translation, we get the following:

> **For I know that my redeemer lives. And that in the end he will stand upon the Earth. And after my skin has been destroyed, Yet in my flesh I shall see God.**

Handel's *Messiah*, of course, has made this passage famous as a proof text for the resurrection of the body. Since that time, many conservatives have seen these verses, which are called the *Goel* passage because that is the Hebrew name translated as "Redeemer" in verse 25.

In another Job passage, this time at 14:12, the author speaking of *Sheol* relates:

> **So he lies down and does not rise, until the Heavens are no more, people will not awake or be aroused from their sleep.**

The same view of extinction can also be seen at Job 7:21, which asks,

> **Why do you not pardon my offenses and forgive my sins. You will search for me, but I will be no more.**

In these two passages from Job, we see the overall general view of survival after death in the Hebrew Bible or Old Testament—When you die, you are dead, and you stay that way.

By the time we get to the biblical Book of Daniel, however, probably from the second century BCE, we find this at chapter 12:1–3:

> **Those who sleep in the dust of the Earth shall awake. Some to everlasting life. And others to share in ever-lasting perdition [or contempt]. Those who are wise will shine like the brightness of the Heavens, and those who lead many to righteousness, like the stars forever and ever.**

It should be clear that in these verses from the Book of Daniel, the author is endorsing a belief in the resurrection of the body at the end of time. That is what makes these verses an outlier regarding survival after death.

Another exception to the extinction view on survival after death in the Hebrew Bible or Old Testament can be found at the Prophet Isaiah's book, at 26:19. There the prophet tells us:

> **But your dead will live, Lord; their bodies will rise—let those who dwell in the dust wake up and shout for joy—your dew is like the dew of the morning; the earth will give birth to her dead.**

Needless to say, there have been many scholarly attempts to make sense of what Isaiah 19:26 could possibly mean, but one view that could be put forward is that, like the Book of Job's 19:25 and 26, the verse in Isaiah 19:26 may be arriving at the same conclusion. That is, at the end of time, the bodies of the dead shall rise.

Another passage that is sometimes seen as an outlier regarding the extinction view is known as the "Dry Bones" pericope in the Prophet Ezekiel's book at chapter 37:1–14 (NIV), where the Prophet Ezekiel is led by God into a valley filled with dry bones. The Lord instructs the prophet to prophecy to the bones, saying that,

> **God will make breath to enter, and you will come to life. I will attach tendons and make flesh come upon you and will cover you with skin.**

There have been many interpretations of the Dry Bones passage over the years. Some have believed that the bones stand for Israel. In fact, in the previous chapter, number 36, Ezekiel proclaimed the blessing over all of Israel, that it will produce fruit, even though now they are in desolation. That one day, the Jews will reinhabit their towns and see their ruins rebuilt.

During the time of Ezekiel, the Babylonians had laid waste to the nation of Israel. They took several of their people captive, such as the Prophet Daniel and his friends. The Babylonians destroyed the Jewish temple, and restoration now seemed impossible. Israel was under the yoke of a powerful empire, and they themselves were the poorest of the poor, as Second Kings 24:14 indicates.

In essence, Israel was like the Dry Bones, a dead nation full of absolutely no sign of life that the nation would have a recovery. It would take an absolute miracle for them to rebuild, and this is when the Dry Bones vision of Ezekiel 37 occurs. Ezekiel himself had witnessed the Babylonian destruction of the temple. He knew it was just as impossible to raise Israel from the dead as it was to bring life again to the Dry Bones.

The Prophet Ezekiel, however, also understood that only God could bring someone, or even a nation, back to life. Then Yahweh commanded Ezekiel to prophecy over the bones, commanding them to attach themselves to one another. When they did so, skin, tendons, and muscles covered the bones, but they still had no life in them.

Next, God commanded Ezekiel to breathe the breath of life into the dead bodies as he did to Adam at Genesis 2:7, and when Ezekiel said the bodies sprang to life, they stood on their feet, enough of them that they could form a great army.

Many other scholars have suggested a variety of other interpretations of Ezekiel 37:1 to 14, as well. One of those, not surprisingly, is that some have viewed the Dry Bones passage as a confident and positive belief that the author of the Book of Ezekiel was assenting to the idea of the resurrection of the body of individual Jews at the end of time.

It seems more likely, however, that the reconstitution of the nation of Israel after the Babylonia captivity is the proper understanding of Ezekiel 37:1 to 14.

The vision of the Dry Bones passage has been used in several cultural manifestations over the centuries. One of the images of the *Vision of Tundale*, a twelfth-century vision of hell by an Irish knight named Tundale, shows Tundale in *Sheol* standing next to an angel.

Novelist Anthony Powell named his seventh novel *The Valley of Bones*. James Weldon Johnson's well-known spiritual "Dem Bones," also known as "Dry Bones," was inspired by Ezekiel 37:1 to 14. Gustave Dore produced an engraving called *The Vision of the Valley of the Dry Bones*. The woodcut was completed in 1866.

Marc Chagall completed a painting in 1931 titled *Jacob Weeps over Joseph's Tunic*, in which Jacob is surrounded by four of the *Rephaim* in the afterlife. These ghouls are all standing and have pale masks and open mouths on their faces.

Although we have seen several outliers regarding the views of the afterlife in the Hebrew scriptures, the overall understanding of that issue appears to have been that death is final, and that the life of the *Rephaim*, or Shades, in the underworld was murky, quiet, dark and dry, with little that might be called "Life."

This brings us to the major conclusions we have made in this third chapter, followed by Chapter Four, in which we will explore the idea of hell in the twenty-seven books of the New Testament.

Conclusions

We divided this chapter of this history of views on hell into three main sections. In the first of these, we had two tasks. First, to speak of the idea of the translation of the Hebrew noun *Sheol* in modern English translations, beginning with the 1611 rendering of the Old Testament in the King James Version.

The other task was to discuss the three most popular theories about the origin of the Hebrew noun *Sheol*. In that discussion, we put forth three views that the word *Sheol* is connected to the verb "to ask." A second theory argues it comes from an adjective that means "hollow." The third theory we have endorsed and argued by William F. Albright, one of our former mentors, ties the word *Sheol* to the Old Babylonian term *Sualu*, meaning "beneath the Earth."

In the second and central section of Chapter Three, we attempted to answer the question, "What goes on in *Sheol*?" We then suggested that five different kinds of comments regarding *Sheol* or the Underground are found in the Hebrew Bible or Old Testament.

In the second section, we argued that these five kinds of remarks about *Sheol* in the Hebrew Bible or Old Testament are the following: First, comments about the direction of *Sheol*. Second, comments related to the physical conditions of *Sheol*. The third variety of remarks about *Sheol* spoke of the conditions of the human *Rephaim*, or Shades, in *Sheol*.

The fourth kind of remarks about *Sheol* found in the Hebrew Bible or Old Testament are those places where the Jewish underworld is spoken of as personifications of anthropomorphically, where *Sheol* is spoken of as if it were a person.

Finally, we also suggested in the second section of this third chapter of this history of views about hell that are very general remarks that do not seem at first to meet any of the other four categories. Among these remarks, as we have seen, are the views that people may "suddenly go there," that it is a land that is "difficult to satisfy," that even God "may be found in *Sheol*," and that it is possible for God to "ransom" and "redeem" the *Rephaim* from *Sheol*.

In this chapter's third and final section, we have attempted to answer another question about the ancient Jewish underworld. That is, do the sixty-six references to it imply a view of personal survival after death?

The short answer to our question is *No*. Most views that the Hebrew Bible or the Old Testament provides about our question is that death means extinction, or when you die, you are very dead, and you stay that way.

At the end of section three, we introduced several texts that we labeled "outliers" with respect to personal survival of death. Among these texts were the Book of Job's *Goel* passage at 19:25 and 26. Another outlier, as we have suggested, is the Prophet Isaiah's 19:26 that, like the passage from Job, may imply Resurrection of the Body at the end of time.

A third passage, at the second-century BCE's Book of Daniel, Chapter 12:1 to 3, provides the clearest evidence in the Hebrew scriptures that "the dead shall be raised, some to everlasting life and some to perdition."

In a final text from the Hebrew scriptures, this one from the Prophet Ezekiel, 37:1 to 14, known as the "Dry Bones" narrative, we also have seen what is, perhaps, another indication of the idea of the Resurrection of the Body at the end of time.

In our discussion of Ezekiel's Dry Bones passage, however, we concluded that it is more likely that the Dry Bones allusion is a symbol for the survival of the nation of Israel during the reign of the Babylonians of the Jews.

At the close of chapter three, we have shown a number of Western cultural manifestations in which artists, philosophers, and exegesis have utilized Ezekiel's Dry Bones.

Our final conclusion, however, about these "survival outliers" is that none of them seem convincing enough to establish that the ancient Jews believed in personal survival after death in their scriptures.

In the final section of Chapter Three, we discussed the two Classical Hebrew nouns, *Nefesh* and *Ruah*, which are generally translated as "Soul" and "Spirit." But even in that discussion, we have pointed out that the uses of these nouns suggest more of a psych-somatic monism or fusion of ideas and that the *Nefesh* or *Ruah* could not exist without a body that works.

In the fourth chapter to follow, we will treat the ideas of hell and after death in the context of the twenty-seven books of the New Testament. For one thing, the New Testament has many more names for the notion of hell than just the single *Sheol* we have seen in the Hebrew Bible or Old Testament.

As we shall see in Chapter Four, many names and terms for "hell" are found in the New Testament, including *Sheol* and *Abaddon*, to which we shall turn next.

Dionisius, *Descent into Hell*. Ferapontov Monastery, Russia.

Chapter Four
Hell in the New Testament
Hades, Tartarus and Gehenna

I translated Dante's Inferno in order to
discover some of my ancestors.
—Antoine de Rivarol

I would prefer an intelligent Hell to a stupid Paradise.
—Blaise Pascal

Hell is always other people.
—Jean-Paul Sartre

Introduction

The purpose of this fourth chapter is to describe and discuss the places in the New Testament where hell and after death is a topic of conversation. We will begin this chapter with some introductory remarks on the English word "hell," as well as its Western predecessors. These will be followed by a summary of the Koine Greek vocabulary on words related to hell and punishment after death. As we shall see, there are at least six different names and words for hell in the twenty-seven books of the New Testament.

In the third and central section of the chapter, we will explore where the many names for hell in the New Testament are employed in the earliest Christian sources, the four Gospels, the Letters of Paul, and the other remaining books of the New Testament.

There is a total of one hundred and sixty-two verses in the New Testament that speak of unrepentant people going to a place of punishment. In seventy of these, Jesus is the speaker warning people to live good lives or they will be consigned there after death to receive punishment.[94]

The King James Bible translators render the word *Sheol* thirty-one times as "hell" in the Old Testament and two Koine Greek nouns as hell on twenty-three occasions in the New Testament. More modern Biblical translators, such as the New International Version (NIV) and the Revised Standard Version (RSV), for example, tend to translate only the word *Gehenna* as hell in the New Testament.

This modern tendency can also be seen in the New American Bible (NAB), the New King James Version (NKJV), and the NASB or New American Standard Bible. Each of these more modern translations only renders the word *Gehenna* as "hell" in the New Testament and thus either twelve or thirteen times, depending on the translation. Most modern English translations of the New Testament also use *Hades* or its equivalents when the original text uses *Sheol*.[95]

This brings us to a discussion of the origins of the modern English word "hell" and its many cognates, the subject matter of the first section of this fourth chapter.

Hell in English and Other Cognates

The modern English word hell is derived from the Old English *hel* or *helle*, which was first attested around 725 CE to refer to a Netherworld of the dead, reaching into the Anglo-Saxon period of the development of the English language.

The English word hell is a cognate of the words "hole" and "hollow." It is a substantive form from the Anglo-Saxon, *helan* or *behelian* that implies "to hide." The verbal form has the same function as the Latin *occulere* and *celare*, as well as the classical Greek *Kalyptein.* Thus, by etymology, the English word hell denotes a "dark" or "hidden place."[96]

In Early Norse mythology, the goddess *Hel* was the unpopular deity of the underworld. Only those who fell during battles went to Paradise, called *Valhalla*, another cognate of the English word hell, but everyone else goes down to *Hel* in the underworld. *Hel* was both a goddess and a giant. Her name means "hidden" or a "hiding place."[97]

According to thirteenth-century Icelandic writer Snorri Sturluson, *Hel* is the daughter of the God *Loki* and his giant wife *Angrboda*, a name from the Old Norse *Angrbooa* that means anguish-boding. This also makes the goddess *Hel* the sister of the wolf god *Fenrir* and a demon known as *Jormungand.*[98]

Jormungand was also called the "Midgard Serpent," for he was a snake or dragon living in the ocean surrounding Midgard, the visible world. His body is so enormous that it forms a circle around the entire world of the senses. Thus *Hel* was part of a most disreputable family.[99]

The goddess *Hel* was generally presented as being rather greedy, harsh and cruel, as well as being diffident toward both the living and the dead. Snorri describes *Hel* as half-black and half-white, with a perpetual grin and fierce expression on her face. Thus, *Hel* was an ambiguous figure in her presentation to humans.[100]

The only surviving Norse myth about *Hel* is where she is featured prominently in the story of the "Death of Baldur," in which *Baldur*, another god, was slain by *Hel*'s father, *Loki,* but he was first held captive in *Loki*'s castle. The other Norse gods send an emissary named *Hermod* to get *Loki* and *Hel* to release *Baldur*. *Hel* tells him *Baldur* would only be released if everything in the universe wept for him first.

So the Norse gods and their representatives went all around the universe to get creatures to weep for *Baldur*, but one large giant, who was probably *Loki* in disguise, refused, so the terms of *Hel*'s offer were not met.

The Norse name *Hel* is derived from the same root in the Proto-Germanic language, which is the ancestor of both Old Norse and Old English. That Proto-Germanic root was the word *Haljo*, meaning "a concealed place." Words stemming from this root were used to designate the underworld in virtually all Germanic languages. So hell in German is *Holle*. In Norway, Denmark, and Sweden, the word for hell is *Hel*, as well as the Anglo-Saxon *Helan* and the Old English *Hel*. The Frisian word for hell is *helle*, a language spoken on the North Sea in the north of the Netherlands.[101]

Ultimately, even earlier, the English word hell derives from the Indo-Aryan language and specifically from the word *Kel*, a word in Sanskrit that meant "to conceal," "to hide" or "to cover." In origin, then, "hell" is thus a "concealed place." This same root, *Kel*, also gave us other words that "cover" or "conceal" things, such as hole, hall, hollow whole, helmet, and even the Nordic *Valhalla* that literally means the *Holl* [Hall] of the *Valr*, or the "slain."[102]

According to the *Oxford English Dictionary* (OED), a variety of modern English expressions were first attested to that include the word hell in them. Thus, the expression, "hell breaks loose," was first employed in the 1630s. "Hell in a handbasket" is first attested in 1867, and "going to hell in a handbasket" in 1853.[103]

The *Oxford English Dictionary* first attests to "hell or high water" in 1874. Apparently, it is a derivation of "between the devil and the deep blue sea." Shakespeare uses "go to hell" in *The Merchant of Venice* around 1596 or 1597, and the idea of a "snowball's chance in hell" is attested in 1931 in American English. The expression "until hell freezes over," however, derives from British English first attested in 1832.[104]

If one just does something "for the hell of it," it may mean just for fun. It was first attested in American English in 1921. "Hell for leather" is another American expression from 1899, initially referring to riding on horseback, or so the OED tells us. "Hell on wheels" comes from 1843 and was originally the name of a steamboat on the Mississippi River. And even earlier, a "hell-wain," attested in Scotland in the 1580s, was a "phantom wagon seen in the night sky." At least according again to the OED.[105]

Distinct from a religious context, the word "hell" was considered to be profanity in America. Though its use was commonplace in American English, it was not heard on American television until after the 1970s. Many Americans still consider it a rude word.[106]

The expression "cold as hell" is most likely related to the fact that the deepest portion of hell in Dante's "Inferno" is a frozen lake into which the devil is frozen. Finally, another English word related to the Indo-Aryan *Kel* is "cellar," which is related to the Gaelic *ceilid*, meaning "to hide," "a place to hide things" or "a place of concealment."[107]

This brings us to the second section of this fourth chapter in which we will introduce and discuss the many Koine Greek names for hell in the twenty-seven books of the New Testament, in addition to the use of the Hebrew Bible's or Old Testament's *Abaddon*, which appears once in the Book of Revelation, at chapter nine, verse eleven, as well as to the other five words for hell in the New Testament.

Names for Hell in the New Testament

In the New Testament texts, there are several Koine Greek names for hell. Among these names are the following six:

1. Hades
2. Gehenna
3. The Lake of Fire
4. The Second Death
5. Tartarus
6. Abaddon

In this second section of Chapter Four, we will discuss these names for hell in reverse order, providing some background information on these New Testament Greek terms. The name *Abaddon*, which we saw in Chapter Three, was a parallel term for *Sheol* in that chapter. It only appears once in the New Testament, at the Book of Revelation 9:11. It informs us:

> **They had as King over them, the Angel of the Abyss, whose name in Hebrew is Abaddon, and whose name in Greek is Apollyon, that is Destroyer.[108]**

The "them" in Revelation 9:11, presumably, are the "locusts" mentioned at verse seven of the same chapter: "The locusts who looked like horses prepared for battle." This would make *Abaddon* both the king over the locusts and the "Angel of the Abyss," that is, an angel over a bottomless pit.

Revelation 9:11 goes on to equate *Abaddon* with the Greek *Apollyon*. The Hebrew *Abaddon* is employed at Psalm 88:1, which asks, "Is your love declared in the grave, your faithfulness in Destruction [*Abaddon*]." The rabbis of the Talmud made *Abaddon* the nethermost part of the two regions into which the Jewish underworld *Sheol* is divided.

This makes it very clear that the angel is not the Abyss, which is very clear in the Greek text. Both *Abaddon* in Hebrew, as well as *Apollyon* in Greek, mean "Destruction" and or "Destroyer."

In Chapter Three, we also saw that the six uses of *Abaddon* in the Hebrew Bible or Old Testament, at the Book of Job's 26:6, 28:22, and 31:12, as well as Psalm 88:11 and Proverbs 15:11 and 27:20, are all parallel to the idea of *Sheol*, which also means "Destruction."

The Greek name *Tartarus* is a name that goes all the way back to Greek mythology, where it is the name of a deep abyss used as a dungeon of torments for the Greek Titans. In his *Theogony*, Hesiod mentions *Tartarus* in the context of punishing the Titans. Plato, in his dialogue called the *Gorgias*, from around 400 BCE, suggests that *Tartarus* is where souls are judged after death and where the wicked receive divine punishment.[109]

Hesiod asserts that if a bronze anvil was dropped from the Heavens, it would not strike the Earth for nine days, and if it was dropped from the Earth, it would take another nine days to reach *Tartarus*. In Homer's *The Iliad*, around the eighth century BCE, tells us that *Tartarus* "is as far beneath Hades as Heaven is above the Earth." Apollodorus, who lived in fifth-century BCE Athens, makes the same point: "Tartarus is as far beneath Hades as Heaven is above the Earth." He adds, "It is a gloomy place, South of Hades, as far a distance from Earth as the Earth is from Heaven."[110]

For the ancient Greeks, *Tartarus* was considered to be a primordial force or god alongside entities such as the Earth, the Night, and Time. In Greek mythology, *Tartarus* was both a deity and a place in the underworld, or *Hades*. For the Greeks, *Tartarus* appears to have been the deepest part of the underworld.

In classical Greek, the verb *Tataroo* and the noun form *Tartarus* are both used. As a noun, it is the name of a subterranean region, doleful and dark, regarded by the ancient Greeks as the "abode of the wicked dead." Here, the wicked dead suffer punishment for their evil deeds. It is the Greek complement to the Hebrew *Gehenna*.

Second Peter 2:4 to 6 uses the word *Tartarus*, referring to a place of judgment where evil angels are judged. Jude, at verse six, also speaks of the same place for sinning angels. He calls it a place where "everlasting chains" may be found. We will say more about this passage in Second Peter in the next section of this fourth chapter.

Earlier, *Tartarus* can also be found in First Enoch 20:2, where it tells us that God placed the angel Uriel "in charge of the Land of Tartarus." It was generally believed at the time in Judaism, sometime between 400 and 200 BCE, that *Tartarus* is the part of Hades where the fallen angels have been sent.

In *Anead,* Virgil describes *Tartarus* in great detail in Book VI. He describes it as an "expansive space with a triple-walled perimeter to prevent sinners from escaping." Virgil also says that the River Phlegethon surrounds *Tartarus*, and its entry is guarded by a great Hydra with "fifty, black, gaping jaws," that sits behind columns waiting to defend the Land of Tartarus and keep the dead from escaping it.

Again, we will say more about the New Testament uses of *Taturoo* and *Tatarus* in the following section of Chapter Four. It is enough now, however, to point out that these terms are used twice in the New Testament. This brings us to the idea of the Second Death in the New Testament.

The idea of a "Second Death" is an eschatological expression in Judaism and Christianity, usually related in one way or another to punishment in the afterlife. The expression is not found in the Hebrew Bible or Old Testament but is found in several Hebrew and Aramaic Targumim, or Targums.

The Targum Neofiti, for example, related to the Targum on Deuteronomy, suggests that the expression "Second Death" refers to punishment after death and that the "First Death" is physical death.[111] The Targum Isaiah, an Aramaic paraphrase, at 22:14 contains the phrase, "until you die the second time," with no indication of what that means. The same text, at Isaiah 65:6, also refers to the Second Death.

The expression "Second Death" is also found in the Targum Jeremiah and the Targum on Psalms. Many of the readings of Psalm 49:11, such as in the Paris manuscript [number 10] and the Montefiori manuscript [number seven], contain the Aramaic translation, "He sees men wise in wickedness who die a Second Death."

There are two extant Rabbinic opinions about the meaning of "Second Death" in Judaism. The first is from Rabbi David Kimchi

(1160–1235), and the other is from twelfth-century Jewish philosopher and contemporary of Kimchi, Moses Maimonides (1138–1204). Kimchi believed the "Second Death" refers to the "death of the soul [*nefesh*] in the world." Maimonides declares in his *Thirteen Principles of Faith* that the "Souls of the wicked would be punished in annihilation," and that is what is meant by the "Second Death."

The term "Second Death" also occurs four times in the New Testament, all in the Book of Revelation. These come at 2:11, 20:6 and 14, and 21:8. We will say more about these four verses in the next section of this chapter. It is enough to say now that the term "Second Death" in the New Testament is employed these four times to speak of *Thanatos*, or "Death." This brings us to the idea of the "Lake of Fire."

The notion of a "Lake of Fire" can be found in ancient Egyptian texts among what are called the "Coffin Texts," as well as several papyri discovered in archaeological digs. The *Papyrus of Ani*, for example, which was written around 1250 BCE and is a version of the *Egyptian Book of the Dead*, has a description of a lake of fire guarded by four large baboons. The lake is red and appears to be filled with some sort of fiery liquid. More modern Egyptian scholars suggest that any influence of this text on the mentions of the Lake of Fire in the New Testament seems unlikely.

Many contemporary Christian denominations have their own peculiar observations about the New Testament's "Lake of Fire." The Jehovah's Witnesses, for example, believe that the passages in the New Testament imply complete annihilation of the soul after death. A similar view may also be found among the Seventh-day Adventists. They say the Lake of Fire refers to extinction and not to punishment after death.[112]

The Book of Mormon, at a passage known as Jacob 6:10, speaks of "Going to a Lake of Fire and Brimstone whose flames are unquenchable, and whose smoke ascends forever." It also tells us that the "Lake of Fire" and the "Second Death" are either related ideas or identical ideas.

The Catholic Portuguese mystic Lucia Santos reported that the Virgin Mary, the Lady of Fatima, gave her an opportunity to view hell, and she reported that it looked like a "Sea of Fire." Santos related, "Our Lady showed us a great sea of fire which seemed to be under the Earth, and plunged into the fire were demons and souls in human forms."

The idea of a lake of fire and ideas associated with it in the New Testament can be seen in the following texts:

Revelation 20:7–10 and 11–15
Revelation 21:8 and 15
Matthew 18:8
Matthew 25:41
Mark 9:43–48
Jude 1:7

Again, we will say far more about these New Testament passages on the "Lake of Fire," as well as related passages in the third section of this fourth chapter on the ideas of hell and after death. We will move now to some background material on the New Testament Greek word *Gehenna*.

The Koine Greek noun *Gehenna* is derived from an earlier Hebrew noun *Ge Bene Hinnom*, or "The Valley of the Sons of Hinnom," which was a deep, narrow glen in the south of Jerusalem, where some idolatrous Jews practiced child sacrifice to the Canaanite god *Moloch*. This fact is established at Second Chronicles 28:3 and 33:6, as well as Jeremiah 7:31 and 19 and 19:2 to 6. All of these passages condemn the child sacrifices to the god *Moloch*, which were eventually forbidden in the reforms in Judaism instituted by King Josiah in the seventh century BCE around 641 BCE.

The Second Book of Chronicles records that Josiah became king at the age of eight and his reforms began at that time. In modern scholarship these reforms are known as the Deuteronomic Reform.

It is important to point out that the idea of *Gehenna* began as a place where the worshippers of the Canaanite god *Moloch* sacrificed their children there. See Chronicles 28:3 and 33:6. To the Jews, this place of pagan idolatry and cruelty was an utter abomination. It appears that even apostate Jews followed the path of the Canaanites by practicing their own sacrifice of children as Jeremiah 7:31 and 32 and 19: 2–6 seem to indicate.

Thus, from the very beginning, the idea of the *Gehinnom* in Hebrew and the *Gehenna* in Koine Greek had both metaphysical and cultic overtones. *Gehenna* was a place of sacrifice as well as a place of filth. It was regarded as "unclean" in a religious sense. Things regarded as ritually unclean were dumped there—the carcasses of unclean dead animals, the bodies of executed criminals, and trash and refuse could all be found burning there.

To return to our discussion of the use of *Gehenna* in the New Testament, this same Valley of Hinnom afterward became the "Dump" for the city of Jerusalem. Here the dead bodies of animals, trash and garbage, as well as other refuse of the city were consumed in an everlasting fire. So over time, the site became synonymous with the idea of everlasting destruction.

The translators of the King James Version of the Bible routinely translate *Gehenna* as "hell." The Jewish historian, Josephus, does not mention the word *Gehenna*, nor does the second-century BCE translation of the Hebrew Bible, the Septuagint, but it renders the New Testament *Gehenna* with the Classical Greek word *Hades*.

Second Temple period literature and the Talmud mention the words *Gehinnom* and *Gehenna* many times. The Babylonian Talmud, at *Sukka* 42b, uses the Hebrew expression *Tzorh Rotachat*, or "boiling excrement," to describe the conditions of souls who have committed certain sins. He does this in the context of discussing *Gehinnom*. If it is not the most severe punishment in the afterlife, it is very close. Individuals sentenced there are not even given relief during *Shabbat*.

Rabbi Joseph Karo of Toledo (1488–1575) also discusses what he calls the *Sitra Achra*, or "Other Side," and he suggests that idol worship is the most "unforgivable sin," and that is precisely what those Jews who sacrificed their children to Moloch were doing. Rabbi Yehuda Lowe of Prague (1520–1609) points out that *Tzorh Rotachat* is the "lowest of the low" in *Sheol* the exact opposite of the "pure reason" used by God.

In the New Testament, the word *Gehenna* is employed twelve times in twelve different verses. These come at:

Matthew 5:22
Matthew 5:29
Matthew 5:30
Matthew 10:28
Matthew 18:9
Matthew 23:15
Matthew 23:33
Mark 9:43
Mark 9:45
Mark 9: 47
Luke 12:5
Letter of James 3:6

In the King James Version of the Bible, the word *Gehenna* appears thirteen times in eleven verses as "the Valley of Hinnom," the "Valley of the Son of Hinnom," and the "Valley of the Children of Hinnom." In Modern Hebrew, the name for the valley surrounding Jerusalem's Old City, including Mount Zion, from the west and the south, where it merges with the Kidron Valley, the other major valley around the Old City, near the southeastern corner of the city.

Again, we will make many comments on these New Testament verses that mention the Koine Greek noun *Gehenna* in our general discussion of the next section of this fourth chapter on the ideas of hell in the twenty-seven books of the New Testament. This brings us to our final New Testament name for "hell" the classical, as well as the Koine Greek word *Hades*.[113]

Our final name for "hell" in this section of Chapter Four is the word *Hades*, which we introduced in a previous chapter as the name of a Greek god, as well as the Greek underworld. The origin of the word is a bit obscure. Most scholars believe it is derived from the prefix *a* or "not" and the verb *dein* or "to see." Thus, it would mean a place that cannot be seen. Other scholars suggest the word *Hades* comes from the classical word *hado* which indicates something like "all receiving." This would suggest that after death, all go to the same place—*Hades*.[114]

In the New Testament, *Hades* is used for the general abode of the dead, whether good or evil. In the New Testament, Jesus affirms that he possesses the "keys" to the opening of death at the Book of Revelation 1:18. The writer of the Apocalypse sees "death riding a pale horse" followed by *Hades* at Revelation 6:8. Both Death and *Hades* will come to an end says Revelation 20:13 and 14, when the graves will "give up their bodies," a clear reference to the Resurrection of the Body at the end of time and the Second Coming of Jesus Christ.

The word *Hades* is translated at least three ways in the New Testament. First, as a synonym for the "grave," the place of bodily decay.[115] Second, as a place of punishment for the wicked. And finally, as a general designation for the unseen realm of the dead.

The word *Hades* is employed eleven times in the New Testament. In ten of those, the KJV translates it as "hell." The eleventh mention is at First Corinthians 15:55 (KJV), where the 1611 translators render the noun as "grave." This text asks us:

O death, where is thy sting? O grave [*Sheol*] where is thy victory?

The other ten employments of the word *Hades* come in the following places in the New Testament:

Gospel of Matthew 11:23
Gospel of Matthew 16:18
Gospel of Luke 10:15
Gospel of Luke 16:23
Acts of the Apostles 2:27
Acts of the Apostles 2:31
Revelation 1:18
Revelation 6:8
Revelation 20:13
Revelation 20:14

We will discuss all of these New Testament verses that mention *Hades* in our discussion that follows this section of Chapter Four on the names for hell in the New Testament. In fact, we will move to that discussion now.

Detailed Discussion of Hell in the New Testament

In this final section of Chapter Four, we will again reverse the order of our discussion of these passages in the New Testament, this time in the order in which they are listed originally in the second section of this chapter.

As we indicated earlier, the word *Hades* is employed eleven times in the New Testament. In one of those, at First Corinthians 15:51 (KJV), Paul renders *Hades* as "grave." Of the other ten uses of *Hades*, three are in the Gospels, one in Acts of the Apostles and four in the Book of Revelation. At Matthew 11:23, the writer speaks of being "brought down to *Hades*," and at 16:18, we are told that the "Gates of *Hades*" will "not prevail against the Church."

At the Gospel of Luke 10:15, we are told that the people of Capernaum "shall be thrust down in *Hades*." At 16:23, in the story of the rich man, while in *Hades*, he lifted up his eyes and being in torment, he sees Abraham from afar and Lazarus in his bosom, probably a reference to being "gathered to his fathers" we saw in Chapter Three.

The story of the "Rich Man and Lazarus" at Luke 16, if nothing else, is a parable about survival after death in early Christianity. Jesus tells his disciples and some Pharisees a narrative about a rich man and a poor beggar named Lazarus. Some say the point of the parable is that the poor man Lazarus is treated better in the afterlife than the rich man. Whatever the proper intentions of the narrative, it provides more information about survival after death in the New Testament.

The Acts of the Apostles 2:27 and 2:31 tell us about *Hades*:

> **Because you will not abandon me to the realm of *Hades*, you will not let your holy one see decay... And seeing what was to come, he spoke of the resurrection of the Messiah that he would not be abandoned to the realm of Hades, nor did his body see decay.**

The four references to *Hades* in the Book of Revelation come at 1:18, 6:8, 20:13 and 20:14. In the first of these the writer tells us that Jesus "has the keys of *Hades* and of Death." At Revelation 6:8, the writer sees a pale horse, and Death sat on it, and *Hades* follows them. Again, this verse speaks of Jesus having power over death.

At chapters 20:13 and 14, the writer of the Book of Revelation sees *Hades* delivering up the dead," and at verse 14, the text implies that after "Death and *Hades* are cast into the Lake of Fire," there will be no more Death nor *Hades*. The writer calls this the "Second Death."[116]

The word *Gehenna* is used thirty-six times in the New Testament. Twenty-two of those come in the Gospels, with twelve in Matthew, four in Mark, two in Luke, and three in the Gospel of John. Paul does not use the word G*ehenna*. He prefers *Hades*. Jude and James have single references to *Gehenna*. There are three in the Acts of the Apostles and seven mentions of *Gehenna* in the Book of Revelation.

If there is an overall theme in the uses of *Gehenna* in the New Testament, it is that nearly half of them are used in the context of the New Testament writers' desire to have early Christians live pious lives and that if they don't, they will suffer the punishments found there.

Among the passages of the New Testament where this theme may be seen are the following passages:

Matthew 5:22, 29 and 30
Matthew 10:28
Matthew 18:19
Matthew 23:15 and 33
Mark 9:43, 45 and 47
James 3:6

Earlier in this chapter, we introduced the idea of the Lake of Fire in the New Testament. Altogether, there are fourteen references to the phenomenon in the New Testament. Half of these are in the Book of Revelation. See, for example, 19:20, 20:10, 13, 14, 15, and 21:8. Matthew uses the expression "Lake of Fire" four times. These come at 13:42, 18:8, and 25:41 and 46.

The Gospel of Mark employs the idea of the Lake of Fire at 9:47 and 48, Paul uses the expression only at Second Thessalonians 1:8 and 9, Luke uses it once at 16:23, and the Gospel of John does not use Lake of Fire at all. The expression can be found, however, at Second Peter 2:4.

Many of the examples of a Lake of Fire in the New Testament are concentrated in the Book of Revelation, as we have indicated earlier. Revelation 20:14 identifies the Lake of Fire with the "Second Death." Revelation 20:10 associates the Lake of Fire with "having been deceived by the Devil." Revelation 20:15 relates that if your name does not appear in the Book of Life, "then you will be thrown into the Lake of Fire."

The idea of the Book of Life is a notion in both the Old and New Testaments, where it is believed that God has a "Roll" or ledger in which are written all the names of those who will be saved at the end of time. In the Hebrew Bible, this idea can be seen at Exodus 32:31 to 33, the Book of Daniel 12:1, Malachi 3:16, and Psalms 56:8, 69:27 and 28 and 139:16.

The psalmist, at 69:27, relates that the wicked will be "blotted out of the Book of Life." At 56:8, we find another possible reference to the Book of Life. In the NIV translation, the psalmist says:

Record my misery. List my tears on your scroll—Are they not on Your record?

In the New Testament, other references to the Book of Life may be seen at Luke 10:20, Hebrews 12:22 and 23, Philippians 4:3, as well as several other verses in the Book of Revelation, including 3:5, 13:8, 17:8, and 21:27. Luke 10:20 speaks about names recorded in Heaven, but it does not explicitly mention the Book of Life. At Philippians 4:3, Paul mentions his fellow workers who have shared the Gospels alongside him, and their names will be written in the Book of Life.

At Revelation 19:20, context mentions the beast, false prophets, deception, and the "mark of the Beast." These people are also thrown into the Lake of Fire that "burns with brimstone."

The passage in Second Peter 2:4 speaks of the idea of the fallen angels and how they were cast into a "furnace of fire" and "pits of darkness" reserved for judgment. The Gospel of Matthew 18:8 tells us that if one's hands or feet cause one to stumble, "they should be cut off and thrown into the fire."

As indicated earlier in this fourth chapter, the New Testament idea of a Second Death can be seen three times, all of these in the Book of Revelation. These come at 2:11, 20:6 and 14. In the first of these, the text reports, "Whoever has ears, let them hear what the Spirit says to the churches. The one who is victorious will not be hurt at all by the Second Death." This passage tells us little about what the Second Death might be.

We are provided a little more information from the two verses in chapter twenty of Revelation: 20:6 tells us that "The Second Death will have no power over those who share the First Resurrection." Presumably, this means the resurrection of Jesus Christ. At Revelation 20:14, the text again identifies the Second Death with Death and Hades. In fact, it tells us, "The Lake of Fire is the Second Death."

We have suggested earlier in this chapter that the Greek noun *Tartarus* is used at Second Peter 2:4 to 6 to speak of the punishment of the fallen angels who are cast into a place called *Tartarus*. This same text relates that these angels are chained in darkness that was only reserved by God for their judgment. The passage ends by making a point about those who wish to lead "ungodly lives."

Another verse in Jude's epistle also speaks of the place of the sinning angels. He calls it a place of "everlasting chains, for judgment on the Great Day." Presumably, this means the Second Coming, the day of the Resurrection of the Dead, and the life of the world to come.

It may be that *Tartarus* is the same as the Abyss or the Pit. It clearly is a place of judgment for wicked beings, angels and humans, but the translation of "hell" for *Tartarus* is probably not appropriate.

Finally, as we have indicated earlier, the name *Abaddon* is only employed a single time in the New Testament. It comes at the Book of Revelation's 9:11, which tells us, "They had as king over them the Angel of the Abyss, whose name in Hebrew is *Abaddon* and in Greek is *Apollyon*, that is, 'Destroyer.'"

In this verse, an angel named *Abaddon* is the head of an army of locusts. The Hebrew word *Abaddon* appears six times in the Hebrew Bible or Old Testament. These come at Job 26:6, 28:22 and 31:12; Psalm 88:11; and Proverbs 15:11 and 27:20. In all of these, *Abaddon* is either in parallel to *Sheol*, or it is translated as "Destruction."

Even when the Classical Greeks used the name *Tartarus*, it was employed as both the name of a deity and the name of a compartment of *Hades*. In ancient Orphic sources, as well as in the Greek mysteries tradition, *Tartarus* is an unbounded first existing from which the Light of the Cosmos can never be seen.

For Hesiod, *Tartarus* is as far from Earth as Earth is from Heaven. As Homer in the *Iliad* puts the geography, "Tartarus is far beneath

Hades, as Heaven is above the Earth."[117] In his poetry in the fifth century BCE Athens, Apollodorus relates that "*Tartarus* is as gloomy a place in *Hades*, and as far distant from the Earth as Earth is from the Heavens."[118]

In the New Testament, *Tartarus* is clearly a place of punishment, and the ultimate punishment for even the greatest of sinners is to be cut off from the possibility of communicating with God. Even in Classical times, the sins of the Titans—figures like Cronus and Sisyphus, for example—were sent to *Tartarus* so they could atone for their sins.

Cronus was punished for his imprisonment of the one-eyed Cyclops. Sisyphus defiled one of the favorite human maidens of Zeus, so his punishment was to push a boulder up the plane of a hill, only to have it roll to the bottom again. And this punishment goes on for all eternity.

In this more detailed discussion of the uses of words for "hell" in the New Testament, we may make the following conclusions. First, there are at least six names for hell found in the New Testament. Second, some of these names, like *Hades*, *Tartarus* and *Abaddon*, are related to traditions inherited from the Hebrew Bible or Old Testament. Third, other names for hell, like the Second Death and the idea of the Lake of Fire, seem more peculiar to the New Testament writers.

Fourth, although the Hebrew Bible or Old Testament mentions the place called *Gehinnom*, the Septuagint rendered it as Hades when it translated it into Greek, and when it was employed in the New Testament, it was used again to designate the place as *Gehenna.*

A fifth conclusion that may be known regarding our detailed discussion of the names for hell in the New Testament is many of these places designated as *Hades*, *Tartarus*, *Abaddon* and *Gehenna* in the New Testament are designated as places for punishment, both of fallen angels and of fallen human beings.

This brings us to the major conclusions we have made in this chapter, followed by Chapter Five, in which we will concentrate on views on hell and after death in early Judaism from the Apocryphal books of the Hebrew Bible until the period of the Talmud and the Mishnah, or from the second century BCE until the fifth century CE.

Conclusions

We began this fourth chapter with some observations on the origins of the modern English word "hell." In the process, we gave many cognates in other European languages, as well as the Germanic origins of the word and, ultimately, its derivation from the Indo-Aryan *Kel*, as we have shown in that first section of the chapter.

We also indicated in the first section that many modern English words are cognates of the Sanskrit *Kel* and the Old Norse and Old German *Hel*. Among these English words are hollow hole, whole and cellar.

Finally, in the first section of Chapter Four, we discussed a variety of modern English expressions with the word hell in them and the attestations of each found in the *Oxford English Dictionary*.

In the second section of Chapter Four, we introduced six separate names for hell found in modern English translations of the New Testament: *Hades*, *Gehenna*, the Lake of Fire, the Second Death, *Tartarus*, and *Abaddon.*

In this section, we discussed what these six names mean in the context of the New Testament, as well as where in the text the six are employed and how often. Indeed, we have shown that the words *Hades* and *Gehenna* are the most used terms in the New Testament to designate an eternal place of punishment.

In the second section of Chapter Four, we also summarized how our six names for hell have been translated in modern English translations of the New Testament, from the King James Version's translation from 1611 until the present time. The word *Hades*, for example, was translated three separate ways in the early seventeenth century, as we have indicated.

In the third and central section of Chapter Four, we conducted a detailed discussion of the places in the New Testament where these six names for hell are located and the contexts in which they have been placed. Thus, we have shown how these six names for hell are to be understood in the New Testament and how they have been translated.

As we have seen, some of these names, like *Hades* and *Gehenna*, are employed many times. Others, like *Tartarus* and *Abaddon*, are utilized infrequently, while Second Death and the Lake of Fire are used less often than *Hades* and *Gehenna* but more often than *Tartarus* and *Abaddon*.

In this third and final section of Chapter Four, we indicated that many of the connections between these six names for hell can be found in earlier ancient cultures, such as Egypt and Classical Greek culture, for example, and ancient Israel.

This brings us to Chapter Five, in which the subject matter shall be early Judaism from roughly the second century BCE until approximately 500 CE and the end of the early Rabbinic period. This will include Jewish Apocryphal books of the period, as well as mentions of hell and after death found in both forms of the Talmud and in the Mishnah. It is to early Judaism, then, to which we turn next.

Part II
Hell in the Medieval World

Hieronymus Bosch, *The Garden of Earthly Delights*, ca. 1480–1505.
Triptych center panel, oil painting on oak panel.
Museo del Prado, Madrid Spain.

Chapter Five
Hell in Early Judaism

A man is born and dies alone. And he experiences the good and bad consequences of his karma alone. And he goes alone to hell or the Supreme Abode.
—Chanakya

I imagine hell like this: Italian punctuality, German humor, and English wine.
—Peter Ustinov

Hell is not other people. Hell is yourself.
—Ludwig Wittgenstein

Introduction

The purpose of this fifth chapter is to make some observations about the ideas of *Sheol*, hell, *Gehenna*, and punishment after death in Jewish history from roughly the second century BCE until the end of the Rabbinic period around 500 CE. This goal will be accomplished by looking at three separate kinds of ancient Jewish writings.

First, we will explore what non-canonical Jewish books had to say about *Sheol*, hell, *Gehenna*, the afterlife and punishment after death. This will be followed by the second section of this chapter on the places in the Talmud where discussions of these issues at hand may be found. Finally, we will explore many of the places in the Mishnah where *Sheol* and the possibility of an afterlife and punishment after death may be found. We move next, then, to non-canonical literature.

The Idea of Hell in Non-Canonical Jewish Literature

By the word "non-canonical," we mean the ancient Hebrew and Aramaic religious texts that did not make it into the canon of the Hebrew Bible or Old Testament, which was most likely decided sometime between 300 BCE and 100 CE. Many of these non-canonical texts make references to, or simply discuss, the ideas of hell and after death in Judaism.

The Second Book of Maccabees is an ancient Jewish text that focuses on the Maccabean Revolt of the second century BCE against Antiochus IV Epiphanes, and it ends with the defeat of the Seleucid Empire under General Nicanor in 161 BCE by Judas Maccabeus, the hero of the tale. The style of Second Maccabees suggests it was probably written in Koine Greek, probably in Alexandria, a generation after the episodes depicted in the book.[119]

Second Maccabees is important for our purposes because chapter seven of the work speaks of what is known as "The Martyrdom of a Mother and Her Seven Sons." One after the other, the seven sons die by torture and executions. When the fourth was near death, he says this about his impending demise:

> **It is my choice to die at the hands of mortals with the hope that God would restore me to life, but to you [his executioners], he says, "There will be no resurrection to life."**

After describing the death of the seventh brother, all of whom would not give up their faith, the mother says in the same Chapter at verses 22 and 23:

> **I do not know how they came to be in my womb, it was not I who gave you the breathe and life, nor was it I who arranged the elements you are made of. Therefore, since it is the Creator of the Universe who shaped the beginning of humankind and brought about the origins of everything, He, in His mercy, will give you back both breathe and life, because you now disregard yourselves for the sake of His law.**

From these two passages in Second Maccabees 7, we learn the following things. First, it is ultimately God alone who is responsible for the giving of "breathe and life." Secondly, if there is survival after death in the Maccabean Revolt, the form of it shall be Resurrection of the Body, the same view found in another text, possibly as a response to the Seleucids, the Book of Daniel 12:1 to 3 written around the same time in the 160s BCE.

In a second non-canonical text known as Fourth Maccabees, particularly in chapters 9 and 17, we see more references to the phenomena of survival after death in early Judaism. Fourth Maccabees is written in the form of a homily or a philosophical discourse that, among other things, praises reason over passion. Like Second Maccabees, Fourth Maccabees was also most likely completed in Greek in Alexandria, Egypt, in the second century BCE. Although Fourth Maccabees is not canonical for the Jews, nor for most Christian churches, it is part of the canon in the Greek and Romanian Orthodox churches.

At 9:8 of Fourth Maccabees, the text suggests a connection between the suffering of believers and a prize for the endurance of that suffering. The writer of the text relates,

> **For we, through this severe suffering and endurance, shall have the prize of virtue and shall be with God, on whose accounts we suffer.**

The "shall be with God" part of the verse may well be an assent to survival after death at the end of time, as in Second Maccabees, resurrection of the body.

In Fourth Maccabees 17:15, we see a return to the theme of endurance with suffering, and at verse 18 we see the reward,

> **Because of which they now stand before the divine throne and live the life of eternal blessedness.**

Here the form of survival after death, however, is not the Hebrew resurrection of the body, but the Greek idea of immortality of the soul, for the soul is already experiencing the survival.

In chapters 4 and 8 of a third non-canonical Jewish text, Second Esdras, we see other references to survival after death. Second Esdras is the name of an apocalyptic book in many English Bibles. It is ascribed to Ezra, a scribe and priest from the fifth century BCE. More modern scholars, however, date the book somewhere between 70 CE and 218.

At chapter 4:7–8, Ezra encounters the angel Uriel, and they have a conversation about Paradise and the underworld. Uriel asks,

How many dwellings are in the depths of the Sea, and how many springs are at the source of the Great Abyss. And how many paths are there above the dome, or which are the exits of Paradise?

The "Great Abyss" is most likely a reference to the underworld. Ezra answers:

I have not descended into the Abyss, nor as yet into hell, nor have I ascended to Heaven. But I have only asked you here about fire and wind and the day you have passed through, things you can't exist without, and you have not answered me about them.

The word for "hell" in the original Hebrew is the noun *Sheol*. The *BibleGateway* group uses the KJV translation for their website, so this is one of those many places where the seventeenth-century English translators chose to render *Sheol* as "hell."

In Second Ezdras 8:53–54, we may see another non-canonical reference to the afterlife and/or hell. The verse relates:

The root of evil is sealed off from you, weakness is abolished from you, and death is hidden; the Netherworld and decay have fled to oblivion. Sorrows have passed, and the treasure of immortality is displayed to the end.

In this non-canonical pair of verses, the form of survival of death is again immortality of the soul, as it was in Fourth Maccabees 17. These verses also make the claim that the Netherworld and the decay of the bodies that could be found there have "fled to oblivion," though we cannot be sure of just what the writer means by that expression.

Another passage from Fourth Esdras 7: 32–38, which was written in Hebrew but was then translated into Greek and then into Latin and now we only have the Latin Version that is extant, speaks of "And the Earth shall give up those who are asleep in it." This appears to be a reference to the Final Judgment at the end of time.

Then the same text goes on to speak of:

Then the pit of torment shall appear and opposite it shall be a place of rest And the furnace of hell shall be disclosed and

opposite it the Paradise of Delight. Then the Most High will say to the nations that have been raised from the dead, "Look now and understand whom you have denied, whom you have not served, whose commandments you have despised. Look on this side and then on that. Here are delight and rest, and there are fire and torments. Thus, He will speak to on the day of Judgment.

This Latin version of Fourth Esdras, which was translated from the Greek, renders the "furnace of hell" in verse thirty-six as *elibanus gehennae*. *Gehennae*, of course, in the Latin transliteration of *Gehenna*, which in turn is the Greek transliteration of *Gehennom.*

There are also several passages in Books III and V of the *Sibylline Oracle*, a collection of oracular utterances written in Greek hexameters ascribed to a prophetess named Sibyls who made clear her revelations in a very frenetic way. Fourteen of her books and several fragments of the *Sibylline Oracles* survive. The earliest extant editions are from the sixth and seventh centuries CE.

Many of the passages of the *Sibylline Oracles* appear to be forerunners of the most apocalyptic passages in the Book of Revelation. One famous passage is an acrostic spelling out a Christian code with the first letter in successive lines.

For our purposes, Book III: 393 and Book V: 58 and 178 are the most important passages. In Book III, Sibyls speaks of,

An aged mortal man, a false writer and from a doubtful native land, and in his eyes the light shall fade away for he will have great skill when it comes to immortality, as well as Resurrection.

In this passage, she mentions both the Hebraic view of Resurrection and the Greek perspective of surviving death by immortality of the soul.

In Book V of the *Sibylline Oracles* at section 58, she tells us of "the immortal Thunderer in Heaven and those who worship stones and beasts instead of God and thus they deny the immortality that the Thunderer can impart on them." Here, it appears to be Immortality as the form of survival. The "Thunderer" is most likely God, but we cannot be sure about that identification.

At Book V: 178, the oracle gives this advice that includes some thoughts about Resurrection:

> **Escape not fate unseemly, but shall we, worn and weary unto death, him from foreign dust that of Nemea's flower, and he shall hide a corpse; and after him, he shall be decked with a silver helmet and he has been resurrected.**

Among non-canonical books with observations about the afterlife are three "Testaments"—The Testament of Levi, the Testament of Benjamin, and the Testament of Reuben. Levi's comments comes at 4:5; Benjamin's at 9:5; and Reuben's at 4:5.

The Testament of Levi was originally an Aramaic work, most likely completed sometime near 100 CE. There are many connections between this document and texts discovered among the Dead Sea Scrolls, as well as many theological affinities to the Essene community near the Dead Sea at Qumran.

The Testament of Levi at 4:5 to 7 gives us the following assurance:

> **Work righteousness, therefore, my children, upon the Earth that you have it as a treasure in Heaven. And sow good things in your souls that you may find them in your life. But if you sow evil things, you shall reap every evil and affliction.**

Although this passage speaks about souls, it is not clear whether the reward spoken of in Heaven is by immortality of the soul or Resurrection of the Dead.

The Testament of Benjamin is another Aramaic texts most likely written at the end of the first century CE. The text may have originated in Jericho, or in Jerusalem, where the tribe of Benjamin settled.

At the Testament of Benjamin's 9:5 to 10 speaks of eternal reward. This text explains:

> **Nevertheless, the Temple of God shall be your portion and this last Temple shall be more glorious than the first. And the twelve tribes shall be gathered together there and all the Gentiles until the Most High shall send forth salvation in the visitation of an only begotten Prophet. And he shall enter into the first Temple and there shall the Lord be treated with outrage, and he shall be lifted up upon a tree... And He shall ascend from Hades and shall pass from the Earth into Heaven. And I know how lowly he shall be upon the Earth, and how glorious he shall be in Heaven.**

The Testament of Reuben is also an Aramaic text completed at the end of the first century CE. The text mostly deals with the problem of sexual promiscuity. This is most likely because Genesis 35:22 tells us that "Reuben defiled his father's bed" by sleeping with his father's concubine. The writer of the Testament of Reuben uses these events to admonish his readers not to fall into similar practices.

Even though this is the major theme of the work, in the Testament of Reuben at chapter 4:5 to 7, we find more confirmation of survival after death:

> **Therefore, my children, I say unto you, observe all this whatsoever that I command of you, and you shall not sin. For the pit unto the soul is the sin of fornication, separating it from God and the promise of eternal life. For many have fornication destroyed because a man brings reproach upon himself with the sons of men and derision with Beliar.**

Here, the author distinguished between those who have been promised "eternal life" and those who have brought "reproach upon themselves" and will end up in the company of *Beliar*, another name for Satan in the Second Temple period.

Another interesting non-canonical text that speaks of the afterlife is Second Baruch chapter 56:6, which speaks of Sheol as a personified deity in search of blood revenge. This verse serves as a link between the sometimes-personified Sheol in the Hebrew Bible and the defeated Deceiver that we shall see in the next chapter on hell in the earliest patristic sources.

Finally, several passages in First Enoch, as well as in *The Wars* of Josephus, also speak of a hell-like state and punishment after death. The text known as First Enoch is a Hebrew apocalyptic text ascribed by tradition to Enoch, the great-grandfather of Noah. The book contains unique information on the origins of demons and giants and why some angels fell from Heaven while others did not.

In the opening of chapter 27 of First Enoch, he asks the angel Raphael what the purpose shall be of the Valley of Hinnom. The angel responds this way:

> **Here they will be gathered together and will be their place of Judgment. And in the Last Days there shall be a spectacle of**

> **Judgment upon them, In front of the righteous forever. For her the Merciful will bless the Lord of glory, the Eternal King.**

In this non-canonical passage from the Book of Enoch, we see what is perhaps the best distinction between the fate of the sinners and the fate of those who follow the Eternal King. The former will be damned, while the latter have been promised Resurrection and eternal life at the end of time.

In his *The Wars*, the Jewish historian Josephus also makes sporadic comments on *Sheol*, *Hades*, and the fate of the dead. At Book II, section 162, and Book XVIII, section one to three, the Jewish scholar addresses these issues. There is also something known as "Dissertation V: Concerning Hades, Wherein are Contained the souls of the Righteous and the Unrighteous."

Josephus begins this essay this way:

> **And this is the discourse concerning daemons. Now, as to Hades, wherein the souls of the righteous and unrighteous are detained, it is necessary to speak of it. Hades is a place in the world not regularly finished; a subterraneous region, wherein the light of this world does not shine... This region is allotted as a place of custody for souls.**

Josephus goes on in the same essay to speak of a region "in which there is a certain place set apart as a 'Lake of unquenchable Fire.' Here the unjust go and those who have been disobedient of God." These people, Josephus relates, "will be adjudged to this everlasting punishment, while the just shall obtain an incorruptible and never fading kingdom." These people are also confined in Hades but not to the same places as the unjust.

Josephus then relates that the just reside in the "bosom of Abraham in preparation for an eternal, new life in Heaven." But the unjust are dragged by force by the angels allotted to minister punishment in Hades. This is a place "whose gate we believe there stands an Archangel with a host of angels appointed over souls."

In section 6 of the *Dissertation*, Josephus tells us that the end of time, "the just, as well as the unjust, shall be brought before God and He, the Father, will be committed to 'all judgment.'" It is clear that the

Jewish historian Josephus is referring to the idea of judging both the just and the unjust at the end of time when "the bodies of all human beings shall be resurrected."

Thus, in this material we have presented on non-canonical views on survival after death, we may make the following conclusions. First, there are many Jewish texts of this type that speak of a hell-like state and/or punishment after death. Secondly, some texts appear to endorse the Hebraic idea of Resurrection of the Body. Thirdly, some texts also appear to confirm the idea of immortality of the souls after death. Fourthly, some of these non-canonical texts we have examined in this section of Chapter Five seem to combine the two perspectives.

Some of these conclusions are also most likely connected to the ways that *Sheol* and *Gehenna* were employed just before and after the time of Christ. This is the subject matter of the next section of Chapter Five.

Sheol, Gehenna, and the Garden of Eden in the Early Rabbinic Period

The development of notions of life after death in early Judaism must be put within the context of the destruction of the First Temple in Jerusalem in 586 BCE, a period when several of the Israelite prophets, like Amos, Hosea, and Isaiah, for example, all began forecasting a better future for the Jewish people.

After repeated military defeats and episodes of exile and dislocation, the early history culminated with the destruction of the Second Temple as well in 70 CE. Jewish thinkers began to lose any hope in an immediate change. Instead, they began expressing their hope in expectations of a messianic future, as well as beliefs in survival after death. This was linked with incursions of Hellenistic philosophy and ideas related to the soul and immortality.

The catastrophe of 70 CE caused a theological crisis. How could it be that the God of Israel would allow his people to be destroyed and vanquished at the hands of the Roman Empire? The rabbis in the period had a difficult time explaining why good and morally decent individual Jews were made to suffer.

In a section of the Mishnah called the Pirkei Avot at 4:21, Rabbi Ya'akov compared this world to an antechamber that leads to what he called the *Olam-Ha-Ba*, or "The World to Come." He observes, "While a righteous person might suffer in this life, he or she will certainly be rewarded in the next world, and that reward will be a much greater one." Some Rabbis of the period even went as far to say that Jews were made to suffer in this life so that their reward will be that much better in the *Olam-Ha-Ba*.

Several new Hebrew theological terms developed in the period or were augmented in some ways. The term *Gan Eden*, or the "Garden of Eden" began to refer to a heavenly realm where souls reside after physical death. The name itself seems to show that the rabbis wished to return to the period of Adam and Eve in a blissful Paradise.

It was generally believed that the souls of the dead in *Gan Eden* existed in a disembodied state until the time of bodily resurrection in the days of the Messiah. One interesting Talmudic story about *Olam-ha-Ba* when Rabbi Joseph, the son of Rabbi Joshua ben Levi, dies and then comes back to life. Then:

> **His father asked him, "What did you see?" He answered, "I beheld a world the opposite of this world, those who were on top here were below there, and vice-versa." He [Joshua ben Levi] said to him, "My son, you have seen a corrected world."[120]**

Another idea that began to be reinterpreted in the period was the new uses of the idea of *Gehenna*, which now among some Jews began to be seen as a place of punishment and purification. Some Messianic Jews saw *Gehenna* as a place of torture and punishment, and even fire and brimstone. Other Jewish factions imagined it less harshly, as a place where one reviews the words and deeds of one's life, while repenting for past misdeeds.

In another place of the Mishnah, as we shall see later in this fifth chapter, the soul's sentence in *Gehenna* is usually limited to a period of twelve months of purgation and repentance until it is taken to its place in the *Olam-Ha-Ba*. This twelve-month period is also reflected in the year-long mourning cycle, as well as the recitation of the memorial prayer for the dead called the *kaddish*.[121]

The area in Israel known as the "Valley of Hinnom," is also referred to as the *Tophet* or *Topheth*, which was a location in the valley where worshippers, as well as some kings of Judah, burned their children alive as sacrificial victims to the gods Moloch and the Great Baal. After which time the valley was believed to be cursed.

In time in both Judaism and Christianity, *Tophet* became a theological and poetic synonym for "hell." *Gehennom*, or *Gehenna*, became the destination for the wicked in rabbinic literature. Later, the Arabic name for hell in Islam, as we shall see in a later chapter, is *Jahannam*, which comes directly from the word *Gehenna*. In contemporary Israel, the name for the valley surrounding Jerusalem's Old City, including Mount Zion, is the Valley of Hinnom which merges with the Kidron Valley.

Sheol and *Hades* also began to be reinterpreted in the early Rabbinic period of Judaism. They are now regarded as an antechamber of sorts where the soul goes after death to "wait" for the general Resurrection, in which all people will experience the reunion of the body and the soul. For some, *Sheol* or *Hades* also became a place for atoning and for regeneration.

Sheol and *Hades* became the names of places for purgation, purification and cleansing, a place where one atoned for one's sins, and thus, as some rabbis put the matter, "sin itself is burned out of you, like a fire burning consuming rotten wood."

For modern Hasidic Judaism, once purged—whenever that occurs—the soul that is resurrected with its body proceeds on to heavenly happiness in the unceasing Kingdom of God. These *hasids* tend to dismiss the idea of a hell-like state, where wicked people remain eternally and are punished eternally.

This brings us to the third section of Chapter Five where we shall discuss many of the places in the Jerusalem Talmud and the Babylonian Talmud, in which the issues of a hell-like state, survival after death, and punishment after death are the subject matters to be found there.

Hell in the Talmud

There are many comments to be found in the Talmud that deal with the idea of hell and after death. In Eruvin 19b, for example, we are told that all but the most wicked are sent to *Gehenom*, which, according to Berakhot 57b, is a very fiery place."

At Rosh Hashanah 17a, we are told that "The torment of hell [*Gehenom*]" are said to be temporary for most sinners—but instead of ending up in Heaven, they actually end in non-existence. The same tractate, at 16b to 17a, it tells us that on "Judgment Day there will be three groups or kinds of people." Those who were "thoroughly righteous," those who are "thoroughly wicked," and those who "are of an intermediate state."

The first group will receive "everlasting life." The second group will be "doomed to Gehennom." In fact, the text quotes the Book of Daniel 12: 1–3 on the matter. The intermediate group, the Talmud tells us, "will go down to Gehennom and the squeal and rise again," and they will be brought through the fire and it will refine them as silver is refined.

The same tractate, at Rosh Hashanah 17a relates that after twelve months the "body is consumed and the soul is burnt and the wind scatters it under the soles of the feet of the righteous." This idea that life in Gehiennom will only last a period of twelve month at the most, is repeated many times in both the Talmud and the Mishnah.

At Rosh Hashanah 17a, we also learn that while a soul is being purged of its sins in Gehennom, God will forgive the first transgression, but if the person continues to sin, then the sin that had been forgiven God now counts it against the overall slate of the person, and He will mete out punishment accordingly.

The Bava Metzia, in tractate 4, informs us that "Everyone who goes down to *Gehinnom* goes up quickly, except these three: One who had relations with a married woman; one who has not followed the precepts of the Torah; and one who has taken the life of another Jew." The Metzia appears to be at odds with the Rosh Hashanah about how long a person's time in *Gehinnom* shall be.[122]

Another section of the Talmud, this time at Gittin 57a, as well as a companion piece at Tanit 30b, we learn that one way to discover the righteous after burial is by the fact that many of their corpses "do not decompose while in the grave." In fact, the Tanit suggests these bodies do not decompose between death and burial, as well.

The Sotah at tractate 5b explains that "The man who is humble at spirit will have his spirit among those in *Gehinnom* who will eventually experience eternal life at the time of the Resurrection to come.

At section 10a of the Sanhedrin, there is a lengthy discussion of who has priority when a righteous man and a wicked man are in a dispute. The Sanhedrin says the dispute should hinge on witnesses, and their time in the world to come shall be punished or rewarded accordingly. At tractate 99a of the Sanhedrin, it relates that the "Messianic Age," the Age of the Messiah, will only last "seventy years," after which time a "New Age shall be ushered in."

In the Babylonian Talmud 84a suggests that the Sun turns red in the evening because it passes over the entrance to *Gehennom*, where red is also the predominant color in the part of the underworld called *Gehennom.*

Rabbi Eleazer, in Niddah 8b, supplies an analogy for understanding the righteous and the not-so-righteous. He said you should regard them like a tree and the fruit it bears. A good, righteous tree will bear good fruit. And a bad tree does not bear good fruit. "But in the case of a tree that does not bear good fruit, they agree that its sap is considered to be its fruit."

Rabbi Eleazer goes on to compare these two kinds of trees to two kinds of souls in the afterlife. The good souls who, when alive on the Earth bore good fruit, and the unrighteous souls who bear no fruit but their sap. It is the later kind of souls that Rabbi Eleazer believed who are punished in *Gehennom*.

Rabbi Yahonan, at Berakhot 17b, makes similar remarks about the Book of Job, pointing out that all animals and humans shall die. But those who grew up in the Torah and whose labor is in the Torah, and who gives pleasure to his Creator, "and who grew up with a good name and who took leave of this world with a good name, and who was faultless in this life reaches the day of his death on a higher level than he was at the outset."

And for Rabbi Yohanan, this means that they "shall have a higher place in the *Olam HaBa,* [or the World to Come]," as well. The Rabbi tells us that the best places in the afterlife are reserved for those "who have the Torah in their hearts, and who guard their mouths from all transgressions."

In another tractate of the Berakhot, at 34b, Rabbi Yohanan asks, "What is the meaning of he who is far?" He says, "This refers to the full-fledged righteous who was distant from acts of transgression from the beginning." And what is meant by the who was near? Rabbi Yohanan tells us:

> **This refers to the penitent who was close to an act of transgression but has now distanced himself from it, and to whom peace is extended only after it has been extended to him who has been righteous from the outset.**

In the same tractate, Rabbi Yohanan also raises the question of whether the *Gan Eden*, or the "Garden of Eden," and Paradise are the same thing or different things. The rabbi sides with different things on the strength of Genesis 2:10, which speaks of a "river that went out of Eden to water the Garden."

Finally, in another passage of the Niddah, at tractate 30b, the Talmud tells us that before any fetus is born, the angels are assigned to tell the fetuses if they will be righteous or wicked. To the righteous, the angels say, "The Creator gave you a soul that is pure. If you preserve it in its state of purity, all will be well for you. But if you do not keep it pure than I, the Angel, will take it from you."

Thus, in the Talmud, we see many comments about *Gehnnom* and who is to be found there. It states that there are three types of humans who go to the afterlife—the righteous, the sinners, and the intermediate people. Finally, an overall evaluation of the Talmud on the afterlife is that it predominately speaks of the kinds of life that people had lived before their deaths, and they are punished or rewarded accordingly.

This brings us to the fourth and final section of Chapter Five, in which we will introduce and discuss many of the places in the Mishnah where the topics of conversation were a hell-like state or punishment after death.

Hell and After Death in the Mishnah

The Mishnah is the edited record of a complex body of material known as the "Oral Torah" that was transmitted in the aftermath of the destruction of the Second Temple in Jerusalem by the Romans in 70 CE. It was published at the end of the second century CE. Rabbi Judah the Patriarch, also known as Rabbi Judah the Prince and Yehudah Hanasi, undertook the collection and editing of the Halachot, or Oral Law, so that these traditions would not vanish.

There are a variety of passages in the Mishnah about hell and the punishment of souls after death. Many of them confirm judgments about these matters we have seen in the Jerusalem Talmud and the Babylonian Talmud we have seen in the previous section of this chapter.

A text known as the Pirkei Avot, which translates in English as the "Chapters of the Fathers," is one of the best examples of a Mishnah text that speaks of hell and after death. Tractate one of the Pirkei Avot, it tells us about the conditions of the Jews after the destruction of the Temple:

> **Moreover, he saw a skull floating on the face of the water. He said to it, "Because you have drowned others, they now drown you. And in the end, those that drowned you will be drowned."**

About the bodies of the dead, the same tractate continues,

> **The more flesh, the more worms; the more property, the more anxiety; the more wives, the more witchcraft. The more female slaves, the more lewdness. The more male slaves, the more robbery. But the more Torah, the more life in the afterlife.**

In fact, at 1.5 of the Pirkei Avot, we are told:

> **As long as a man engages in too much conversation with women, he causes evil to Himself, he neglects his study of the Torah and in the end, he will inherit *Gehin-nom*.**

In tractate 4 of the Pirkei Avot, the text tells us:

> **The more precious is one hour in repentance and good deeds in this world than all the life in the world to come. And more precious is one hour of the tranquility of the world to come than all the life of this world.**

In the Eduyot, another text of the Mishnah at 2:10, we are told, "The judgment of the wicked in *Gehennom* only continues for twelve months." This, of course, is a judgment we have seen earlier in the Talmud.

Several passages in the Shabbat, a third Mishnaic text, also speak of justice after death. At the Shabbat's 33a, we learn that:

Due to the sin of delay of justice, judges withhold their rulings due to personal considerations and for distortion of justice, that is, judges intentionally distort their verdicts and from this violence and looting abound in the world. As it is written, "And I will bring a sword upon you that shall execute the vengeance of the covenant."

At 63a, the Shabbat informs us that, "All of the prophets only prophesied with regard to the Messianic Age." However, regarding the world to come it was stated, "No eye sees God except You, the faithful."

On the other hand, the Shabbat tells us, "What awaits the sinner in the life to come are not to be depicted, which is why they will be eliminated in the Messianic Age when they will disintegrate to oblivion. Thus, the Shabbat tells us that the righteous will be saved and see the face of God, while the sinners will eventually disintegrate in the life to come.

Tractate 152b of the Shabbat also speaks of the fate of the righteous, as well as the not-so-righteous, in the life to come. Rabbi Hiyya, with support from the Book of Job 14:22, indicates that the dead in Sheol are aware of the pain of his flesh in the grave. Using Ecclesiastes 12:7, Rabbi Hiyya, arguing against those who say that the deceased are aware only until the tomb is sealed, says, "And the dust returns to the Earth as it was and the spirit returns to God who gave It." This indicates that when the body returns to the Earth, the spirit, or *ruah*, also returns to its place and is no longer aware of what is happening to the body.

Tractate 152b of the Shabbat also confirms the existence of the ungodly in the afterlife for whom "There is no peace," for regarding their souls, it states, "they will be projected out as in the hollow of a sling."

Tractate 152b of the Shabbat also contains a debate of sorts about the fate of the righteous after death between Rabbi Ahai and Rabbi Nahman. The former favored the Spirit having consciousness in the afterlife, while the latter, on the strength of Ecclesiastes 12:7, believed that "The dust will return to the Earth as it was."

Several conclusions can be made about this material from the Mishnah in regard to the nature and extent of a hell-like state, as well as punishment after death in the opinions of the Rabbis of the Oral Law concerning righteous humans, as well as sinners in the life to come.

Among these conclusions about this material from the Mishnah on a hell-like state and punishment after death in the Mishnah are the following. First, the Mishnah speaks of the conditions of the bodies of the Jewish people after the destruction of the Second Temple. Secondly, some tractates of the Mishnah speak of the punishment of souls, or *nefeshim*, after death in *Gehennom.*

Thirdly, the Mishnah reiterates the idea that the most time a Jew shall spend in *Gehennom* is twelve months, a judgment we had seen earlier in this chapter regarding the Talmud.

Fourthly, souls who reside in *Gehennom* have the opportunity to atone for their sins in the fires there, the same way that silver may be made pure in the smithing process. This refining of souls is an important process in the Mishnah's views of the afterlife.

And finally, the overall theory that lies behind the views of the writers of the Mishnah regarding a hell-like state and punishment after death is that one's relationship to the Torah and how well one's life on Earth followed its precepts is the number one determination for one's existence in *Gehennom.*

It is important to understand that although the Hebrew Bible or Old Testament texts describe *Sheol* as a permanent place for the dead, in the Second Tempe period, from roughly 500 BCE until 70 CE, a more diverse set of ideas developed, as we have shown in this chapter.

Sheol in the Second Temple period is considered to be the home of both the righteous and the wicked, separated into their own distinct compartments. In some traditions in the period, Gehenna was considered a place of punishment alone meant only for the wicked dead. When the Hebrew scriptures were translated into Greek by the ancient Alexandrian Jews, around 200 BCE, the word *Sheol* was translated as *Hades*, and this becomes reflected in the New Testament views, as we have seen in Chapter Four.

This brings us to the major conclusions we have made in this fifth chapter, followed by Chapter Six where we shall explore what the church fathers in the first five centuries of Christianity have said or have written about the ideas of hell in the afterlife.

Conclusions

We began this chapter by making some observations about what non-canonical texts in the Jewish tradition said about hell and after death. Among the texts we examined in this first section were Second and Fourth Maccabees, Second Esdras, some passages in the Sibylline Oracles, as well as sections of the Testament of Levi, the Testament of Benjamin, the Testament of Reuben, as well as places in Jewish historian Josephus' *The Wars.*

In the first section of Chapter Five, we have seen many observations and discussions about *Gehennom* and the idea of punishment after death in Early Judaism in each of these many non-canonical Jewish sources.

In the second section of Chapter Five, we introduced a number of ideas in Rabbinic Judaism that may be found in discussions of the afterlife. Among these ideas we have introduced are the *Gan Eden*, or the Garden of Eden, and the Greek *Gehenna* that appears in some of these texts.

In the third section of this chapter, we introduced and discussed many of the places in the Talmud where hell and after death is explored in the Talmud, both the Babylonian Talmud and the Jerusalem Talmud.

Among the tractates of the Talmud that we have examined in the third section of Chapter Five were passages from the Berakhot, the Rosh Hashanah, the Eruvim, the Gittin, the Niddah and the Tanit.

In the fourth and final section of Chapter Five, we have introduced and discussed several key passages in the Mishnah, the Oral Law Tradition of Early Judaism where the idea of a hell-like state and punishment after death are the subject matter.

More specifically, we examined tractates from the Pirkei Avot, or the "Chapters of the Fathers," three sections from the Mishnah's Shabbat, at 33a, 63a, and 152a, that also contain a debate of sorts about the fate of the *ruah*, or "spirit," after death. We also have seen in the Shabbat that the stay in *Gehinnom* for any believer will be no longer than twelve months because by that time, one's sins will be "purified," and the soul will be able to experience eternal life in the world to come, or *Olam Ha Ba*.

What we have seen in this material from the Mishnah is that the ancient Jews in the early Rabbinic period during the Second Temple period had begun to incorporate ideas the Jews had borrowed from Greek philosophy. The notion of Immortality of the Soul allowed the Jews to speak of some kind of life in *Sheol* or *Gehennom*, another Greek idea.

Ultimately, the Second Temple Jewish scholars, like their Christian counterparts, began to see the afterlife as a place for punishment after death and ultimately to tie it to the idea of the Resurrection of the Body at the end of time in Biblical texts like the Book of Daniel 12:1 to 3, where "Some will be resurrected to eternal life and some to perdition."

For Rabbinic Judaism, the most fundamental understanding of the afterlife was that one's life on Earth and how one followed the many precepts of the Torah is the final determination of what sort of existence one's *nefesh* or *ruah*—that is, "soul" and "spirit"—will have in *Sheol*, or the "Great Abyss," and *Gehennom*, or the place of punishment, in the afterlife of Rabbinic Judaism.

The subject matter of Chapter Six in this history of views about hell and after death is what the early church fathers, from the first to the fifth centuries, have had to say about hell.

Pieter Brueghel the Elder, *Mad Meg* (Dutch: *Dulle Griet*), 1563. Oil on panel, 115×161 cm. Museum Mayer van den Bergh, Antwerp, Belgium.

Chapter Six
Hell in the Early Church

The darkest places in hell are reserved for those
who maintain their neutrality in times of moral crisis.
—Dante Alighieri

The mind is its own place and, in itself,
can make a Heaven of hell or a hell of Heaven.
—John Milton

Eskimo: "If I did not know about God and sin, would I go to hell?"
Priest: "No, not if you did not know."
Eskimo: "Then why did you tell me about it?"
—Annie Dillard

Introduction

The purpose of this sixth chapter is to examine the many views on hell and after death in the early Christian Church from the first to the fifth centuries. We will fulfill this purpose by looking at separate sections in the chapter on perspectives from the first century CE, the second century, the third, fourth, and fifth centuries, culminating in the work of Augustine of Hippo on the matters at hand. The material from the first and second centuries, for the most part, are works that were completed post the New Testament, so after the year 150 CE, which is where we will begin in this chapter.

Hell in the First and Second Centuries of Christianity

One of the earliest references to hell post the New Testament can be found in the Epistle of Barnabus. The author of the text is unknown, but it clearly was not Barnabus, an associate of Paul who is mentioned in the Acts of the Apostles. The letter was written to help in the conversion of new Christians.

The date of the Epistle of Barnabus is not clear. It is after the destruction of the Second Temple in 70 CE and before a Jewish rebellion in 132 CE, so it was most likely written between 70 and 130 CE.[123] In the text, the author speaks of hell when he says:

The way of darkness is crooked, and it is full of cursing. It is the way of eternal death and punishment.

Another early Christian writer who mentions hell and after death is Ignatius of Antioch, who was a student of the Apostle John, and he followed the Apostle Peter as the Bishop of Antioch. Ignatius is important for our purposes because several of his letters survive that were employed in churches in the first two centuries of Christianity.[124]

In a letter that Ignatius wrote to the Ephesians, he relates,

If a man corrupted by evil reaching the faith of God, for the sake of which Jesus Christ was crucified, a man becomes so foul and will depart into an unquenchable; and so will anyone else who listens to him.

In the middle of the second century, Clement of Rome, who was bishop there between 88 and 98 CE, recorded a sermon that discussed the nature of hell. This letter is now known as Second Clement. At section 5:5 of the letter, Clement tells us this about hell:

But when they see how those who have sinned and who have denied Jesus by their words or their deeds are punished with terrible torture in an unquenchable fire, the righteous who have done good and who have endured tortures because they have hated the luxuries of life, will give glory to their God saying, "There shall be hope for them that served God with all his heart."

Clement of Rome made a similar remark about the residents of Heaven and Hell in the same work, Second Clement at 17:7, as well. And he speaks of hell in several other passages in the work dated by many to have been written around 150 CE.

Around the same time, an anonymous Christian writer wrote a tract entitled the "Martyrdom of Polycarp," sometime around 155 CE. This text at 2:3 also speaks of life in hell. The writer says:

> **Fixing their minds on the grace of Christ [the martyrs] despised worldly tortures and purchased eternal life with but a single hour. To them, the fire of their cruel torturers was cold. They kept before their eyes their escape from the eternal and unquenchable fire.**

Another early Christian named Tatian was an Assyrian believer who moved to Rome while still a pagan and converted to Christianity there later. Tatian became a student of Justin Martyr. In his work *The Ante-Nicene Fathers*, written around 160 CE, at 1:71, relates, "We who are now easily susceptible to death will afterwards either receive immortality with either enjoyment or with pain."

About fifteen years later, a Christian philosopher named Athenagoras of Athens had become a Christian, possibly because of its affinities to Plato's teachings on the soul. Athenagoras wrote two apologetic works, his *Apology*, also known as the *Embassy for the Christians*, as well as *A Treatise on the Resurrection.*[125]

In the former work, Athenagoras speaks of the Christian afterlife and its relation to evil and hell. Around 175 CE, Athenagoras tells us,

> **We are persuaded that when we are removed from the present life we will live another life, better than the present one... or, if they fall with the rest, they will endure a worse life, one in fire. For God has not made us as sheep or beasts of burden who are mere by-products. For animals perish and are annihilated. On these grounds it is unlikely that we would wish to do evil.**

A few years later, around 181 CE, the Patriarch of Antioch, a man named Theophilus, who was Patriarch from 169 until 183, also wrote eloquently about the Christian afterlife in a letter to a friend named Autolycus. At 1:14 of that letter, Theophilus relates the following about his Christian view about survival after death. He tells us:

> **Give studious attention to the prophetic writings in the Bible and they will lead you to a clearer path to escape the eternal punishments and to obtain the eternal good of God... God will examine everything and He will judge justly, granting recompense**

to each according to merit. To those who seek immortality by the patient exercise of good works, He will give everlasting life, joy, peace, rest, and all good things... For the unbelievers an for the contemptuous, and for those who do not submit to the truth but assent to iniquity when they have been involved in adulteries and fornications, and homosexualities, and avarice, and in lawless idolatries, there will be a wrath and indignation, tribulation and anguish; and in the end such men as these will be detained in everlasting fire.

By the close of the century, two other second-century Christian writers, Clement of Alexandria and Tertullian, also wrote extensively about the nature of hell. The former thinker was the first significant scholar from the Church of Alexandria. He was raised with a solid Greek education. Thus, he had a tendency to blend Greek and Christian ideas together and he wrote about and defended Christian doctrine, often basing his views on the Scriptures.

From his *Post-Nicene Manuscript*, a work of his collected after his death, Clement tells us this about survival after death:

All souls are immortal, even those of the wicked. Yet, it would be better for them if they were not deathless... For they are punished with endless vengeance of quenchless fire. Since they do not die, it is impossible for them to have an end put to their misery.[126]

This text of Clement of Alexandria is usually dated around 195 CE, but it was not recorded until two centuries later. At around the same time, the great Christian scholar, Tertullian, in his work *The Apology*, also speaks of the conditions to be found in the Christian afterlife. In sections 18:3 and 44:12 and 13, Tertullian writes specifically about Heaven and Hell.

At 18:3 of his *Apology*, Tertullian tells us the following:

These have further set before us the proofs He has given of His majesty in judgments by floods and fires, the rules appointed by Him for securing his favor, as well as the retribution in store for the ignoring, forsaking and keeping them, as being about at the end of all to adjudge His worshippers to everlasting life, and the wicked to the doom of fire at once without ending and without break, raising up again all of the dead from the

beginning, reforming and renewing them with the object of awarding either recompense or damnation.

At 44:12 and 13 of the same work, Clement of Alexandria's "Apology," he speaks again about the circumstances of the life beyond the grave. Clement tells us this about the Resurrection of the Dead:

Then will the entire race of men be restored to receive its just deserts according to it has merited... There will be no more death nor resurrection, but we shall be the same as we are now... The worshippers of God shall always be with God... But the godless and those who have not turned wholly to God will be punished In fire equally unending, and they shall have from the very nature of this fire a supply of incorruptibility.

Finally, a third place in his Apology, where Clement of Alexandria speaks about survival after death, can be seen at 48:12 of that work. Clement relates the following:

Therefore, after this there is neither death nor repeated resurrection, but we shall the same as we are now and still the unchanged servants of God, ever with God clothed upon with the proper substance of eternity; but the profane and all the untrue worshippers of God, in like manner shall be consigned to the punishment of never-ending fire, and that fire from its very nature directly ministers to their Incorruptibility.

Another significant second-century Christian writer who made observations about hell is Irenaeus, Bishop of Lyons, who was born around 140 CE and died in 203. In his principal work, *Against Heresies*, the French bishop made a variety of comments about the wicked in hell. At I:10.1, for example, he relates:

God will send the spiritual forces of wickedness, and the angels who transgressed and became apostates, and the impiously unjust, lawless, and blasphemous among into everlasting fire.[127]

Three books later, in the same work at IV: 28:2, Irenaeus again speaks of those subject to eternal punishment when he writes,

The penalty increases for those who do not believe in the word of God and who despise his coming... It is not merely temporal, but

eternal. To whomever the Lord shall say, "Depart from me, accursed one into the everlasting fire." And they will be damned forever.

This brings us to several examples from the third century of the Christian Church where the subjects of hell and after death have been discussed, the second section of this sixth chapter.

Hell in the Third Century of Christianity

Several third-century Christian scholars also have made cogent remarks about hell and after death. Among these scholars were Hippolytus of Rome, Felix Minucius, Cyprian of Carthage, Ignatius of Antioch, John Chrysostom, as well as early Christian texts like the Apocalypse of Peter.

Around 212 CE, Hippolytus of Rome was one of the most prolific writers of the early church and was often at theological odds with the early popes and church leaders of his time. He appears to have been a student of Irenaeus and wrote many volumes of history. In one of his works entitled *Against the Greeks*, in section three of that work, Hippolytus speaks of the life of the condemned in hell.

Hippolytus observes about the condemned,

There is an eternal and unquenchable fire that awaits the condemned and a certain fiery worm which does not die, and which does not waste the body but continuously burst forth from the body with unceasing pain.

Hippolytus adds this about the condemned:

No sleep will give them rest, no night will soothe them. No death will deliver them from punishment. And no appeal of interceding friends will profit them in any way.

One of the earliest Latin apologists was a man named Felix Minucius whose work *Octavius* is a dialogue between a non-believer named Caecilius Natalis and a Christian man names Octavius, who was a lawyer, friend, and confidant of Felix Minucius. In his dialogue named *Octavius*, Felix tells us this about the afterlife,

I am not ignorant of the fact that many in the consciousness of what they deserve would rather hope than actually believe that there is nothing for them after death.

Felix continues his analysis about the afterlife at 34:12 of *Octavius*:

They would prefer to be annihilated rather than be restored for punishment... Nor is there either measure nor end to these torments. That clever fire burns the limbs and restores them, wears them away and yet sustains them, just as fiery thunderbolts strike bodies but do not consume.

One of the most important third-century Christian scholars was Cyprian of Carthage who was the Christian bishop of that North African city for many years. His parents afforded him a classical Greek education and he wrote several key letters and treatises in which he discussed many of the doctrines of the church, including the afterlife.

In fact, in one of his letters to a man named Demetrian, in section 24 of that letter, Cyprian turns his attention to *Gehenna* and the punishment of some after death. The Carthage bishop begins his remarks about these matters this way:

An ever-burning Gehenna and the punishment of being devoured by living flames will consume the condemned. Nor will there be any way in which the tormented could ever have any respite or be at the end. Souls along with their bodies will be preserved for suffering in unlimited agonies... The grief of punishment will be without the fruit of repentance. Weeping will be useless and prayer will be ineffectual. Too late will they believe in eternal punishment who would not believe in eternal life.

In another of his letters, this time to a friend named Thibaris, Cyprian again turns his attention to hell and after death. Cyprian tells Thibaris,

Oh how great will that day be in its coming, beloved brother, when the Lord shall begin to count up His people and to recognize the deserving of each one by the inspection of His Divine knowledge to send the guilty to Gehenna.

Cyprian continues the letter to Thibaris at section 55:10,

And to set fire on our persecutors with the perpetual burning of a penal fire, but to pay us the reward of our faith and of our devotion to the Lord.

At around the same time as Cyprian's letters, Ignatius of Antioch, in the same letter to the Ephesians that we saw in the section on the second century, around 250 CE, Ignatius again reiterates his views about the condemned in hell. He tells us about the condemned, "A man becomes so foul that he must depart into an unquenchable fire."

Finally, a text known as the Apocalypse of Peter, was a piece of Christian apocalyptic literature with very heavy overtones of Greek philosophy. This text is mentioned in the Muratorian fragment, the oldest surviving account of the New Testament canon that includes the Apocalypse of Peter.[128]

There are several versions of the Apocalypse of Peter, one in New Testament Greek and several Ethiopic versions. The Greek manuscript was discovered during excavations by Gaston Maspero during an archeological dig in Upper Egypt in 1887 and 1888. Many have dated the Apocalypse of Paul to the end of the second century or, more likely, sometime in the third century.

Scholar Oskar Skarsaune makes a case for dating the Apocalypse of Peter during the Bar Kochba Rebellion around 132 to 136 CE. Other scholars prefer a later date, as do we, in the last quarter of the second century or the beginning of the third century.[129]

The fullest version of the Apocalypse of Peter is a Coptic manuscript version that is now owned by the Coptic Museum in Old Cairo. The Ethiopic version was discovered in an archeological dig in 1910.

The Apocalypse of Peter is important for our purposes because it contains visions of both Heaven and Hell in its text. On the one hand, it supplies this description of those who occupy Heaven:

- People have pure, milky white skin, curly hair and are generally beautiful.
- Heaven blooms with everlasting flowers that do not wilt and spices.
- People there wear shiny clothes made of light, like the angels.
- Everyone there sings in choral prayers.[130]

On the other hand, the punishments in the visions of Peter correspond to the past sins when a person was on Earth, in a retributive justice manner. Thus, the text reveals:

- Blasphemers are hung by their tongues.
- Women who adorn themselves for the purpose of adultery are hung by their hair.
- Men who practiced adultery are hung by their feet.
- Lesbians are driven off a great cliff.
- Women who have had abortions are set in a lake of fire made up from the blood and gore of other punishments in hell.
- Those who lend money and demand usury upon usury are sunk to their knees in a lake of foul matter and blood.[131]

The Apocalypse of Peter shows remarkable similarities to the Second Epistle of Peter, as well as to the Sibylline Oracles. It has been suggested that the Apocalypse of Peter also has been a source for the Acts of Perpetua, an early-third-century Christian convert, as well as the visions to be found in the Acts of Thomas, our two final third century texts in this section.

The Passion of Saints Perpetua and Felicity is a diary purported to have been written by Vibia Perpetua that describes her imprisonment as a Christian in the very early third century. It appears to have been written in 203 CE and after her death was completed by a redactor. In addition to the experiences of Perpetua and Felicity, the text also contains the visions of a man named Saturus, another early Christian martyr. A later editor claims to be an eyewitness to the martyrs of these early saints.

The Acts of Perpetua and Felicity survives in both New Testament Greek, as well as in a Latin version. This text is important for our purposes because it provides some visions of Heaven, as well as some glimpses of life in hell in the beginning of the Christian third century.

Finally, the Acts of Thomas, another early third-century Christian church is one of the New Testament books of the Apocrypha. Early Christian evidence suggests it had circulated in the church in the third and early fourth centuries. Two versions of the text survive, one in Syriac and the other in Greek.

Most contemporary scholars suggest that the Acts of Thomas was originally written in Syriac. Most likely in the city of Edessa. For the most part, the Christian churches have later rejected the Acts of Thomas and the Roman Catholic Church declared it to be heretical at the Council of Trent in the mid-sixteenth century.[132]

This brings us to the third section of Chapter Six in which we will explore several fourth-century Christian scholars who have made observations about hell and after death in Christian literature.

Hell in the Fourth Century of Christianity

In the fourth century of the Christian Church there was also a variety of texts and manuscripts, as well as significant scholars who have commented on hell and after death.

The fourth-century text known as the Apocalypse of Paul, for example, is a non-canonical text considered to be a text of the Christian Apocrypha. It was originally written in Greek, which is now lost, but it does survive in a Latin translation called the Apocalypsis Pauli. The text purports to be a detailed account of a vision of Heaven and Hell experienced by the Apostle Paul. This text is important because it helped to shape the beliefs of the early church about the afterlife.

Some scholars argue that the Apocalypse of Paul was composed at a communal Pachomian monastery in Egypt between 388 and 400 CE. The text primarily focuses on a detailed account of both Heaven and Hell.

The Apocalypse of Paul makes several points about life in hell and how souls arrived there. Among these points are:

1. Pride is the root of all evil.
2. Pride is responsible for most of those who are condemned to hell.
3. Heaven is a land of milk and honey.
4. Hell has rivers of fire.
5. Hell also has rivers of ice.
6. Some of the angels are evil. Thy are dark angels of hell.
7. Among these dark angels is Temeluchus, the Tartaruchi.

8. Temeluchus is the leader of the devils who reside in Tartarus.
9. Human beings reside there, as well.[133]

The lost Greek original was translated into Latin as the Visio Pauli. It appears that the text was widely translated and distributed, and adapted to fit various historical and cultural contexts and necessities. It is likely that the Visio Pauli was a major source for Dante's "Inferno," particularly the description at II:28. Dante speaks of having read the Visio Pauli in the "Purgatorio."

The Visio Pauli may also have influenced the description of the home of Grendel in the Old English version of *Beowulf*, possibly by way of the Old English "Blickling Homily," Section XVI. The Blickling Homilies is the name given to a collection of anonymous homilies from Anglo-Saxon England, written in Old English. These homilies deal primarily with Lent, as well as Passion Sunday, Palm Sunday, and the feast days of various saints.

Among fourth-century Christian scholars who have written about hell and after death, two stand out from the rest. These are Lactantius and Cyril of Jerusalem. Around the year 350 CE, in his Catechetical Lectures, particularly section XVIII, Cyril of Jerusalem made a number of comments about hell, its occupants, and the punishments there.

At XVIII:19, for example, Cyril, the bishop of the church at Jerusalem, tells us this about hell and its residents:

> **We shall be raised therefore, all with our bodies eternal, but not all with bodies that will be alike.**

Bishop Cyril goes on to describe the exalted bodies of those who will be saved and then follows this with this,

> **But if a man is a sinner, he shall receive an eternal body, fitted to endure the penalties of sins, that he may burn eternally in fire, nor ever be consumed.**

A few lines later, at XVIII:28, Cyril again returns to describe the damned. He relates,

> **And as to the damned, these shall go away into eternal punishment, but the life of the righteous shall be life eternal.**

Cyril of Jerusalem goes on to provide more specific details about what life in hell shall be like, in addition to its being fiery.

Lactantius (250–325) was a Roman, Christian philosopher and advisor to the first Christian Roman emperor, Constantine, who established Christianity as one of the empire's faiths. Honorius later made Christianity the official faith of the empire in 395 CE. Lactantius' major work was called *Divine Institutes*, completed around 307 CE.

In *Divine Institutes* at VII:21, the Roman philosopher turns his attention to those in hell. About them, he observes:

> **The sacred writings inform us in what manner the wicked are to undergo punishment. For because they have committed sins in their bodies, they will again be clothed with flesh, that they may make atonement in their bodies. And yet, it will not be that flesh with which God clothed man, like this our Earthly body, but indestructible and abiding forever, that it may be able to hold out against tortures and everlasting fire, the nature of which is different from the fire of ours, which we use for the necessities of life and which is extinguished unless it is sustained by fuel of some material. But that Divine fire always lives by itself, and flourishes without any nourishment.**

The Roman philosopher Lactantius completes his analysis of hell.

> **The Divine fire, therefore, with one and the same force and power, will both burn the wicked and will form them again, and will replace as much as it will consume of their bodies, and will provide itself with eternal punishment. Thus, without any wasting of bodies, which regain their substance, it will only burn and affect them with a sense of pain. But when He shall have judged the righteous, He will also try them with fire.**

The notion of the "trying with fire" of the righteous, as mentioned by Lactantius, is related to the idea that even the souls of the righteous will be tested and tried the way precious metals are tested and tried in their smelting. If the believer comes out of the other side of the testing and trying, then a soul, at least in the view of Lactantius, will indeed be numbered among the righteous.

This brings us to the fourth and final section of Chapter Six of this exploration of views on the history of hell and after death in the world's history in which we will examine and discuss the views of fifth-century Christian thinkers on our issues at hand. Among these views, as we shall see, are those of Saint Patrick and Augustine, the Bishop of Hippo, in the fifth century.

Hell and After Death in the Fifth Century Christian Period

By the beginning of the fifth century, the doctrine of hell was taught throughout Western Christianity. It was reaffirmed officially by popes and church councils throughout the Middle Ages, as we shall see in a later chapter, such as the Council of Florence that made comments on hell in Session Six on July 6, 1339, and in Session Eight on November 22, 1439. It also issued a third pronouncement about hell in Session Eleven on February 4, 1442.

There also is extant a variety of fifth-century Christian thinkers who have made extensive comments on hell, punishment after death, and life in hell. In this section we will speak specifically about three of those fifth-century Christian apologists—Saint Patrick, Augustine of Hippo, and Saint Jerome, the fifth-century Latin translator of scriptures called the Vulgate.

Saint Patrick was a fifth-century Roman-British Christian missionary and Bishop of Ireland. In fact, he is considered to be the patron saint of Ireland and is known as the "Apostle of Ireland." The dates of Saint Patrick's life have not been fixed with any certainty, but there is a broad agreement that he was active in his apostolate to Ireland for much of the fifth century.[134]

Only two of Saint Patrick's writings have survived, his Latin *Confessio*, or "Confession," a kind of autobiography, and a *Letter to the Soldiers of Coroticus* that also provides details of his life and beliefs.[135]

In the *Letter to the Soldiers of Coroticus*, written sometime around 425 CE, Saint Patrick makes several comments about hell and the residents there. In the context of the murder of some converts that he had brought to the faith, the fifth-century Roman Catholic Bishop tells us, "In everlasting punishment they [the soldiers who murdered my new converts] will become slaves of hell along with Coroticus."[136]

A few lines later, in the same letter, Saint Patrick adds, "For truly, who so ever commits a serious sin becomes a slave of sorts and becomes what is called a 'Son of the Devil.'" It is clear that Saint Patrick has a fairly traditional view of what goes on in hell, as well as who are the residents there.

A second fifth-century Christian writer who made many observations on hell, who resides there, and what punishment goes on there is Saint Jerome (342–420), who was a protégé of Pope Damascus the First and the translator of the Christian scriptures from the Hebrew and Koine Greek to the Latin language.

Jerome rendered the Hebrew *Sheol*, as well as the Greek *Hades*, as *Infernus*, the word from which the name for Dante's work is derived. Secondly, much of what Jerome had to say about hell was derived from the teachings of Saint Augustine of Hippo. Thirdly, because of his nasty tempter toward many of his enemies, many of his comments about hell came in the context of these remarks. For example, many times Jerome made comments on women he believed were too salacious or alluring and he responded to them by saying they will someday be residents of hell because of that behavior.

Along the way, Saint Jerome also made some general or random remarks about hell such as the following comment, "The Gates of hell are sins and vices, especially the teachings of heretics." On another occasion he made a similar remark when he wrote, "Heretics and hypocrites of every sort will be burned in the fires of hell."[137]

At another time, Jerome related that,

> **The devil is not busy in pursuing infidels and such men who live outside the bosom of the Holy Church because he considers them already to be residents of hell he has won over.**

Saint Jerome also mentions hell in several of his extant letters, including his letter number thirty-nine, addressed to a young woman named Paula. In this letter, Jerome cautions the young woman against "falling into many of the traps that the devil uses to secure more residents of his Kingdom."[138]

Our final Christian figure who wrote extensively on hell and after death is fifth-century Bishop of Hippo of North Africa, Saint Augustine

(354–430). Augustine made many remarks about hell over the years, particularly in his two major works—*The Confessions* and the *City of God.*

One of the general remarks that Augustine makes many times about hell is the remark in the *City of God*, "There is no salvation outside the Church." The church he had in mind, of course, is the Roman Catholic Church. He often repeats this idea thar those who are not believers in the true church will someday be residents of hell. In another section of the *City of God*, we find the same judgment when the North African saint wrote, "The Church is the gate to Paradise, opened by Christ on Easter Sunday, through which believers alone may pass."[139]

In yet another place in the *City of God,* Saint Augustine again speaks of the exclusivity of salvation when he observes, "Without that faith [the Roman faith], man cannot live piously and uprightly." In the same section of the same work, Augustine remarks, "Unless we believe in Scripture, we can neither be Christians nor can we be saved."[140]

A second remark about hell and after death that Augustine frequently repeated is the idea that many of the heretics of his day will find their final resting places in hell. In the *City of God*, the North African bishop tells us, "Heretics from the very fact that they left the Church, are certainly damned." He adds, "heretics are rebels against God and against His Church."[141]

In another place of the *City of God*, Saint Augustine tells us:

> **Heresies are embraced only by those who, had they persevered in the faith would be lost by the irregularity of the irregularities of their lives.**[142]

In another place where Augustine makes this same point about heresy and hell, the Bishop of Hippo says in the *Confessions*, "There is no one so far removed from the presence of God as a heretic."

Augustine also spoke of hell in the context of the Gospel story of "The Rich Man and Lazarus" in the Gospel of Luke 16:19 to 31. He reasons that while the rich man was unmistakably confined to hell for his sins, Lazarus was in close proximity, yet "comforted in the bosom of Abraham."[143]

In another section of the *City of God*, Saint Augustine, relates, "The misery of the devils would never have been had not their malice not been great, for otherwise, it would not be proportional." Augustine goes on to say that every serious sin is tacit or expressed contempt of the Divine will, so the proper place for these kinds of sinners is that they should wind up as far from the presence of God as they can be. And that place is hell.[144]

Of all the comments that Saint Augustine makes about hell and the residents there, this notion of being "cutoff from God" is the most fundamental idea of the North African bishop's teachings about hell.

This brings us to the major conclusions we have made in Chapter Six of this study of the history of attitudes toward hell and after death. The subject matter of Chapter Seven to follow is an analysis of what medieval Judaism has had to say about the ideas of a hell-like state and punishment after death.

Conclusions

The purpose of this sixth chapter has been to explore what Christian scholars have had to say about the issues of hell and after death in the first five centuries of the Christian Church from some of the earliest Christian scholars in the first and second centuries to the time of Saints Jerome and Augustine of Hippo in the fifth century.

We began the chapter with observations about what some first and second centuries manuscripts and texts, such as the *Epistle of Barnabus* and the *Martyrdom of Polycarp*, have revealed about what the authors of these texts thought about hell. This was followed by a series of first and second-century Christian scholars have had to say about the issues at hand—hell and the idea of punishment after death.

Among the Christian scholars we examined in the first section of Chapter Six have been Ignatius of Antioch, Clement of Rome, Tatian an Assyrian Christian, Athenagoras and his *Apology*, as well as Theophilus, the Patriarch of Antioch in the second century.

Additionally, in the opening section of Chapter Six, we also examined some of the views on hell and after death of three of the greatest Christian philosophers of the second century. That is, Clement of Alexandria, Tertullian, and Irenaeus, Bishop of Lyons in France.

In the second section, we have turned our attention to the scholarly work of two noted third-century Christian scholars—Hippolytus of

Rome and Cyprian of Carthage. In the case of Hippolytus, we have analyzed some selections from his work entitled *Against the Greeks*. In the case of Cyprian, we have employed a few of his extant letters to ascertain what the Bishop of Carthage believed about hell.

In the second section of Chapter Six we also introduced a third-century Christian scholar by the name of Felix Minucius and his dialogue called *Octavius* that contains a lengthy description, as we have shown, about the afterlife.

Additionally, in the section on the third century, we introduced and discussed three other Christian texts that have provided information about third-century Christian views on the afterlife. These texts were the apocalyptic *Apocalypse of Peter*; the *Acts of Thomas*, a book of the Christian Apocrypha; and the biographical texts *The Passion of Saints Perpetua and Felicity*.

The most important thing that these three third-century Christian texts had in common is that each of them provides a kind of travelogue of the hereafter. Indeed, each contains a description of Heaven, as well as one of hell.

In the third section of this sixth chapter, we introduced and discussed two fourth-century Christian scholars—Lactantius and Cyril of Jerusalem who also have written extensively on the ideas of hell and after death in the Early Christian Church.

In addition to our remarks about Lactantius and Bishop Cyril of Jerusalem, we employed some observations from a text called the *Apocalypse of Pauli*, that purports to be another travelogue of the Apostle Paul in a tour of both Heaven and Hell in the course of the text.

We also suggested in the third section of Chapter Six that the original Greek version of the *Apocalypse of Paul* is now lost, but it survives in the Latin text known as the *Visio Paili*. We indicated that the *Apocalypse of Pauli* was one of the chief sources for Dante Alighieri's "Inferno," as well as the Old English text, *Beowulf*.

In the fourth section of Chapter Six we turned our attention to three major fifth-century Christian thinkers on the issues of hell and the phenomenon of punishment after death. These Christian scholars were Saint Patrick, Saint Jerome, the great Biblical translator, and perhaps the greatest Christian scholar in the first thousand years of the Church, Saint Augustine of Hippo.

Each of these three men have made valuable observations about the idea of hell and the punishments that go on there after death. Saint Patrick, the Apostle to Ireland, made some extensive remarks on hell in his *Letter to the Soldiers of Coroticus*.

Saint Jerome did not undertake a specific treatise devoted to hell, but he did make extensive, general comments about these issues in many of his writings. We also have indicated that much of the theological foundations for Saint Jerome's general remarks about hell came from the two major works of Saint Augustine—the *Confesions* and the *City of God.*

More specifically, we have shown that Saint Augustine's remarks about the phenomena of hell and after death that goes on there are divided among three distinct but related categories.

This first of these varieties of comments on hell by Saint Augustine are those that suggest that all those people outside believers of the Roman Catholic Church will be eternally punished in hell.

Augustine's second category of remarks about hell and after death has to do with the fate of heretics, particularly in the time of Saints Augustine and Jerome. Neither man had much that was good to say about heretics of their time Thus, when the two mention them, it is usually in the context that their final resting place will be in hell.

Finally, the third variety of remarks about hell and its residence—a theological type shared by Augustine and Saint Jerome—is that the most important theological point about the souls in hell is that in that location, both theologically and morally, those souls are as far from the presence of God as they could possibly be.

For both Augustine and Jerome what it meant to be in hell is to be as far as a union with the Divine as it is possible to be. One could not be farther from God, at least according to Saints Augustine and Jerome.

This brings us to the next chapter and a discussion of what figures in medieval Judaism have had to say about *Sheol Gehinnom*, or *Gehenna*, and the idea of punishment after death, the subject matter of Chapter Seven of this study of the history of views on hell and after death.

Peter Paul Rubens, *The Fall of the Damned*, ca. 1620.
Oil on canvas, 112.5 x 88.1 in. Alte Pinakothek, Munich, Germany.

Chapter Seven
Hell in Medieval Judaism

Heaven and Hell seem out of proportion to me.
The actions of men do not deserve so much.
—Jorge Luis Borges

The torture of a bad conscience is the hell of a living soul.
—John Calvin

There is no greater hell than to be a prisoner of fear.
—Ben Johnson

Introduction

The goal of this seventh chapter is to make some observations about what medieval Judaism has had to say about a hell-like state, as well as punishment after death from the tenth century until the fifteenth century.

We will fulfill this goal of this chapter by looking carefully at the work of several medieval Jewish philosophers and theologians, as well as what the movement known as the Kabbalah and some representative examples of that movement, have had to say about the soul, punishment after death, and *Sheol* and *Gehennom* in the period.

Among the Jewish medieval philosophers and theologians we will examine in this seventh chapter are the following:

1. Saadiah Gaon (882–942)
2. Yehudah Halevi (1075–1141)
3. Abraham Ibn Ezra (1092–1164)
4. Moses Maimonides (1138–1204)
5. Moses Ben Nahman (1194–1270)

As indicated earlier, we will also explore the medieval Jewish views on the soul, resurrection and survival after death among representatives of the movement in the thirteenth to the fifteenth centuries.

Thus, this chapter will unfold in six separate sections, one each of the five Jewish philosophers and a sixth on the perspectives of the Kabbalists on the *Olam Ha Ba*, or the "World to Come" in Classical Hebrew. We will begin with a short introduction to each figure or movement followed by what he, or it, has had to say about the afterlife in the medieval Jewish tradition. We begin then with Saadiah Gaon.

Saadiah Gaon on the Soul, Resurrection, and Survival after Death

Saadiah ben Joseph al-Fayyum, or better known as Saadiah Gaon was the first important medieval Jewish philosopher. He was also the first to write extensively in Arabic. He is considered to be the founder of Judeo-Arabic literature. He is also known for his writings on Classical Hebrew linguistics, Jewish Halakha, as well as Jewish medieval philosophy. His Jewish philosophy is also sometimes known as his "Jewish *Kalam*," a classical Arabic word for what today would be called "Philosophy of Religion."[145]

Saadiah Gaon's principal work of *Kalam* is called his *Book of Beliefs and Opinions*. This was the first attempt at a marriage or integration of ancient Greek philosophy, with Jewish Biblical thought and theology. Saadiah was born in Upper Egypt, but he spent most of his life living, writing, and teaching in Babylonia.

Saadiah left home around the age of twenty when he left Egypt to study under renowned Torah scholars of Tiberius. There he began work on his first great treatise, a Hebrew dictionary which he entitled *Agron.* In 928, at the age of forty-six, Saadiah was called to take up residence in Babylonia and to become the "Gaon," or "exalted teacher" there.[146]

In Babylonia, Saadiah completed his *Sefer-ha-Mo'adim*, or "Book of Festivals," in which he refuted many of the theological beliefs of his enemies. Saadiah's most important work for our purposes is his *Book of Beliefs and Opinions*, also sometimes called "The Book of Doctrines and Beliefs."[147]

This book of Saadiah's is composed of ten chapters, in six of which he makes observations about the soul, death, reward and punishment after death in this world and the resurrection and redemption of Israel. Saadiah shows a clear belief in survival after death and has an obvious assenting to the idea of the soul tinged, as we shall see, with Greek philosophical ideas.

Saadiah's philosophical method looks very much like what will develop in Italy three centuries later in the work of Thomas Aquinas who will be discussed in Chapter Eight of this study. In both of their philosophical methods, they begin in a negative way by first introducing counterarguments to their views, and then, more positively their actual theological positions. Saadiah also employs this method when speaking of the nature of the soul and its fate after physical death.[148]

In fact, Saadiah mentions seven different arguments about the nature of the soul, and he finds all of these theories unsatisfactory. The names that Saadiah gives these seven theories are the following:

1. Soul as one of the Accidents.
2. Soul consists of Air.
3. Soul consists of Fire.
4. The Soul is Dualistic with two Parts.
5. The Soul consists of two kinds of Air.
6. The Soul is to be identified with the Blood.
7. The Soul is known by logical Inference.[149]

Although Saadiah Gaon rejects the first six theories, he employs the seventh theory as a starting point of his major observations about the Soul and the possibility of it surviving in the Afterlife.

He begins his analysis on the nature of the Soul by suggesting pointing to several Biblical references. According to Saadian when God created man, He also created the Soul in the heart of man. He quotes Zechariah 12:1, "Then God formed the spirit of man within him." In addition, Saadiah also set a limited time for the existence of the soul and the body. They will be separated for a while from each other. Then, later, they will be united again, according to the Gaon.[150]

Saadiah also claims to have tools for determining the nature of the soul: logic and inference. From these two sources, he concludes that the soul is "a substance even finer, clearer, purer, and simpler than any of the celestial spheres."[151]

Another Biblical passage that Saadiah employs regarding the nature and extent of the soul is the Book of Daniel 12:3, which tells us, "The wise shine as the brightness of the firmament." In other words, the righteous soul will have a refined purity that the heavenly creatures do, as well.[152]

Saadiah argues that the true nature of the soul may be determined by an analogy to the celestial sphere. He says the body "loses everything" after the soul disconnects from it. This tells us that the soul is not made of the same substance as the body. Saadiah goes on to suggest that the soul, in order to perform its acts, must have three different, distinct elements. He calls these three abilities "discernment," "appetite," and "courage."

Saadiah also points out that the Classical Hebrew language also has three different words for the soul or spirit. These are *nephesh*, *ruah*, and *neshumah*. He explains each of these three terms with a verse from Scripture. For *nephesh*, which he identifies with the faculty of appetite, he gives Daniel 12:20, "Because your soul [*nephesh*] has desires."

Saadiah identifies the faculty of courage with the noun *Ruah*, or "spirit." He gives the Book of Ecclesiastes 7:9 as the Biblical quote associated with this function. "Be not hasty in your spirit [*ruah*] in order to be angry." Saadiah also gives Proverbs 39:11 as another Biblical line associated with courage and *ruah*, "A fool will spend all of his spirit."

Neshamah is the faculty of discernment. This word in Classical Hebrew usually means "breathe." Saadiah gives two verses from the Book of Job to explain the function of discernment, Job 32:8 and 26:4. "And the breathe of the Almighty gives them understanding," and, "Whose breath came forth from Thee."[153]

For Saadiah, all three of these functions reside as single soul. For him, the soul resides in the heart which is in the middle of the body. For Saadiah, human beings are in the center of the universe and the heart has the soul in the central point of the body.[154]

The belief in the afterlife, according to Saadiah Gaon, is a necessity. For humans to achieve genuine happiness, joy, and pleasure, there must be another abode after death. The world of the senses cannot be the ultimate resting place for humans, so there must be some other realm where souls reside after death.[155]

Saadiah says if human beings live moral and respectful lives in their bodies, and since it seems impossible that they always get their just rewards in this life, then it follows thar there must be another life, a world, he thinks, about which the Torah speaks. For Saadiah, there are two reasons that the Torah speaks about the world to come: reward and punishment. By logic, humans figure out the ideas of reward and punishment. And the second reason has to do with what Saadah calls, "the habit of prophecy."[156]

What Saadiah means by the "habit of prophecy" is that people tend to think more about closer goals than they do long-term goals. The habit of prophecy is to do just the opposite—to think about long-term goals like the afterlife rather than short-term goals like what is going on in the present life.[157]

Saadiah Gaon classifies Biblical passages about the soul and survival after death into seven different types. Saadiah gives these as the seven types:

1. The passages related to survival after death.
2. Where God distinguished the just from the unjust.
3. God records all that humans do.
4. God will judge after death.
5. Judgment will be based on behavior on Earth.
6. There will be a "Day of God" in the future.
7. Actual reward and punishment after death.[158]

For each of these seven categories, he supplies several examples:

1. Ezekiel 18:20, Psalm 16:11, and Proverbs 15:21.
2. Deuteronomy 6:25, Proverbs 1:7, and Isaiah 58:8.
3. Exodus 32:32, Isaiah 65:56.
4. Genesis 4:7 and Ecclesiastes 3:7.
5. Deuteronomy 32:4, Psalm 9:8 and 9, and 145:17.
6. The Book of Zephaniah.
7. Deuteronomy 5:26, Psalm 31:20, and Ecclesiastes 8:12.[159]

The fate of the soul, Saadiah says, after departing the body is based on what the tradition says. The angel who separates the soul from the body and the breath departs as well. He establishes this from First Chronicles 21:16. After this separation, the body goes to the grave and may undergo torture at torture time. This torture, according Saadiah, will be "more or less how the person behaved on Earth."

Saadiah believes, however, that the soul and body will only be separated temporarily. The good souls, according to Saadiah, will be stored by God until the Day of Judgment. Their temporary storage place is in Heaven, while the souls of the unjust will be tortured in *Sheol*. Saadiah Gaon used Daniel 12:1 to 3 and Ecclesiastes 3:21 as proof texts for the place of souls after death.[160]

Saadiah Gaon also suggests that the Final Judgment also will occur simultaneously with the reestablishment of the Jews in Israel. So, for him, the End Times for Saadiah will be the Final Judgment and also the reconstitution of the Nation of Israel in the Middle East. This brings us to the points of view on the soul and survival after death of Rabbi Yehuda Halevi.

The Soul and Survival in Yehuda Halevi

Rabbi Judah Halevi (1075–1141) was a Spanish, Jewish physician, poet, and philosopher. He was most likely born in Toledo and died shortly after arriving in the Holy Land in 1141. He is considered one of the greatest Hebrew poets of both religious and secular poems. His greatest philosophical work is entitled the *Kuzari*, a King of the Khazars, and his dialogue with a rabbi, who was the guide for the king in his seeking of religious truth.[161]

Halevi's *Kuzari* is divided into several essays. He makes most of his comments on reward, punishment, the soul, and the afterlife are the first and fifth of those essays. At the beginning of the first essay, the rabbi sets the tone for the dialogue. He says:

> **We believe in the God of Abraham, Isaac, and Jacob, Who took the Jews out of with great wonders and miracles, Who sustained them in the desert and God sent Moses to give His Torah and later thousands of prophets throughout history who exhorted the**

populace to follow the Torah and Who taught about the great reward for those who observe it and the arduous punishment for those who violate it.[162]

Thus, for Rabbi Halevi, reward and punishment first a Jews depends on how he or she practices the teachings of the Torah. Halevi does not mention, however, when the reward and punishment will occur. The king then asks the rabbi about the reward and punishment, and he points out that other religions have much richer guarantees than Judaism. Before we look at the rabbi's response, we first must say something about Rabbi Halevi's view of Creation.[163]

In classifying God's creatures, Halevi divides them among five separate kinds, from the inorganic things at the lowest level, to the prophetic, or highest level. Halevi's five levels of creatures look like this:

1. The Prophetic Level
2. The Angelic Level
3. The Human Level
4. The Animal Level
5. The Inorganic Level[164]

Art the highest level of existence in the Universe, the Prophetic Level, one communes with God. All humans have a desire to achieve prophecy, but only the Chosen Nation of Israel can succeed in doing so. Contact with a true prophet on Earth, Halevi argues, gives one the opportunity for spiritual renewal, and an individual may depart from the human level to the Angelic Level. A soul who has experience prophecy, or that has been in contact with a prophet, will return to its source and will be free from the fear of death.[165]

At this point in Rabbi Halevi's analysis, he introduces the idea of Divinity. One's reward or punishment he says is how close he or she is to Divinity. This point of Halevi's is reflected in one of his most famous poems:

Toward the source of life, of truth, I run
Impatient with a life of vanity.
To see my Master's face is all I want.
None other do I fear, none other revere.

If only I could see Him in a dream,
I'd sleep at ease, not caring if I died.
I could see His face within my heart.
My eyes would never turn their gaze outside.[166]

Since God is the Giver and source of life, to see Him and have the experience of prophecy is his only aim in life. Even seeing Him in a dream is enough to have a better life in the World. Halevi accepts the fact that the Bible did not say enough about the life to come, and he tries to fill in the gaps with rabbinic materials.

Rabbi Judah Halevi mostly speaks of his ideas about the soul in his fifth essay. He accepts the existence of the soul and that can be known through movement and sensation. The soul is divided into three parts. He calls these the "vegetative," the "living" part that has the power of locomotion, and the "speaking soul" which is unique in humans for their ability to verbalize.[167]

Halevi believes that the soul has an ethereal nature like the angels. For him, the soul resides in the human heart because the Divine Soul, God, needs a way to connect to the spirit of a man like the connection between the flame and the wick. The heart of the human is like the Temple of God. The secondary repository for the soul is the brain, but most of its activity is directed by the heart.

Although the body needs the soul to exist the soul does not need the body. Halevi gives an analogy of an old man. When the body gets older, the soul becomes stronger than it used to be. The soul has an infinite capacity, and it can exist independently of the body. Since the soul is not perishable, its activities of mobility, sensual perceptions imagination, and memory, although they cease with the death of the body, are nevertheless aspects of the self that the soul is always familiar.

Ultimately, the goal of the soul is to attach itself to Divinity either by being a prophet on Earth, or by being in contact with a prophet in this world. If the soul is attached with Divinity, it will be free of any other attachments and bring itself reward in the *Olam Ha ba*, or "World to Come."

Rabbi Halevi also believed that Divinity may be communed with in the land of Israel. God is present there. In fact, Halevi defines

Israel as the place where the *Shechinah*, or "Presence of God" may be found. In fact, in his poetry, Rabbi Halevi frequently turns his pen to descriptions of how God is "Present" in the Holy Land. In fact, one of his poems is called the "Ode to Zion."[168] Halevi says:

> There the Shechinah dwelt in thee; and He
> God, thy Creator, lo, He opened there
> Toward the gats of heaven, the gates of Thee.

In another part of the poem, he says of Zion:

> Thy God desired for you a dwelling place;
> And happy is the man whom He shall choose
> And draw him nigh to rest within thy space.

In another stanza of the same poem, Rabbi Halevi says that:

> Zion, O perfect is Thy beauty found.
> With love bound up, with grace encompassing,
> With thy soul try companions souls are bound.

Thus, Judah Halevi believed there was a connection between the soul of Zion and the soul of the observant Jew. This connection may be interpreted as a correlation between the destiny of the Holy Land and the destiny of God's Chosen People. For Halevi, Jerusalem is the place where God opens the Gates of Heaven for those who really follow Him.

Thus, Rabbi Judah Halevi believed in the existence of the soul in the afterlife, but the life of the Nation of Israel is far more important than any individual human life. One may achieve immortality of the soul if one has been a prophet on Earth, or if one associates with a prophet. This brings us to the views on the soul and the afterlife of Abraham Ibn Ezra, the topic of the next section of Chapter Seven.

Abraham Ibn Ezra on the Soul and Survival After Death

Abraham Ibn Ezra (1092–1167) was one of the most distinguished Jewish Biblical scholars and philosophers of the medieval period. He was born in Tudela, in northern Spain, in the province of Navarre. At the time the town was under Muslim rule. Later, Ibn Ezra moved to Córdoba. Ibn Ezra was a close friend of Judah Halevi. In fact, Ibn Ezra may have been Rabbi Halevi's secretary. Later, Ibn Ezra moved to Italy.[169]

Abraham Ibn Ezra completed a total of twenty-nine commentaries of Hebrew Bible or Old Testament books, including the five books of the Torah, only Isaiah of the major prophets, twelve of the minor prophets, and among the Wisdom Books, Psalms, Proverbs, and a very fine commentary on the Book of Job.

Ibn Ezra was a prolific writer. He wrote commentaries on Biblical books, Hebrew grammar and philology, books in what today would be called philosophy of religion, and books on mathematics. He also authored several books of poetry and a major tome on astrology called the *Mishpetai ha-Mazzelot*, or *The Judgments of the Zodiacal Signs*.[170]

Regarding the soul and survival after death, Ibn Ezra saw the soul as having component parts, what he calls the "vegetative," the "animal," and the "rational" parts of the soul. Ibn Ezra says he based this conclusion on what he calls in Hebrew the *Hakhnei ha-ra-ayot*, or "claims upon truth." What he appears to us by this is that the behaviors of animals differ from that of humans because the latter possesses logical reasoning while the former does not.[171]

The angels possess rationality and the animal function but not the vegetative for they do not have physical bodies. For Ibn Ezra, God is "pure reason," so that is the only function of His soul if He possesses one.[172]

Ibn Ezra also employs the tripartite scheme and terminology related to the soul we have seen earlier in this chapter such as in Saadiah Gaon's thinking. Thus, he uses *nefesh* to indicate appetites and lusts, *ruah* to designate "sensation," and *neshumah* to indicate "wisdom."[173]

In a book of Abraham Ibn Ezra's entitled *Yesod Mora*, or the *Foundation of Reverence*, the Spanish philosopher assents to two of our theories on why the innocent suffers. First, Ibn Ezra suggests that God uses evil and suffering to "test the characters of believers, or to make these characters better."[174]

Secondly, regarding the Akedah narrative of Genesis 22:1–19, Ibn Ezra relates that it is sometimes permissible for a prophet to "suspend the normal moral regulations" for certain activities in Jewish theological circles, and that may have been at plat in the Akedah or Sacrifice of Isaac narrative. Thus, Ibn Ezra assents to Soren Kierkegaard's *Teleological Suspension of the Ethical Theory*.[175]

This brings us to the views of twelfth-century Jewish philosopher, Moses Maimonides, and his understanding of the subject matter of the fourth section of this chapter of this history of views about hell, the soul, resurrection and survival after death in general.

Moses Maimonides on the Soul, Hell, and the Afterlife

Moses ben Maimon (1138–1204), also known as Moses Maimonides, was a medieval Sephardic Jew, philosopher, and physician of Saladin, mostly in Morocco and Egypt, though he was born in Cordoba, Spain. In his lifetime he was also one of the premiere scientists of his day, particularly in the discipline of astronomy.[176]

During his lifetime, Maimonides' writings on Jewish law and ethics were acclaimed and honored as far away as the southern part of the Arabian Peninsula, as well as Palestine and parts of India. Maimonides is sometimes called *Ha Nesher ha Gadol*, or "the Great Eagle," in recognition of his preeminent place as an exponent of the Oral Law in the Jewish faith.

In addition to being revered by Jewish scholars, Maimonides' views also figure very prominently in the history of the Arab sciences, as well as his influences on Muslim philosophers such as al-Farabi, Avicenna, and his contemporary, Averroes. Maimonides is also quoted by Albert the Great and Thomas Aquinas in the Christian Middle Ages, and even beyond that time.

Moses Maimonides believed that the human being is most fully human when the soul and the body are united. Thus, for him, people are most human while on Earth and then again after the Resurrection of the Dead at the end of time.

For Maimonides, the resurrection of the dead is only a temporary, intermediate stage in the journey of the soul. It is followed by what the Spanish philosopher calls a "second death," after which those who had lived properly on Earth will live forever as bodiless souls. The wicked, on the other hand, at least according to Maimonides, are "cut off" from God and their souls disintegrate to nothingness.

For Rabbi Moses Maimon immortality is not an inherent property of the human soul, but rather a consequence of righteous behavior. He did not speak of the "*nizhiyut ha-nefesh*," or "eternality of the soul." Every morally good human soul, for Maimonides, deserves a recompense in the *Olam Ha Ba*, or "World to Come." He thought this was demonstratable because God is sincerely Good and Just. If He is, and if many people do not receive justice in this life, then they must receive it in the life to come.

The two places where Moses Maimonides speaks of the soul, resurrection, punishment and reward after death are in his *Guide for the Perplexed* and in his work the *Mishneh Torah*. In the latter work, he tells us that a human is most human when the body and soul are united. For him, only a body and soul together have human free will, and only together can they be said to be in the image of God.[177]

To explain the union of body and soul, Maimonides offers an analogy. A blind man and a lame man decide to invade an orchard with succulent fruit. The blind man can reach the fruit but does not see it. The lame man sees it but cannot reach it. Thus, the lame man tells the blind man to carry him across the field just before the orchard, with the lame man directing him to the fruit.[178]

After eating some of his fruit, the outraged orchard owner appears and begins to question them. The blind man says, "I could not take the fruit. I cannot see." The lame man said, "I could not take the fruit, I cannot walk." The owner then thinks for a moment and then forces the lame man to hop onto the shoulders of the blind man. Only then, when the two were together, had the owner found his culprit. And he beat them both.

The human self is like the analogy. It can only be most human if the body and soul are united. Thus, for Maimonides the body has a crucial place in the human self. The kind of body possessed by humans after the Resurrection of the Body, however, is not a corruptible body. It is a kind of "Spiritual Body," an idea also found in Paul's First Letter to the Corinthians.

Just as there can be no punishment or reward for the lame man alone, there can be no punishment or reward for the soul alone. Alone, it cannot sin. A soul only sins in its body. Only with the blind and the lame together can, and should, justice be meted out. Similarly, for Maimonides true punishment and reward after the Resurrection can only be ministered in a just way after the soul and body have been rejoined.

In several sections of the *Mishneh Torah*, Maimonides says of the life to come, "No eye has ever seen it. The world to come is inconceivable, even a prophet cannot describe it. It is beyond the comprehension of a created creature." In this sense, Maimonides appears to be assenting to a version of the Divine Plan Theory, whereby in the afterlife justice will be accomplished simply because God is All-Knowing and All-Good.

Maimonides employs an idea he calls "total being," a "set of accomplishment of actually being able to comprehend Absolute Existence." And for Maimonides, that comprehension is only possible with the whole being, that is, the body and the soul. This brings us to Moses ben Nahman and his views on the soul, immortality, and punishment and reward after death, the subject matter of section five of this chapter.

Nahmanides on the Soul and Survival After Death

The Spanish-born, Jewish scholar, Nahmanides (1194–1270), also called Moses ben Nahman, was the first outstanding rabbi to declare that the resettlement in the Land of Israel was a Biblical precept, a moral requirement, that binds all Jews. Among Nahmanides' other achievements are two other most important ones. First, he reorganized and revivified the study of the Talmud in Spain. And secondly, he profoundly influenced Jewish Biblical theology through his exegetical works.[179]

It was in this second area that his mystical leanings and in his Kabbalistic traits can be seen, starting with his Neoplatonic view of the Soul. Like Plato, Nahmanides thought that the soul has three parts—the appetitive, the spirited, and the rational parts. Again, like Plato, Nahmanides believed that only the rational element of the soul survives death. The term that Nahmanides uses is the *Sefirot*, or the "inner life."[180]

For Nahmanides, the rational part of the soul is the part that knows the Divine and the element that displays wisdom. His fullest description of his view of the soul is in the final chapter called *Shaar ha-Gemul* of his work, *Torat ha-Adam*, which deals with mourning rites and burial customs. In the final chapter, Nahmanides turns his attention to reward and punishment, resurrection, the nature of the soul, and related matters.[181]

Moses ben Nahman believes that the rational element of the soul is the part of the soul that received Divine intervention. He says that if God is truly Just, then there must be reward and punishment in the afterlife because it does not work that way on Earth.[182]

The appetitive part of the soul is shared by all living creatures. It is one's biological element, as well as one's emotions, passions, and feelings. The spirited element of Nahmanides and Plato's soul is the rules of society and church. The rational element of the soul is reason. It is to rule the other two elements of the soul.[183]

At death, Nahmanides believes the rational part of the soul disconnects from the body and goes to *Gehinnom* to be punished, or Heaven to be rewarded. At the Resurrection of the dead the soul will be reunited with a new body, and then experience eternal reward or eternal perdition.

For Nahmanides, the Final Judgment will take place only after the coming of the Messiah and the reestablishment of the Nation of Israel. For Moses ben Nahman, like Maimonides, he believes the new "body" given by God in the Resurrection will be a method for conforming itself into a "pure essence" that will be eternal. Thus, for Nahmanides, the reunion of body and soul, at least for morally good people, will receive eternal life.

For the not-so-morally good, on the other hand, the souls of the unrighteous, in Nahmanides' view, will disintegrate into oblivion. They will cease to exist, and thus, there is no survival for morally imperfect.[184] This brings us to the final section of this seventh chapter on medieval

Jewish views of the soul and survival after death—what the Kabbalah and its adherents have to say about the issues at hand.

The Soul and Survival in the Kabbalah and its Followers

The Kabbalah, a word that means "reception," or "tradition," in Hebrew is the esoteric and mystical wing of the Jewish faith. One who practices the Kabbalah in Judaism is traditionally known as a *Mequbal*. The followers of the Kabbalah, and there have been many, have written and spoken much about the idea of hell and the afterlife.

In this final section, we will examine these Kabbalist views related to four different issues. First, the views in Kabbalist literature to be found about *Gehennom*, or a hell-like state in Judaism. Second, what the Kabbalists have had to say about the nature of, and parts of, the soul. Third, we will examine what the Kabbalists say about survival after death. And finally, what they have to say more specifically about the idea of *Gilgul*, or Reincarnation.

Because ancient Jewish sources suggested that there are seven levels of Heaven, many of the Kabbalist also believe that there are seven levels, or compartments, or habitations, in the Jewish underworld. In most followers of the Kabbalah, we can find the following structure of the underworld:

1. *Sheol* (the underworld)
2. *Abaddon* (doom or perdition)
3. *Be'er Shachat* (pit of corruption)
4. *Tit ha-Yaven* (clinging mud)
5. *Sha'are Mavet* (the Gates of Death)
6. *Tzalmavet* (the Shadow of Death)
7. *Gehinnom* (Valley of Hinnom or Purgatory)

For believers of the Kabbalah, *Gehinnom* is not "hell," but it was originally the grave and later became a kind of Purgatory where one is judged based on one's life deeds, or rather, it is where one becomes aware of one's own moral shortcomings. The Kabbalah explains that *Gehennom* is a kind of "waiting room," for all souls not just the wicked ones. The longest any soul will spend time in *Gehennom* is the maximum of twelve months, though there has been occasional exceptions.

Some of the followers of the Kabbalah describe *Gehinnom* as a "place of forging," in which the soul is "purified" by expunging the memory of ashamed deeds. After purification, the soul is completely obliterated or goes on to be present with God, or the *Shechenah*, ultimately to live an eternal life in bliss.

Among the Kabbalist, like Isaac Luria, for example, there are five levels of Souls and Worlds. These five levels are the following:

1. *Yechidad* (the Single One or God)
2. *Chaya* (the living one or world of emanations)
3. *Neshamah* (breathe of life or world of creation)
4. *Ruah* (the spirit or World of Formation)
5. *Nefesh* (the soul of vitality or World of Action)[185]

Any given soul may travel up this scale of "Soul Worlds," eventually reaching the top level where one is in community with the Divine. Immediately after physical death, for the Kabbalists, the soul travels to Gehennom, where it is purged of its sins over time. Or the soul of the individual is reincarnated into another human body. If the soul goes through this process, the soul is now subject to the "law of Gilgul, a Hebrew word that means "cycle," or "wheel."

Among the Kabbalists, souls are believed to cycle through a series of lives or reincarnations are attached to different human bodies over time. Which body they ultimately become attached to depends on their tasks in the physical world. This series or rebirths in Kabbalistic Thought is tied to the idea of the Messianic Age, of the Cosmic *Tikkun,* that will usher in the end of time, the coming of the Messiah, and the reestablishment of the Jews in the Nation of Israel.[186]

The most important Kabbalist text regarding Gilgul is known as the *Sha'ar Ha'Gilgulim*, or "The Gate of Reincarnations." It was written by Rabbi Isaac Luria and codified by his student, Rabbi Chaim Vital. The book describes the complex laws of reincarnation. One idea that arises in the book is that every Gilgul is parallel to the notion of human pregnancy also in some complex fashion.[187]

Luria, Vital, and their like-minded compatriots add several things to the idea of survival after death in Judaism. First, that there are seven levels of the underworld, just as their seven levels of hell. Secondly, there are different distinct levels or "worlds" related to the Souls, and these five levels have requirements for reaching the next level.[188]

And finally, the Kabbalists believe in survival after death, but they also maintain that the soul may undergo a process of transmigration of the soul or reincarnation. This brings us to the major conclusions of Chapter Seven, followed by Chapter Eight in which we will describe and discuss what the Late Middle Ages Christian world had to say about the soul, Heaven and Hell and punishment after death from Gregory the Great in the late sixth century to Thomas Aquinas in the thirteenth century.

Conclusions

We began this seventh chapter on the history of attitudes toward hell and after death by introducing five separate Jewish scholars or movements, between the tenth and the fifteenth centuries who have written about the Soul, a hell-like state, or punishment after death.

The first of these thinkers was philosopher and exegete Saadiah Gaon, the first great medieval Jewish philosopher. As we have seen in the first section of this chapter, most of what Saadiah has to say about the Soul, Resurrection, and survival after death can be found in his book, *The Book of Beliefs and Opinions*.

In this tome, we have pointed out that Saadiah Gaon, when speaking of the Soul, first gives an analysis of six, Jewish understandings of the soul that he did not believe in. We also have shown that next, he turned to his views on these issues, using as the background foundations for his perspectives the Hebrew Bible and the use of logical inference to arrive at his conclusions.

From the Biblical materials, Saadiah had arrived at the conclusion that there are three different Hebrew words for "soul" and "spirit," and those words are associated with different aspects and functions of the human being. These words are *nefesh*, *ruah*, and *neshumah*.

Also, in regard to the Biblical materials, Saadiah concludes that there are seven different types of comments on the Soul, Resurrection, and survival after death in the Hebrew Bible. In introducing these seven categories, he also supplies two or three examples of each to be found in the text.

Above all, what we have seen in discussing the views of Saadiah on the afterlife is that he claims that a human being is most fully human only when the body and the soul are united. For him, after death, the souls of the righteous enter a temporary stay in Heaven, while the souls of the unjust will travel to Gehinnom, where these souls will be purged.

For Saadiah, at the end of time and the coming of the Resurrection, the Soul and the body will be reunited, in a period that will establish the age of the Messiah and the reestablishment of the Nation of Israel in the Middle East. This brings us to the views of Rabbi Yehuda Halevi, the subject matter of the second section of Chapter Seven.

We have shown that the most important remarks that Spanish philosopher and exegete Rabbi Halevi has to say about the soul and survival after death comes in his dialogue known as the *Kuzari*, an exchange between a learned rabbi and a king of the Khazers.

We also have shown that Rabbi Halevi has a peculiar view of living things from the inorganic level all the way up to the prophetic level of existence. It is only at the prophetic level, Rabbi Halevi tells us, that communication with the Divine can take place.

Like many of his Jewish contemporaries, Halevi also believed that the Resurrection of the Dead will follow the Messianic Age and the reestablishment of the Nation of Israel in the Middle East. We also have shown that he thought the bodies at the Resurrection will be more "ethereal" than the physical bodies on Earth.

In the third section of Chapter Seven, we turned our attention to the scholarship of twelfth century Spanish philosopher and Bible scholar Abraham Ibn Ezra. Ibn Ezra's views on the soul, for the most part, follow a Platonic path, particularly regarding his parts of the soul, vegetative, animal, and rational.

We also have shown in the section of Chapter Seven on the views of Abraham Ibn Ezra assented to two different theories about why the innocent suffer. What we have called the "Test View," and a version of what Soren Kierkegaard would later call the "Teleological Suspension of the Ethical." By this, Ibn Ezra means that sometimes the prophets of Israel may circumvent the moral rules and duties of the faith, if the prophet deems it acceptable.

Moses Maimonides and his views on the Soul and survival after death has been the subject matter of the fourth section of Chapter Seven. In this section, we have shown Maimonides' debt to Aristotle's account of the parts and functions of the Soul. We indicated that Maimonides, like many of his contemporaries, believed that a human is most human when his body and soul are united.

In the fifth section of Chapter Seven, we explored the views of Spanish philosopher Moses ben Nahman, or Nahmanides, on the soul and survival after death. In that section, we showed the affinity of Nahmanides' view of the soul with that of Plato. Ultimately, for Nahmanides the soul disconnects from the body at death and reconnects at the Resurrection. For him, the souls of the righteous in their new bodies will be reunited with God. But the unjust souls in the afterlife will disappear to oblivion.

In the final section of Chapter Seven, we introduced and discussed the rather peculiar views of the Kabbalists, like Isaac Luria. Among those peculiar views are: The Jewish underworld has seven compartments; that there is a hierarchy of levels of religious enlightenment; and that the Kabbalist believed in both immortality of the soul and Transmigration of the Soul, or Reincarnation.

The material to follow in Chapter Eight is a companion piece to Chapter Seven, in that we will explore the Christian views on hell, the Soul, and survival after death from the time of Gregory the Great in the sixth century to the time of Thomas Aquinas in the thirteenth century and Dante in the fourteenth century.

El Greco, *Adoration of the Holy Name of Jesus*, 1577–1579.
Oil on canvas, 55 x 43 in. Monasterio de El Escorial, Madrid, Spain.

Chapter Eight
Hell in Medieval Christianity

The road to hell is paved with adverbs.
—Stephen King

Hell is not merely paved with good intentions. It is walled and roofed with them. Yes, and furnished too.
—Aldous Huxley

Hell was made for the inquisitive.
—Saint Augustine

Introduction

The purpose of this eighth chapter is to explore the phenomena of hell and after death in the Christian tradition from the sixth to the fourteenth centuries. Among the Christian sources we shall examine in this chapter are the following:

1. Saint Brendan (484–577)
2. Gregory the Great (540–604)
3. The Venerable Bede (673–735)
4. John Scotus Eriugena (800–877)
5. Peter Lombard (1100–1160)
6. The Vision of Tundale (1149)
7. Christian Medieval Mystery Plays (twelfth century)
8. Thomas Aquinas (1225–1274)
9. Dante Alighieri (1265–1321)

The material in this chapter will be organized into the following parts:

1. Sixth to the ninth century
2. Twelfth and thirteenth centuries
3. Dante and the fourteenth century

Hell in Christianity: Sixth to the Ninth Century

In this first section, we will examine the views on hell of four, early medieval Christian thinkers—Saint Brendan, Gregory the Great, the Venerable Bede, and John Scotus Eriugena. As we have in the previous chapters, we will make some introductory comments on each of these four figures and then talk about what they have to say about the phenomena of hell and after death.

Brendan of Clonfert (484–577), called Saint Brendan by the Roman Church, was also called "Brendan the Navigator" and "Brendan the Voyager." He has also been called one of the "Twelve Apostles of Ireland." He was born in the town of Tralee in County Kerry in the Province of Munster. He was ordained a priest at the age of twenty-six. Afterward, he founded a number of monasteries in Ireland and Scotland.

Saint Brendan is primarily known for a legendary journey to the Isle of the Blessed in his journal which was published in the ninth century. Many versions of the journal exist about this voyage on the Atlantic that some say was to America, while others maintain it was the Canary Islands. Brendan's voyage is usually dated to 512 to 530 CE.[189]

The Latin name of Brendan's journal is *Navigatio Sancti Brendani Abbatis*, or *The Voyage of Saint Brendan the Abbot*. We have listed Brendan first in our list because he lived before the other thinkers in the same period, even though his journal did not appear until three hundred years after his death.

In Brendan's journal he and his companions visit what they call "The Island of the Fire Giants."[190] He tells us,

> **It was a very rugged, rocky, and covered with slag, without any sign of trees or plants, but full of the forges of smiths.**

Then Brendan says to his companions,

> **Truly brothers, I am distressed about this island.**
> **I do not want to go onto it or even approach it.**

Eventually, however, Brendan does enter the island and a short time later, he sees one of its inhabitants. Brendan gives us this description of the man:

> **He was very hairy yet blackened**
> **and covered with flames.**[191]

Saint Brendan goes on to tell us that "All the seas around the island were boiling," and that the island was headed by Judas Iscariot. Later, on the island, when the Sun went down, the Roman Irish saint relates:

> **When the evening hours cast its shadows, behold innumerable multitude of demons eclipsed the face of the Sun, crying out and saying, "Depart from us, man of God, for we cannot approach our comrade until you move away from him."**[192]

Again, this is a reference to Judas Iscariot, and Saint Brendan responds by telling the followers of Satan that they are cursed, even though they believe that he is the one being cursed.

The importance of the tale should be clear for our purposes. Saint Brendan went to the island of hell and he and his fellow monks experienced a harrowing place full of demons led by Judas Iscariot.[193]

Our second figure in this first section of Chapter Eight is the early Roman pope, Gregory the Great (540–604.) Gregory was pope from 590 until the time of his death in 604. In many ways, Gregory the Great was one of the true founders of the Christian Middle Ages, both through his policies and his widely read writings.

Gregory the Great was born into a prominent Roman family. In 573, he became the Prefect of Rome, a position that made him the highest civil servant in the city. Afterwards, he renounced his political career, and turned instead to the church. In 579, when the city was under siege by the Lombards, Pope Pelagius II recruited Gregory as a special envoy to Constantinople. After six years, he returned to Rome and in 590 he was elected to the papacy.

Gregory's most important text for our purposes is his four volume *Dialogues* in which he comments about the fate of souls of ordinary Christians poses to him by a young disciple name Peter. His responses appear in the final volume of his *Dialogues*.[194]

Gregory begins his responses to his student Peter, a fellow monk, by telling us that Peter was from Spain, and that "before he sought the wilderness, he had died during a sickness of the body, but he was later mysteriously restored to life." He claimed, Peter did, that he had visited and had seen the punishments of hell, and he now was going to tell Gregory the Great about them.

Peter tells Gregory about what he saw as the geography of hell:

> **There were dwellings of different sizes, full of light, including a magnificent house, which seemed to have been built of gold bricks, but whose house it was he could not tell. Upon the banks of the river were a few more smaller dwellings. Some had a stench of dripping vapor, others reeked from the rising river.**[195]

Peter speaks of a bridge on the river that he had to cross. If the unjust attempted to cross it, they would slip and fall into the black and fetid river. Peter was accompanied by a soldier who was there to help to punish the residents. Peter also encountered another man named Stephen who slipped on the bridge and fell with half his body dangling from the bridge. The story goes on to tell us, however, that Stephen's soul returned to his body on Earth after he had seen the many domains of hell. This brings us to the Venerable Bede and his views on hell.

The Christian scholar known as the Venerable Bede (672–735) was born in Monkton in Jarrow, Northumbria, England. He was canonized in the Roman Catholic Church in 1899 and his feast day is celebrated on May 25. Bede is numbered among the greatest of the Anglo-Saxon theologians, historians, and chronologists. He is best known for his work the *Ecclesiastica gentis Anflorum*, or *The Ecclesiastical History of the English People*.[196]

This work of Bede's is also an important piece for understanding the conversion to Christianity of the Anglo-Saxon tribes Bede's reputation is mostly based on his commentaries of Scripture, copies of which found their way to most of the monastic libraries of Western Europe in the late medieval period.[197]

Very little is known of Bede's family background nor his childhood. One tradition has it that he was taken to the monastery of Saint Peter of Wearmouth, near Durtham, to whose care he was entrusted. By 685, Bede had moved to another monastery near Saint Paul's in Jarrow. He was ordained a deacon at nineteen and became a priest at age thirty.[198]

Bede's written works fall into three main categories: grammatical and scientific works, Scriptural commentaries, and his historical and biographical works. His treatise on "The Reckoning of Time," was composed in 725. An earlier work called *De Temporibus*, or "On Time," was completed in 703. Bede's most famous Bible commentary is his treatment of the Book of Revelation, written from 703 until 709.[199]

The Venerable Bede also completed a work on poetry from 705 until 716; a biography of the life of St. Cuthbert, the Bishop of Lindisfarne; and his *Historia Abbatum*, or *The Lives of the Abbots*, finished in 725. By 732, Bede had also completed his *Historia Ecclesiastica*, the text with which we are most concerned for our purposes.[200]

Bede's *History* is unique because it provides an account of Purgatory, a word invented by Gregory the Great, as well as a lengthy description of hell itself. Bede gets these descriptions from a fellow monk named Fursa, who has fallen ill and a day later was revived and told of his visits to Purgatory and Hell.[201]

Fursa tells us that he had a guide in Purgatory who "had a shiny countenance and a bright garment and they traveled silently" until they came to a site of "dreadful flames." On the other side of the flames were "violent hail and cold, flying in all directions." Both of these places were "full of men's souls."[202]

When the wretched could no longer endure the excess heat, they leaped into the midst of the cold, and finding no rest there, they leaped back again into the middle of the unquenchable flames. Fursa commented to his guide that this surely must be hell, but he was wrong about that. Bede continues the narrative of Fursa:

> **I was led into an even darker place. When I came into it, the darkness was so thick that I could see nothing but the form of he who led me. I saw a great many balls of black fire rising up out of**

a deep pit and falling back again. Then I saw that there were souls trapped inside these balls of fire.

Then the Venable Bede further relates:

The smell that came out of the pit was unbearable. He who led me to this place now went away. So I stood there in great fright, not knowing what to do. All at once I heard behind me voices crying and lamenting most forcefully. I heard other voices mocking and laughing. These voices came nearer and nearer, and grew louder and louder. Then I saw that these souls were crying and laughing with demons who were dragging along with them the souls of men who were howling and lamenting. Then I saw a man and a woman whose souls were being dragged into the pit, but I could not hear their voices very well.

Bede continues the narrative of fellow monk Fursa:

After a while, some of the dark spirits again came up from the pit. They ran forward and came around me. I was frightened by their flaming eyes and the stinking fire which came out of their mouths and nostrils. They seemed as though they wished to lay hold of me with burning tongs. I looked around for help but all I saw was a star shining in the darkness.

Bede tells us that the light had come from Fursa's guide and "When the light came very near, the devils went away." Then the guide told Fursa,

That fiery stinking pit which you saw is the mouth of hell, and whoever goes into it shall never come out again. Go back to your body and live among men again. Examine your actions well and speak and behave so that you may be among the blessed in Heaven.

"And when he said this," Bede reports, "All of the sudden I saw myself alive again among men."

It is interesting in Bede's account of Fursa's narrative that at first impression the latter appears to have gone to Purgatory and Hell. But on further analysis we find that he had only arrived at the outskirts of hell, at the "Mouth of Hell" as Bede put the matter. This brings us to John Scotus Eriugena, our next thinker in this first section.

John Scotus Eriugena (800–877) was an Irish theologian, Neoplatonist philosopher, and poet. He succeeded Alcuin of York as head of the Palace School at Aachen. He authored a number of works but is best known for his *The Divisions of Nature* that some call the "final achievement of the ancient world."[203]

John Scotus Eriugena also wrote many commentaries on the works of Augustine of Hippo, as well as those of a scholar now known as "Pseudo-Dionysius." He was also one of the first Christian scholars to know Greek well, apparently having studied in Byzantine Athens. One tradition about his life that is now believed to be spurious is that he was murdered by his own students with the stylists they used as pens.

John Scotus Eriugena is important for our purposes for four reasons. First, he was a "Universalist," that is, he thought that everyone shall be saved. John Scotus says,

> **Whereupon, the word of Christ returns to God, unifying man and woman into genderless humankind, and through humankind, the entirety of creation, returns to unity in the undifferentiated One. In the end, all will be saved, both saints and sinners.[204]**

Second, John Scotus Eriugena was the first Christian thinker to suggest that "hell is not a place." Rather, it is a "condition of being in eternal pain and suffering." Third, Eriugena believes that Heaven and Hell are primarily about a person's nearness or farness from God. And lastly, the Irish Neoplatonists thought that "Heaven must, in fact, be bifurcated, in the same way that torment is bifurcated from bliss."

This brings us to the second section of Chapter Eight in which we will analyze and discuss views from the twelfth and thirteenth centuries on the ideas of hell and after death. Figures in this section will begin with Peter Lombard and his *Book of Sentences.*

Hell in Christianity: Twelfth and Thirteenth Centuries

Peter Lombard (1100–1160) was born in Novara, Lombardy, in Italy, but he spent most of his adult life in Paris. He taught in the Cathedral School of Notre Dame, where in 1144 he became a canon, or a staff clergyman. Lombard was present at the Council of Reims in 1148 that was called to examine the theological works of French theologian

Gilbert de la Porree. In June of 1159, he was consecrated as Bishop of Paris and died a year later.

Although he wrote sermons, letters, and commentaries of books of the Bible, Lombard's most important and most influential work is his *Four Books of Sentences*, an assembled collection of the teachings of the Church Fathers and the opinions of medieval masters of the faith. Until the sixteenth century, the *Sentences* was the official textbook in theological classes throughout Europe.[205]

Book One of the *Sentence* deals with the issues of God, the Trinity, evil, and predestination, among other issues. Book Two is about Creation, the good and bad angels, and the Fall of Adam and Eve. Book Three deals with the Incarnation, Redemption, the virtues, and the Ten Commandments. And Book Four is mostly concerned with the sacraments, as well as death, judgment, Heaven and Hell. It is in this fourth book that Peter Lombard makes many observations about the issues of hell and after death.[206]

Among these observations about hell, Peter Lombard tells us:

1. Some of the demons descend into hell every day and lead souls there.
2. Other demons are responsible for punishment there.
3. Lucifer is the head of the demons in hell.
4. Christ descended into hell after his death, so that he might lead forth the Just who are held there.[207]

Additionally, and perhaps most importantly, Peter Lombard followed Augustine's dictum that hell is a real fiery place with physical torments added to those of the mind and the spirit. So, Lombard's view is at odds with that of John Scotus Eriugena. This brings us to a discussion of the *The Visions of Tundale*, a popular mid-twelfth-century Christian text.

The Visions of Tundale was written in the mid-twelfth century by an Irish monk who had traveled to Regensburg in Bavaria.[208] This extended vision is more than ten thousand words and was very popular in the late Middle Ages and it was translated into at least fifteen languages. *The Visions of Tundale* is also related by Helin and Vincent of Beauvais. Their version appears to be indebted to the *Apocalypse of Paul* and the *Voyage of Saint Brendan*, two texts we have discussed earlier in this study.

Tundale was an Irish knight who was most likely on the road to hell. He appears to have been a true sinner who was struck dead, but a few signs of life on his left side prevented his comrades from burying him. In the meantime, like many of the other "visions" we have seen in this study, his soul was met by a guiding angel who leads the Irishman on a tour of Heaven and Hell.[209]

As Tundale is lead through hell he is severely punished in a hell that is strictly divided according to offenses committed against God. These seems are enumerated beginning with murder. This account of hell is more fully developed than any other before Dante who will be discussed at the end of this chapter.

In Tundale's hell, many traditional features are present, like pits of fire, mountains of fire and ice, a horrible beast belching fire, valleys of fire, narrow bridges, the forge of Vulcan. All the souls in the upper regions of hell are not finally judged, so these regions serve as places of purgation, as in Gregory the Great's thought.

Lucifer gives a full and careful description of the different areas of his kingdom. After hell, the angel takes the Irish knight on a gradually rising path visiting better and still better souls who reside in green fields and pavilions. They traverse walls made of precious stones and unusual metals. Finally, they come to a great gate.

Throughout the entire journey, Tundale and his guiding angel maintain a running discussion that centers on the nature of Divine grace, mercy, and justice. They also speak of the needs for masses, prayers, and alms for the dead which are also included in many of the other visions from the same period such as *The Vision of John, Monk of Saint Lawrence* dated around the same time as *The Visions of Tundale*.[210]

There are also many visions of hell to be found in medieval mystery plays, the subject matter of the next item of this eighth chapter of this study of the history of perspectives on hell in Judaism, Christianity, and Islam.

Mystery plays in medieval Europe were one of the three principal kinds of vernacular drama during the Middle Ages. The plot of mystery plays usually represented Biblical subjects, first developed and produced by medieval Christian churchmen. These plays depicted scenes from the creation of the world until the Last Judgment. By the thirteenth century, the task of producing these dramas was taken over by various guilds and they were produced in the vernacular languages, often at sites removed from churches and cathedrals.

There are extant in England four nearly complete collections of Biblical dramas. These are the following:

1. The York Cycle (48 pageants)
2. The Townley Cycle (32 pageants)
3. The Wakefield Cycle (24 pageants)
4. The Chester Cycle (24 pageants)

These mystery plays often had multiple stages, where different parts of the story were told. Heaven usually had a ladder leading skyward and there may have been stages of different locations on Earth like Jerusalem, the wilderness, etc. But by far, the best of these stages was the depictions of hell.

The hell stage in these medieval mystery plays were usually fully decorated completed with a hell mouth that sometimes were built around the stage. The action in hell of ten happened inside the jaws of hell. In productions that were less fancy, the hellmouth was built on scaffolding over the stage and the action occurred beneath it, in the belly of the beast, as it were.

As time went on, the idea of the hellmouth became progressively more ornate complete with flaming sulfur, cannons, and jaws that could open and close, and large crews beneath the hellmouth to operate mechanical devices and serpents and allow them to spit fire.

One way, then, that knowledge of hell was gained by the common people was to attend these dramatic pageants that often showed Heaven and Hell in dramatic and existential ways often depicting hell as an enormous hellmouth. This brings us to Thomas Aquinas' understanding of hell, our next figure in this second section of Chapter Eight.

Thomas Aquinas (1225–1274) was an Italian Dominican philosopher and theologian and perhaps the most influential medieval Christian thinker. He was born in the Italian town of Aquino, near his family home, Roccasecca, at the time in the Kingdom of Sicily. He was canonized a saint by the Roman Catholic Church in 1323.

The body of the work completed by Thomas Aquinas is enormous. In addition to his two major works, *The Summa Theologica* and the *Summa Contra Gentiles*, he also completed a number of Biblical commentaries, including a significant work on the Biblical Book of Job.

Most of what Thomas Aquinas has to say about hell and what goes on there can be found in Question 69, 1–7 of the supplement to his *Summa Theologica*, as well as Question 97, articles one to seven of volume one of the same work, where the Italian philosopher raises seven question about hell.[211]

In the *Supplement to the Summa Theologica*, Thomas sketches out what might be called his view of the "Geography of Hell." He suggests there that *Infernus*, his word for hell, consists of four compartments. He calls these:

1. Gehenna
2. The Limbo of Children
3. The Limbo of the Fathers
4. Purgatory[212]

The first of these—Gehenna—is hell in the strict sense. It is a place of punishment for the damned, both of human beings as well as the fallen angels. *Limbus parvulorum*, the second compartment of hell, is reserved for unbaptized babies who died in the state of original sin. Since they were without mortal sin, they now enjoy, Thomas tells us, a place of "natural beatitude without the sensation of pain."

For Thomas, the *Limbus Patrum*, or the "Limbo of the Fathers," is the place where the souls of the Old Testament saints now reside before Christ awaited their admission to Heaven. The *Limbus Patrum* is also called "Abraham's Bosom." The residents there also enjoy natural beatitude and are without any sensation of pain. The Limbo of the Fathers is now vacant, for they are now enjoying Heavenly bliss.

The fourth compartment of hell for Thomas Aquinas is known as the *Purgatorio*, or Purgatory. This is a place where the righteous who died in venial sin may be found, for these residents still owe a debt of temporal punishment for sin. They are being cleansed of their sins by suffering before their final admission to Heaven, at least according to Thomas Aquinas.

In Question 97, articles one to seven of Part One of the *Summa Theologica*, the Italian philosopher raises seven questions about the nature and extent of hell. These may be summarized this way:

1. Are the damned tormented with the sole punishment of Fire?
2. Is the worm by which they are tormented corporeal?
3. Is the weeping of the souls there corporeal?
4. Is the Darkness in hell material?
5. Is the Fire of hell corporeal?
6. Is the Fire of hell the same species as the Fire on Earth?
7. Is the Fire of hell beneath the Earth?

Thomas Aquinas begins this discussion by raising three objections about raising a positive answer to question one in the above analysis. He then goes on to quote Basil the Great and the *Wisdom of Solomon* 5: 21 to conclude that the answer to question number 1 is yes.

In article 2 of Question 97, Thomas again begins by raising three objections to answering our question number two in a positive manner. He then replies to these objections by relating:

> **The damned will pass from the most intense heat to the most intense cold without giving them any respite because they will suffer from external agencies, not by the transmutation of their bodies from their original natural disposition; and the contrary passion affording a respite by restoring an equitable or moderate temperament that happens now by the spiritual. In the same way that sensible objects act on the senses being received by impressing the organ with their forms according to their spiritual and their material being.**

In other words, Thomas again answers the second question of Question 97 in the affirmative. About the third question, Thomas only raises two objections and then he speaks at length about what he calls "corporeal weeping" and their "dissolving into tears." He then goes on to answer question three with a resounding "yes," as well.

Thomas then turns his attention to whether the damned are in "material darkness." Again, he raises three objections and then on the authority of the Gospel of Matthew 22:13, as well as the writings of Basil the Great. Thomas final remarks on question three is that the "Darkness of Hell" is caused by the many bodies of the damned together in hell, which indeed is a "Material Darkness."

Regarding "Whether the Fire of Hell will be corporeal?" Thomas Aquinas again mentions three principal objections, but he ends article five of Question 97 by suggesting that "The Fire of hell is indeed corporeal."

When Thomas raises the question in article six of Question 97 in which he asks if the Fire of Hell is of the same species as the Fire on Earth, he raises four objections to answering the question in the positive, but he adds that the Fire of Hell "has certain properties that the Fire on Earth does not have, so they are of different species."

Finally, in regard to the question of whether hell is beneath the Earth, Thomas again raises four cogent arguments that suggest the question should be answered in the negative. Thomas answers these objections by referring to passages in the Book of Job, Athenagoras, Saint Augustine and the Biblical Book of Lamentations. Ultimately, however, he agreed that hell is to be found "deep beneath the Earth."

This brings us to the third and final section of Chapter Eight, views of hell in the fourteenth century and more specifically those of Dante Alighieri and his notion of what he calls the "Inferno."

Hell in Fourteenth Century Christianity: Dante's Inferno

Dante Alighieri (1265–1321) is the author of the *Divine Comedy*. He was born a Roman Catholic in the Italian city of Florence. He died of malaria in Ravenna on September 13/14, 1321. His body is buried in Ravenna, although there is an empty tomb in Florence dedicated to him.

Dante was successful as a poet and in politics. Early on, he fell in love with a woman named Beatrice who died young in 1290. Both Dante and Beatrice married other people, but the poet wrote a series of poems to honor Beatrice that he called *La Vita Nuova*, or "The New Life."[213]

Dante was a member of a political group known as the "Guelfs," but when the group split into rival factions, Dante joined the "White Guelfs" who were opposed to the pope and wished for Florence to be free from papal authority. The "Black Guelfs," on the other hand, supported the pope and were willing to do his bidding in Florence. Pope Boniface VIII supported the Black Guelfs and sent troops into Florence to take over the city in November of 1301. Some date Dante's exile from Florence on that date, but he was not technically banished from the city for another two months in January of 1302.

While Dante was in exile he lived in Ravenna, and it was during this period that he completed the *Divine Comedy*. Dante never returned to Florence and died in Ravenna in 1321 at the age of fifty-six, suffering from malaria.

Dante's masterpiece *The Divine Comedy* is an imaginative journey through the afterlife. Dante finds himself in a magical dark wood and he meets the poet Virgil, the author of the *Aeneid*, who serves as Dante's guide. Together, the two travel through the Inferno, or hell, and then ascend the Mountain of Purgatory to the Forest of Eden. There, Dante is met by his beloved Beatrice who now becomes Dante's new guide. The two ascend together to the sphere of Paradise, until aided by the Blessed Mother Mary, Dante is able to see God face to face.

Dante and Virgil climb down to the center of the Earth where Lucifer is punished, then they continue to climb up the other side of the world where they come to Mount Purgatory. Dante's hell is shaped like a funnel that extends all the way to the center of the Earth. It is situated underneath the city of Jerusalem, which is at the center of the Northern Hemisphere.

The funnel is made with nine circles. The first circle is the widest and the circles get progressively smaller until the ninth circle, the smallest. This is because fewer people reside in the ninth circle. These nine circles of Dante's "Inferno" look like this:

1. Limbo
2. Lust
3. Gluttony

4. Greed
5. Anger
6. Heresy
7. Violence
8. Fraud
9. Treachery

Limbo, Dante' first circle, is the residence of noble pagans and unbaptized babies. They live in a castle with seven gates that symbolize the seven cardinal virtues. Dante placed many prominent figures from classical antiquity in Limbo such as Homer, Socrates, Aristotle, Hippocrates, and Julius Caesar.

In his second circle of hell, the circle of Lust, Dante and Virgil find people who were overcome by lust in their lives on Earth. The souls of the lustful are punished by being blown violently back and forth by very strong winds, preventing them from ever finding true peace. In this circle, the two poets find Cleopatra, Tristan, and Helen of Troy, who all were adulterous during their lives.

When Dante and Virgil reach the third circle of hell, they find the many souls of gluttons who are overseen by a worm monster named Cerberus. The souls in this circle are being punished by being forced to lie in a vile slush that is produced by a never-ending icy rain. In this third circle, Dante speaks to a man named Ciacco, who discusses with him the fate of the two factions of Guelfs mentioned earlier.

The fourth cycle of hell for Dante is Greed. This circle is divided into two groups—those who hoarded their possessions and those who spent too lavishly on Earth. These two groups are guarded by Pluto, the ancient Roman ruler of the underworld. Dante says at this level he met many prominent clergymen, including cardinals and popes.

The fifth circle of Dante's hell is where the wrathful and the sullen are punished for their sins. To arrive there, Dante and Virgil had to take a boat from Phlegyas. While on their voyage, the two poets see furious fighting on the River Styx. The punishment again reflects the nature of the sin. Among the inhabitants of the fifth circle, Dante finds Filippo Argenti, the man who confiscated Dante's property after he was exiled from Florence.

Heresy is the sixth circle of Dante's hell. There the two poets see many heretics of history and of their own times. Epicurus, Frederick II, and Byzantine Emperor, Anastasius I were all occupants of the sixth circle of Dante's hell.

Violence, the seventh circle of Dante's hell is divided into three rings. The outer ring houses murderers. Dante placed Alexander the Great in this ring, as well as Dionysius of Syracuse and many other mythic and historical figures. In the inner ring of circle seven of Dante's hell may be found blasphemers, and sodomites. They reside in a desert of burning sand and burning rain that falls from the sky.

The Fraudulent can be found in Dante's eighth circle of hell. To reach this circle the two poets had to travel on the back of Geryon, a flying monster with different natures just like people who commit fraud. This circle of hell is divided into ten *Bolgias*, or "ditches," with bridges between them. These different ditches contain the souls of panderers, seducers flatterers, those who commit simony, sorcerers, false prophets, alchemists, and hypocrites, among others.

Finally, circle nine is the place of residents in Dante's hell for those souls who committed treachery on Earth. The ninth circle is divided into four parts according to the seriousness of the sins and crimes. All the residents in the ninth circle are stuck in a frozen, icy lake. The first part of circle nine is named for Cain who killed his brother Abel.

The second part of circle nine of Dante's hell is named after Antenor of Troy, who was Priam's counselor during the Trojan wars. Part three of circle nine is named after Ptolemy, the son of Abubus. And the final section of the ninth circle of Dante's hell is named after Judas Iscariot, the man who betrayed Jesus with a kiss.

This brings us to the major conclusions we have made in Chapter Eight of this study of the history of views on hell. The subject matter of Chapter Nine of this study is what the religion of Islam has had to say and believe about *Jahannam*, the classical Arabic word for hell.

Conclusions

The overall goal of Chapter Eight has been to examine views on hell and after death in the Christian tradition from the fifth to the fourteenth century. We have met this goal by treating this period into three, distinct times. These were:

1. The sixth to the ninth century
2. The tenth to the thirteenth century
3. The fourteenth century and Dante's "Inferno"

In the first of these sections of Chapter Eight, we examined the perspectives on four prominent Christian scholars. That is, Saint Brendan, Gregory the Great, the Venerable Bede and his *Ecclesiastical History*, and John Scotus Eriugena, ninth-century Irish philosopher. In our analysis of these figures, we have seen that each of them relates quite a bit of information about what people in the Dark Ages thought about hell.

Saint Brendan provided a travelogue of being in hell. Gregory the Great, in his *Dialogues*, made many comments about the nature and extent of hell, as well as inventing the word "Purgatory." Gregory also provided an account of a monk named Peter who he said had died and then gone to hell. Much like the Harrowing of Hell in the New Testament.

Similarly, the Venerable Bede reported on a vision by a fellow monk named Fursa who became ill, died, and was then revived. Bede also provided, in this first section of Chapter Eight, an account of Fursa's vision that is strikingly similar in content and extent to those of Saint Brendan and Gregory the Great.

John Scotus Eriugena, ninth-century Irish Neoplatonist was the final Christian thinker we examined from the Dark Ages. Scotus' view of hell, as we have seen, was very different than those of the other thinkers of his time in that he did not believe that hell was a physical place. Rather, he saw hell as a condition, a condition of being absent from the presence of God.

In the second section of this chapter, we examined and discussed several Christian thinkers and movements in the Christian tradition from the tenth to the thirteenth centuries, a period known as the High Middle Ages. In this section, we have introduced and discussed the thoughts of Peter Lombard and his comments about hell in his *Sentences*, the twelfth-century *The Visions of Tundale*, hell as seen in medieval mystery plays, and the perspectives to be found on hell and after death in the work of Italian philosopher, theologian, and exegete Thomas Aquinas.

In Book IV of his *Sentences*, Peter Lombard made extensive comments on the nature and extent of hell, as well as punishment after death. We have shown in this second section that Lombard followed Augustine's lead that hell is a physical and a fiery place.

The twelfth-century *The Visions of Tundale*, as we have seen, is perhaps the most extensive vision or travelogue of hell before the time of Dante. Tundale and his guiding angel maintained a running discussion about the ideas of forgiveness, Divine grace, mercy, and justice during Tundale' journey with his angel guide.

Medieval mystery dramas and their depictions of hell was the subject matter of the next part of Chapter Eight. We have introduced the four major mystery cycles popular in England in the period, from York, Townley, Wakefield, and the Chester Cycle. We also described and discussed the use of character, plot, and stage production in these mystery dramas.

Finally, we examined the perspectives on hell and after death to be found in the work of Thomas Aquinas, principally in his *Summa Theologica*. Indeed, we have shown that the Italian saint believed that hell had four separate compartments or regions. He called these:

1. Gehenna
2. The Limbo of Children
3. The Limbo of the Fathers
4. Purgatory

After explicating what goes on in each of these four parts of hell, we went on in section two of Chapter Eight to speak of seven separate questions that Thomas Aquinas raises in part one, Question 97, articles 1 to 7 of his *Summa Theologica*.

In that analysis, we have seen that for the most part, Thomas Aquinas answers these seven questions about the nature and extent of hell with affirmative responses. Among these questions were:

1. Are the damned tormented with Fire?
2. Is the worm by which they are tormented corporeal?
3. Is the weeping of sous in hell corporeal?
4. Is the darkness in hell material?
5. Is the Fire of Hell corporeal?
6. Is the Fire of Hell of the same species as the Fire on Earth?
7. Is the Fire of Hell beneath the Earth?

In the third and final section of Chapter Eight, we have introduced and discussed the ideas and content about hell to be found in the fourteenth-century work of Dante Alighieri's "Inferno." In our analysis, we have shown that Roman poet Virgil was Dante's first guide through hell, and that later on he was replaced by Beatrice, Dante's muse who eventually leads him to see the face of God.

We have also given a clear analysis of the nine circles of hell to be found in the "Inferno," as well as the view that the punishments in each of the circles is primarily associated with the sins that any particular soul has committed on Earth.

We have shown that for Dante, hell is shaped like a funnel, with each circle becoming progressively smaller because the number of occupants in each circle also gets smaller. Finally, we pointed out that Satan himself is to be found in the ninth circle of hell, where his feet are stuck in the ice there and he cannot escape.

The subject matter of Chapter Nine of this study of hell to follow is what the Islamic tradition has written and said about the phenomenon of *Jahannam*, the classical Arabic noun for hell. As we shall see, the Muslim tradition has much to say about *Jahannam* and *Al-Nar*, or "The Fire."

Botticelli, *Map of Hell*, 1480–1490. Vatican Library.

Chapter Nine
Hell in the Islamic Faith

Hell is empty. All the Devils are here on Earth.
—William Shakespeare

A man from hell is not afraid of hot ashes.
—Dorothy Gilman

If you want to enter hell, don't complain about
the dark. You cannot blame the world for
being unfair if you start on the path of a rebel.
—Liu Xiaobo

Introduction

The purpose of Chapter Nine is to examine the phenomena of *Jahannam*, or hell, in Arabic and the idea of punishment after death in the Islamic faith. We will fulfill that purpose by looking at the following sections in this ninth chapter. First, we shall look at the etymology and classical Arabic vocabulary of words and phrases connected to the Islamic views on hell.

In the second, and principal section of this chapter, we will discuss the many places and ways in the Muslim Holy Book, Al-Qur'an, where the subjects of hell and after death may be found. As we shall see, the number of these examples in Al-Qur'an about these matters is considerable and we will examine over forty passages from Al-Qur'an that speak about hell and after death in Islam.

In the third section of Chapter Nine, we will enumerate many of the places in traditional hadith literature where *Jahannam* and related terms are mentioned, both among traditional Sunni collectors of hadith, as well as those of Shiite Islam. Among these hadith collectors on *Jahannam* we shall examine will be Abu Bukhari, Abu Hurayra, Sahih Muslim, and many other medieval collectors of hadith literature on hell.

And in the fourth and final section, we will explore the ideas of hell and after death to be found among many of the prominent Islamic philosophers from the period of the High Middle Ages, or the tenth to the fifteenth century. Among the philosophers we shall examine shall be al-Farabi, al-Ghazali, poet Jalal Rumi, and philosopher Ibn Tamiyyah. This brings us to section one of Chapter Nine, arabic etymology and vocabulary related to *Jahannam* and associated terms.

Etymology and Arabic Vocabulary of Hell in Islam

The classical Arabic terms *Jahannam* and *Jannah* are related to earlier ancient Hebrew words we have seen previously in this study. Those words are *Ge Hinnom* and *Gan*. The Arabic *Jahannam*, or hell, is related to the Hebrew *Ge Hinnom* that we have discussed thoroughly throughout this study. The Arabic *Jannah*, or "Heaven," is connected to the Hebrew *Gan*, a Classical Hebrew word that means Paradise, as well as *Gan Eden*, or the Garden of Eden in Classical Hebrew.

Throughout Al-Qur'an, there are many references to *Jahannam*. Often these are associated with seven different names for hell in Islam. It is not clear, however, is these seven are synonyms, or the names of seven different compartments or sections of the Islamic hell. Others suggest these seven names are related to seven different "Gates" of *Jahannam*.

These seven names related to *Jahannam,* and their English equivalents, are the following:

1. Jahannam (a pit of some sort)
2. Jahim (a blazing fire)
3. Sa'er (a lighted or kindred fire)
4. Saqar (intensely hot)
5. Laza (blazing flames)
6. Hawiyah (a deep Abyss)
7. Hutama (broken into pieces)[214]

As mentioned earlier, it is not clear whether these seven names are all synonymous, whether they are the names of seven different levels of hell in Islam, or whether they are the names of the seven "Gates" of hell in Islam. The classical Arabic word for "Gate" is the female noun *Bawaaba*.

What is clear is that the words *Jahannam* and *Jahim* come from the same Semitic root, JHM, or GHM, [*jeem ha* meem] from which the Classical Hebrew word *Gehinnom* rises, and that the Arabic word for Heaven, *Jannah*, comes from the same Semitic root, GNN, as the Hebrew *Gann*, or Paradise.

Regarding the seven levels of *Jahannam* mentioned above, some Islamic traditions suggest that the non-monotheists are to be found in level one, the Jews at level two, the followers of Christianity at level three of *Jahannam.* The Sabians, in these same traditions, suggest they are to be found in level four of the Islamic hell, while the polytheists are at level five of *Jahannam*. And, perhaps most importantly, the soothsayers and hypocrites are assigned to the sixth and seventh levels of the Islamic hell.

The word *Jahannam* is used seventy-seven times in the Muslim Holy Book, Al-Qur'an. It is related to the Arabic term *jahm* that means the "darkest part of the night." It is also related to the classical Arabic expression *fahashabu Jahannam*, meaning that "*Jahannam* is sufficient for him," referring to the fate of the disbeliever in Islam.

Several other classical Arabic words are also associated in Islam with the idea of hell. Among these is the word *Al-Naar* that implies "The Fire." This word is employed most frequently in Al-Qur'an to designate "hell" in Islam. The word *Al-Naar* is used one hundred and twenty-five times in the Muslim Holy Book to signify hell.

The word *Jahim*, the name at number two in the above analysis, is employed twenty-six times in Al-Qur'an. It also comes from the Semitic root *Jeem ha meem*, or JHM. The word *Jahim* literally means "to stir up a fire."

Finally, the two most important Arabic words for discussing the idea of punishment after death in Islam are *Adhab* and *hudud.* The former is used in Islam as a "punishment for a crime," as well to describe breaking what amounts to the rules of etiquette.

Th Arabic word *Hudud*, on the other hand, is employed to designate the most grievous of crimes. Thus, they are called "Hudud crimes." Robbery and civil disturbance against Islam, for examples, are spoken of in Al-Qur'an at Surah 5, *ayat,* or verse, 33. This text relates:

> **The punishment for those who wage war against Allah and His Messenger, and who strive with might and main for mischief through the land is: execution or crucifixion, on the cutting off of hands and feet from opposite sides, or exile from the land; that is their disgrace in this world, and a heavy punishment is theirs in the Hereafter.**

The crime of illicit consensual sex is referred to in several *ayats* of the Muslim Holy Book, including 24:2, which tells us, "The woman and man guilty of adultery or fornication, whip each of them with a hundred lashes. Let not compassion move you in their case," in a matter prescribed by Allah, "If you believe in Allah and the Last Day." And let a party of believers witness their punishment.

The crime of "accusation of illicit sex or rape against chaste women without four witnesses" is another *Hudud* offense in the eyes of Allah. This judgment is based on the Holy Book's 24:4 and 6, 9:66, and 16:106, among many other verses.

Among the offense subject to *Hudud* punishments are the following with their Arabic equivalents, along with the suggested *Shariah* punishments:

1. Theft (sariqa). Amputation of hand.
2. War against Allah (hirahbah). Crucifixion or amputation of right hand and left foot.
3. Rebellion (baghi/baghat plural). Banishment
4. Apostasy (Riddah). Beaten to death by neighbors.
5. Illicit Sexual Behavior. (Zina) Stoned to death.
6. Drinking of Alcohol (Shurb al-Khamir). Forty to eighty lashes according to the Islamic School.

This brings us to the second section of Chapter Nine in which our goal is to describe and to discuss the many places in the Muslim Holy Book, Al-Qur'an, where the ideas of hell and after death may be found.

Hell and After Death in Al-Qur'an

There are hundreds of passages in Al-Qur'an where the subject matter is hell. Many verses confirm that there are different levels of punishments of this in *Jahannam*. At Surah 4:145, we learn from the Muslim Holy Book that "Hypocrites will be in the lowest depths of the Fire," or *al-Naar*, in Arabic.

Among the hypocrites that the Muslim Holy Book has in mind is the Pharaoh of Egypt. Surah 40:46 tells us, "And on that Day Judgment will be established and We will cast the people of Pharaoh into the most severe punishment." Other types who will be severely punished in the Fire of *Jahannam* include, as 16:88 records, "Those who reject Allah and hinder from the path of Allah. For them will be added punishment to punishment, for they used to spread mischief in the world."

Many of the passages in Al-Qur'an that speak of the punishments in hell speaks of what will happen to the bodies of the occupants of hell. At Surah 5:56, for example, relates, "The Fire of the Almighty will burn the skin of the non-believer. After the skin has been burned, it will be replaced by Allah with a new skin, so that they will feel the full punishment."

Another of the torments of hell will be the "pouring of *al-Hameem* over their heads." This is a term that means "boiling water" that is poured onto the heads of those in *Jahannam*. At Surah 22:19 to 20, we are told about the disbelievers in Allah in hell:

> **As for those who disbelieve, garments of fire will be cut out for them, and boiling water will be poured on their heads. With it will let away or vanish what is in their belies, as well as their skins.**

Another way in which Allah will humiliate the people in hell is by gathering them on their faces, blind, deaf, and dumb on the Day of the Resurrection. As the Holy Book at Surah 17:97 tells us:

> **We shall gather them together prone on their faces, blind, dumb, and deaf. Their abode shall be *Jahannam*. Every time it shows abatement, We shall increase for them the intensity of the Fire.**

This idea that the disbelievers will be punished while on their faces is a common theme that runs through Al-Qur'an. We see the theme, for example, at 27:90, 21:39, 23:104, 14:50, 39:24, and 33:66. The last of these simply tells us, "The day that their faces will be turned upside down in the Fire and they will say, 'Woe to us, would that we have listened and obeyed Allah and His Messenger.'" At Surah 27:90, we find a similar conclusion:

> **And if any do evil, their faces will be thrown headlong into the Fire. Do you receive a reward other than that which you have earned by your deeds.**

At Surah 23:104, we are told that, "The Fire will burn their faces and they will therein grin with their lips out of place." In several other verses of the Muslim Holy Book, it speaks of the souls in *Jahannam* being "dragged along," in some way, such as Surah 54:47 and 48, 40:70–72. In the former, we are told this, "On that Day they will be dragged through the Fire on their faces." And the latter passage, the one in Surah forty, relates that, "But soon they shall know, with the yokes around their necks, and in chains, they shall be dragged along in the boiling still liquid, and they shall be greatly burned."

Several verses in the Muslim Holy Book speak of the occupants of hell having darkened faces, such as at Surah 3:106 and 10:27. In the former, the Qur'an tells us:

> **On that Day when some faces shall be white and some faces will be black; and to those whose faces shall be black, "Did you reject the Faith after earlier having accepted it? Taste the penalty then for having rejected it."**

At Surah 10:27, the Muslim Holy Book again speaks about the faces of those in hell.

> **Their faces will be covered with pieces from the darkest parts of night. They will be companions to the Fire. They will abide therein forever.**

Many passages in Al-Qur'an speak of the idea that Fire will surround the disbeliever's body. At Surah 29:55, for example, it relates that, "On that Day the Fire shall cover them from above and from beneath their feet." Surah 7:41 agrees with this conclusion. "The Fire will surround the *kafir* [a non-believer] on all sides."

Many other passages in the Muslim Holy Book speak of the food that the occupants of hell will have in Islam. Among the passages where this theme may be seen are the following: 17:60, 37:62–68, 44:43, 56:52, 73:13, and 88:5–7. The last of these talks about drink and food for those in hell:

> **They will be left to drink from a scalding spring. They will have no food except a foul, thorny shrub. They will have neither nourishment nor satisfaction of hunger.**

The tree or shrub mentioned here appears again at Surah 17:60 that tells us:

> **And We did not make the sight which We showed you except as a trial for the people, as was the accursed tree mentioned in Al-Qur'an. And We threatened them but it increased them none except for gross impiety.**

The tree mentioned in Surahs 17 and 88 is known as the *Zaqqum* tree that according to Al-Qur'an, "springs out of the bottom of hell." The fruit of the *Zaqqum* tree is shaped like a "Devil's head," at least according to Surah 37:62–68. Most Muslim scholars suggest it is a tree grown in Fire, and the occupants of *Jahannam* are forced to eat it, along with "boiling water."

The fruit of the Zaqqum tree is also mentioned at Surah 44:43–46, where it speaks of the fruit being food in *Jahannam*, calling it "deadly fruit," and that it is to be considered "fruit of the sinful, like molten lead in the belly, like the boiling of burning despair."

The idea of drinking boiling water by those in the Islamic hell is repeated several times such as at Surah 38:57 and 58. That tells us about the fluids available in hell, "They shall taste it, a boiling fluid, and a murky and dark fluid, intensely cold, and other penalties of a similar kind that matches them." Surah 14:16 and 17 tell us that the condemned "will be made to drink boiling, festered water. He will sip it unwillingly and he will find great difficulty in swallowing it."

A few passages of the Muslim Holy Book speaks of the clothing worn by the residents of hell. At Surah 22:19 and 14:49 and 50, we find two prime examples of this theme. The former relates, "But those who disbelieved will have cut out for them garments of fire, and poured upon their heads shall be scalding water." In the verses from Surah 14, *ayats* 49 and 50, we are told:

And you will see the criminals that Day bound together in shackles their garments of liquid pitch and melted copper and their faces covered by the Fire.

There are also a number of places in the Muslim Holy Book where the question is raised about whether the punishment that goes on in *Jahannam* is temporary or permanent. At Al-Qur'an's 5:37 and Surah 2:167, it appears that the time for those in *Jahannam* is permanent and eternal. The former passage relates, "They will long to leave the Fire, but never will they leave there, for theirs will be a lasting torment." Similarly, Surah 2:167 tells us, "And they will never leave the Fire."

Surah 33:64, 72:23, and Surah 7, *ayats* 40 and 41 also agree that the punishment in hell, as 33:64 relates, "will abide there forever." Al-Qur'an's 72:23 also relates that, "Whoever disobeys Allah and His Messenger, then surely for him is the Fire of hell he shall dwell there forever."

Surah 2:81 and 82 also speak of how long *Jahannam* will last. The former verse relates, "Indeed, whoever commits misdeeds and becomes besieged by his iniquities, these are the inmates of the Fire, wherein they will dwell forever." In the very next verse, the Holy Book tells us, "As for those who believe and who do righteous deeds—these are the inhabitants of Paradise, wherein they will dwell forever."

Over and against the view that the punishment in *Jahannam* shall last eternally are other *ayats* like Surah 6:128. At this verse, the Muslim Holy Book tells us about what Allah says to the residents of *Jahannam*, "The Fire is your home, yours to stay in forever, except who Allah wishes to spare. Surely, your Lord is All-Wise and All Knowing." This *ayat* appears to combine the two views—that the fire lasts forever, except those who Allah wishes to spare.

There are also many passages in Al-Qur'an that speaks of the mercy and forgiveness of Allah. One example of this theme may be found at Surah 39:53 that relates the following:

Say o Prophet, that Allah says, "O My servants who have exceeded the limits against their souls, do not lose hope in Allah's mercy, for Allah certainly forgives all sins. He is indeed All-Forgiving and Most Merciful."

This verse and others like it leave open the possibility that the time in *Jahannam* may not be permanent. Thus, the question of whether the punishment of hell in Islam is permanent or temporary, the evidence from the Muslim Holy Book, Al-Qur'an appears to be mixed on the matter.

Another theme that one finds about hell in Islam, particularly in Al-Qur'an, is the idea that *Jahannam* has "Gates," Four verses that mention this phenomenon are: 15:43–44, 39:71–72, and Surah 90:19 and 20. In the first of these—the one from Surah fifteen—the text relates:

And verily, hell is the promised abode for them all. It has seven gates. To each of those gates comes a specific class of sinner.

At the Holy Book's 39:71–72, again speaks of the Gates of *Jahannam*. The former relates, "The unbelievers will be led to hell in crowds until, when they arrive there, its gates will be opened." The next *ayat*, or verse, continues:

To them will be said, "Enter the Gates of hell to dwell there. And how evil is this Abode of the arrogant.

Al-Qur'an's 90:19–20 also relates that, "Those who reject our signs are the companions of the left hand. On them will the fire be vaulted over." In the Muslim Holy Book, the "Companions of the Right Hand" are those who give food and clothing to the needy. Those on the Left Hand, do not. Those who do not follow the rules of Allah are those of the Left Hand.

Another theme about hell that frequently can be seen in Al-Qur'an is that Allah and His Prophet often can be seen in the Holy Book of Islam to warn believers about those who could wind up in *Jahannam*. Two examples of this theme can be seen at Surah 67:6–8 and Surah 5, *ayats* 36 and 37. The former passage provides this warning about hell:

For those who reject their Lord there is the penalty of hell. And Evil is their destination. When they are cast therein, they will hear

> **the terrible drawing in off their breathe even as it blazes forth, almost bursting with fury. Whenever a group is cast into it, its keeper shall ask them, "Did not there not come to you a Warner?"**

The same idea can be seen at Surah 5:36 and 37, where the text tells us:

> **As to those who reject the faith, if they had everything on Earth, and was twice repeated to give as a ransom for their penalty on the Day of Judgment, it would never be accepted by them. Theirs would be a grievous penalty. Their wish will be to get out of the Fire, but never will they get out. Thy were warned early on and now their penalty endures.**

There are also many random *ayats*, or verses in Al-Qur'an that speak of *Jahannam*, as well as the punishment that goes on there. At Surah 66:6, we see a repeat of the view that the fuel of *Jahnnam* is "men and stones." At Surah 21:98 the text points out that if anyone worships anything except Allah, "He will find himself as the firewood of hell."

We learn from Surah 104:6–9 that there are "extended columns in *Jahanaam*." At Surah 98:6, we learn that the polytheists are the "worst of men." And at Surah 4:93, the Arabic text implies that anyone who kills a non-believer, "Allah will send wrath upon him."

Finally, in several passages throughout the Muslim Holy Book, the point is made that whatever punishment that the occupants of the Islamic hell receive those punishments are directly tied to the sins and crimes a person has committed on Earth. As Surah 2:81 tells us, for example, "Whoever earns evil and his sins beset him on every side, these are inmates of *Al-Naar*, or 'The Fire,' and in it they shall abide."

This same point about what might be called Retributive Justice, that is that the punishment should fit the crime, is made many times in the Muslim's Holy Book, such as at Surah 43:74 that relates, "Surely, the guilty shall abide in the chastisement of hell, or *Jahannam*."

This brings us to the third section of Chapter Nine in which we will explore what many of the major hadith collectors have had to say about the ideas of *Jahannam* and punishment after death.

Hell in Hadith Literature

Hadith and its plural, *ahadith*, is an authoritative collection of literature in Islam that has recorded the Prophet Muhammad's words, deeds, and actions, to be used by subsequent Muslims in the Islamic faith. Both the Sunni and the Shiite traditions have their bodies of traditional collectors. The purpose of this third section of Chapter Nine is to identify and to discuss what many of those traditional collectors have said and written about *Jahannam* and related ideas.

Sunni collector, Abu Hurayra, for example, at volume I, hadiths number 536 and 537, relates that:

> **In very hot weather, the *Zuhr* prayer may be delayed until it gets a little cooler because the severity of the heat is from the raging of hell Fire. The fire of hell complained to the Lord saying, 'O lord, my parts are destroying one another.So Allah allowed it to take two breathe, one in the winter and the other in the Summer. The breath in the Summer is at the time when you feel the most severe heat, and the breath in the Winer is at the time when you feel the most severe cold.**

Sunni collector of hadith, Abu Bukhari, in book 76, hadith number 583, relates that:

> **After Judgment, all men and women are made to cross over a deep abyss, when the flames of *Jahannam* leap up, and they come to a thorny bridge so thin that it cannot be seen. Crossing this bridge is such a difficult task because the bridge is as thin as a single hair and as sharp as the sharpest sword. The believers and those destined for *Jannah* are able to cross quickly. They see the bridge as a wide, stone structure. Whereas, those who fall off the bridge fall into *Jahannam*.**

In another hadith from Abu Bukhari, this time at book 72, number 834, the hadith scholar informs us, "Added to the list of the dwellers in *Jahannam*, are the people who become picture makers." This same hadith goes on to say, "A person who drinks from a silver vessel brings the fire of *Jahannam* into his belly." Abu Bukhari continues, "A woman was tortured and was placed in *Jahannam* because of a cat she had allowed to starve to death."

A tradition from Sunni scholar Sahih Muslim quotes the Prophet Muhammad as saying that, "Suicides will reside in *Jahannam* forever." And Imam Malik, in his work, the *Muwatta*, suggests that the Prophet Muhammad uttered the words, "If a man speaks words to which there attaches no importance, then by those words he falls into the Fire of *Jahannam*."

In another hadith from Maalam ul-Tanzil, in his hadith, volume VII, number 45, informs us that the Prophet Muhammad said,

> **A time will come when no one will be left in *Jahannam*. The winds will blow and the windows and doors of hell will shake and make a rattling noise on account of the bowing winds.**

In another hadith from Sahih Muslim, volume I, number 398, a man came to the prophet and asks, "Where is my father?" He answered, "He is in the Fire." When the man turned away, He, the prophet, called him back and said, "Verily, my father and your father are in the Fire together."

At volume IV, number 2130, Sahih Muslim tells us this:

> **The Apostle of Allah visited the grave of his mother and he wept, and he moved others around him to tears. And Muhammad said, 'I sought permission from Allah to beg forgiveness for her but it was not granted to me, and I sought permission to visit her grave and it was granted to me. So, visit the graves of your loved ones, for that makes one mindful of death.**

It is most likely that this hadith from Sahih Muslim is related to the fact that the Prophet Muhammad's non-Muslim parents were believed in Islamic tradition to be two residents of *Jahannam*.

In another unusual hadith from Abu Sa'id Al'khudri, he reports that, "There was a dispute between *Jannah* and *Jahannam*. Al'Khudri continues his tradition:

> **"The haughty and proud are in me," *Jannah* said, "in me are the weak and the humble." Thereupon Allah judged between them saying, "You Jannah are my mercy and through you, I shall show mercy to whom I wish." And then speaking to *Jahannam*, Allah said, "You are my punishment to punish whom I wish amongst my slaves, and each of you will have its fill."**

Many of the ahadith that appear about *Jahannam* are about how far the filth of hell will come up on the bodies of the disbelievers. One Shiite account tells us this:

> **There are some whom the fire will take up to their ankles, others up to their knees, others up to their waists, and others up to their collarbones.**

Another Shiite account from Al-Jannah was Sifaat Na'imiha, volume IV, number 2185, adds, "Up to their necks." Several other ahadith, in both Sunni and Shiite Islam, speak of the intercession of the Prophet Muhammad on the Day of the Resurrection, such as one hadith from Ali Ibn Abi Talib, volume I, number 360, in which he observes that Muhammad said "On the Day of the Resurrection, I will intercede for him so that he is placed in the shallowest portion of *Jahannam*."

Many traditions about hell in hadith literature are related to the seven gates of *Jahannam* and what goes on at each of those gates. Imam As Sa'id, for example, at commenting on a passage about hell in Al-Qur'an observes: "It is called *Sa'er* because it will eat up the flesh of the human being and not his bones."

Sunni collector of hadith, Abu Hurayra observes this about *Jahannam*, "When the month of Ramadan begins and the Gates of Heaven are opened, the Gates of hell are closed, and all the devils there are chained."

Another tradition from Sahih Muslim, from volume IV, number 112, the Sunni collector of hadith observes, "In the Kingdom of *Jahannam* there is never any shade to be found there. This is true of all those in hell who are of the Left Hand." In another hadith from Sahih Muslim, from the same book number 113. He makes the same point that no shade shall be found "in any of the seven levels of *Jahannam*."

Finally, several other ahadith from Abu Bukhari, famed Sunni collector, makes several other observations about *Jahannam* from the Sahih Muslim, book 4, no. 2130, like this hadith:

> **A slave may utter a word which pleases Allah without giving it much importance, and because of that Allah will raise him to a degree of reward. But a slave of Allah may utter a careless word**

that displeases Allah without thinking of its gravity, and because of that he will be thrown into the Fire.

Thus, we have seen in our analysis of hadith literature some comments on the ideas of hell and after death in Islam from Abu Hurayra, Abu Bukhari, Sahih Muslim, Imam Malik, Malaam Ul-Tanzil, al-khudri, as well as other minor collectors in both the Sunni and the Shiite traditions.

This brings us to the fourth and final section of Chapter Nine in which we will explore what medieval Islamic philosophy has had to say about the phenomena of *Jahannam* and punishment after death.

Jahannam in Medieval Islamic Philosophy

There has been a great variety of Islamic philosophers who have written about the ideas of *Jahannam* and punishment after death in the Islamic faith. Because of that fact, we will treat only four thinkers in this final section of Chapter Nine. These four Islamic philosophical thinkers are:

1. al-Farabi (872–950)
2. al-Ghazali (1058–1111)
3. Jalal ad Din Muhammad Rumi (1207–1273)
4. Ibn Tamiyyah (1263–1328)

The first of these philosophers was al-Farabi who was also a prominent jurist in the tenth century. In fact, he was called by some, "The Second Teacher," following Aristotle in al-Farabi's time who was known as the "First Teacher."

Most of what al-Farabi wrote about *Jahannam* is a very straightforward view following Al-Qur'an in most of his observations. He mentions the seven gates of hell, the different punishments in each and follows the Retributive Justice View that these punishments are meted out according to the offenses to which they are tied by the justice of Allah.[215]

al-Ghazali, our second medieval Islamic philosopher, discusses the ideas of *Jahannam* and punishment after death in his work, *Hujjat Al-Islam*, or "The Proof of Islam." The most important observation of the many that al-Ghazali makes about hell is that "Whoever interprets

Al-Qur'an on *Jahannam* according to his own opinion is ignoring the clear, outer meaning of the text.[216]

Al-Ghazali also makes the point that the greatest intercessor for this in *Jahannam* is none other than the Prophet Muhammad. He suggests that all entreaties from those suffering in *Al-Narr*, or "The Fire," should begin with an expression of the faith in Allah and in His prophet.

The Persian philosopher, mystic, poet, and Islamic scholar, Jalal as-Din Muhammad Rumi used the idea of *Al-Narr* as a metaphor for the evil inclinations of the soul that can only be quelled by the Divine Light or the "water of mercy" that "flows from the virtuous heart."[217] He also equated *Al-Narr* to the burning passions of the lover that leads to the annihilation of the self in the beloved of Allah.

Rumi also raised the possibility of whether *Jannah* and *Jahannam* were psychological states and not physical places. Many modern modernist Islamic thinkers have made the same point such as Bangladeshi scholar Jama at el-Islami who has threatened that Muslim women who fail to support his radical organization will ultimately be condemned to the regions of *Jahannam*.

The most controversial thinker of those we have examined in this fourth section is philosopher, Ibn Tamiyyah, who apparently held the unusual view we have seen earlier in this chapter that the punishment in *Jahannam* is temporary and is not eternal. Some even go so far in interpreting Ibn Tamiyyah that the advocate of the Hanbali School of philosophy was also in favor of Universal Salvation.[218]

Among subsequent Islamic philosophers who have affirmed these two beliefs of Ibn Tamiyyah were his student, Ibn Qayyim al-Jawziyyah, as well as Imam al-Kawthari and Ibn al-Wazir. Among those who criticized these views of Ibn Tamiyyah were Ibn Arabi (1165–1240), a man who is considered by many to be the "greatest of all Muslim philosophers."

Several places in Al-Qur'an speak about the fuel that *Jahannam* runs on. One example of this phenomenon is Surah 2:24 that indicates, "Be on your guard against the on which men and stones are the fuel. It is prepared for the unbelievers.

One final feature of the Islamic hell is that those who reside in *Jahannam* will have no respite while they are there. Among the passages of the Muslim Holy Book where this point is made are the following; Surah 2:161 and162; Surah 4:52 and 145; Surah 14:42; and Surah 22:19 to 21. At 14:42, for example, we learn:

And do not regard Allah to be heedless of what the unjust do. He only respites them about their punishment until the day on which the eyes shall do nothing but stare with terror.

At Surah 4:52, the Muslim Holy Book relates about non-believers,

They ae men whom Allah has cursed and those whom Allah has cursed, they will find that they can get no help anywhere.

The same judgment may be found at Surah 2:161 and 162:

Those who reject the faith and die rejecting, on them is Allah's curse, and the curse of the angels and of all mankind. They will abide therein. Their penalty will never be lightened, nor will they ever receive any respite from their plight.

This brings us to the major conclusions we have made in this ninth chapter. The subject matter of Chapter Ten to follow is the phenomena of hell and after death in the Early Modern period: the sixteenth to the eighteenth century.

Conclusions

We began this chapter with the simple goal of describing and discussing how the Islamic tradition has responded to the two theological ideas of hell and after death. We then went on to achieve our goal by dividing the chapter into four parts or sections.

In the first section, we described and discussed the classical Arabic vocabulary connected to the two issues of this chapter—hell and after death. In this first section, we outlined the origins of the word *Jahannam*, as well as its cognates in other Semitic languages.

We also have shown that in the tradition of Islam, hell is said to have seven sections, all with various names related to *Al-Naar*, or "The Fire." As we have indicated, it is not clear whether these seven names are all synonyms, whether they are simply the names of the seven gates of hell, or the names of seven different compartments that make up hell in the Islamic faith.

In the first section of Chapter Nine we introduced other classical Arabic vocabulary of words related to hell and after death such as the words *hudud* and *adhab*—words that mean serious crimes and punishments for certain crimes in the Islamic faith.

The second section has been the central section in the chapter because we have shown and discussed many of the places in the Muslim Holy Book Al-Qur'an, where the phenomena of *Jahannam*, as well as punishment after death are discussed. Altogether, in this section, we have described and discussed forty-two portions of Al-Qur'an that speak explicitly about the ideas of hell and after death.

In that material, we have spoken of the food and drink of the occupants of *Jahannam*, the weather to be found there, the idea that in the Muslim hell the punishment fits the crime, that sometimes souls are "dragged along" in *Jahannam*, that the occupants of hell sometimes have darkened faces, and that the residents of *Jahannam* appear to get no respite from their plight.

We also engaged in a debate in the second section of this chapter about whether the punishments in hell are a permanent state of affairs or merely temporary. As we have seen, most of the evidence from Al-Qur'an is in favor of the eternality of punishment in *Jahannam*, but we have also seen some counterarguments to the effect that the *adhab*, or "punishment," in hell may not be a permanent state of affairs. Among these counterviews, we have provided passages from Al-Qur'an suggesting that hell is a temporary state, as well as *ayats*, or verses that speak of the mercy and forgiveness of Allah.

Along the way, we have also spoken of the Zaqqum Tree, an apparently bitter-fruit tree that provides some of the food for those in Islamic hell. We also pointed to several passages in the Muslim Holy Book that suggest that while humans were on Earth, they were warned by the Prophet Muhammad and his followers if they did not follow the prescriptions of the faith.

In the third section of Chapter Nine our primary interests were to describe and discuss several places in traditional hadith literature where the phenomena of *Jahannam* and punishment after death have been the subjects of conversation or description.

In this section, we introduced the ahadith of Sahih Muslim, Abu Hurayra, Abu Bukhari, Imam Malik, Maalam ul-Tnzil, al-Khudri, as well as several other minor hadith collectors in both the Sunni and the Shiite traditions. For the most part, what we have seen in this material is that the observations of the hadith collectors have mirrored very closely what we had seen in the Qur'anic materials.

In the fourth and final section of Chapter Nine, we began by pointing out that there is a voluminous amount of material in medieval Islamic philosophy regarding the issues of hell and after death in Islam. Because of that fact, we have chosen instead to discuss only four medieval Islamic philosophers and what they have had to say about the ideas of *Jahannam* and punishment after death in the Islamic tradition.

These four figures we have chosen to discuss were:

1. al-Farabi
2. al-Ghazali
3. Jalah as Din Muhammas Rumi
4. Ibn Tamiyyah

In this section, we went on to take these four Muslim thinkers one at a time and to explicate cogent remarks that each of the four Islamic thinkers have had to say about the ideas of hell and after death in the Islamic faith.

For the most part, as we have seen in the final section of Chapter Nine, al-Farabi's comments about hell are almost entirely remarks that can be gleaned from reading the Muslim Holy Book, Al-Qur'an, on these matters. To that end, al-Farabi discussed the seven names or "gates of hell," as well as the overall theological Islamic view that in *Jahannam*, the punishment fits the crime, a version of Retributive Justice or what medieval Christian philosophy sometimes called *Lex Talionis*—or the "Law of Retribution."

Among the comments we have seen that al-Ghazali has made about hell and after death, the medieval philosopher cautions that when it comes to matters regarding the afterlife, it is very important to disregard one's personal opinion when it comes to such matters.

In fact, when it comes to survival after death, the best advice we have gleaned from al-Ghazali on the matter is to stick as closely as possible to the letter of what the Muslim Holy Book, Al-Qur'an, has had to say about these matters.

The major insights about the phenomena of *Jahannam* and punishment after death that we have seen from Persian poet and philosopher, Jalal as Din Muhammad Rumi, were that the idea of *Al-Naar*, or "The Fire," should be understood as a metaphor for the evil inclinations to be found in the human soul. And that these desires can only be quelled by the Light and the Grace of Allah Himself.

We also have seen—perhaps for the first time in Islam—whether *Jannah* and *Jahannam* are, in fact, physical places, or whether they may also simply be psychological states. In fact, we have suggested that this latter view can sometimes be seen in many modernist Islamic philosophers, like Bangladeshi scholar, Jama at Et-Islami, for example.

Perhaps the most interesting of the four medieval Islamic thinkers that we have explored in regard to the phenomena of *Jahannam* and punishment after death is that of Hanbali philosopher, Ibn Tamiyyah (1263–1328). As we have shown, Tamiyyah is important because he raised the possibility that the human's time in *Jahannam* may not be eternal. Rather, he suggests that because of the mercy and forgiveness of Allah, hell may simply be a temporary resting place.

The subject matter of the following chapter of this study—that is, Chapter Ten—is what perspectives on human history can be seen in hell and after death in the Early Modern period of history from the sixteenth century and the Reformation until the end of the eighteenth century.

Part III
Hell in the Modern World

Giotto, *The Last Judgment*, 1306, fresco. Cappella Scrovegni, Padua, Italy.

Chapter Ten
Hell in the Early Modern Period
Sixteenth to Eighteenth Century

Hell is the place where truth is seen far too late.
—Thomas Hobbes

Hell is full of good wishes and countless desires.
—Bernard of Clairvaux

Hell, among other things, is paved with the
skulls of many priests, bishops and other clergy.
—John Chrysostom

Introduction

The purpose of this tenth chapter is to explore and to discuss what Judaism, Christianity, and Islam have had to say about hell, or *Jahannam*, and punishment after death in the period of the sixteenth to the eighteenth century.

We will attempt to accomplish this purpose with separate sections of the chapter devoted to Judaism, Christianity, and Islam, as well as a subsequent section on hell in popular culture in the period in question. We begin, then, with what Judaism has had to say about hell in its Early Modern period.

Hell in Early Modern Judaism

Beginning in the Early Modern period in Judaism, many Jewish apologists began to maintain that there is no explicit Jewish doctrine of the afterlife in general and of the idea of hell in particular. Chaim Pearl and Reuben S. Brookes, for example, in their *Guide to Jewish Knowledge*, in regard to life after death from the Early Modern period observe:

> **Judaism adopted a stand of its own... Having provided the belief of the deathlessness of the soul, the authoritative teachings of Judaism warns us against useless speculation about the details of the afterlife.[219]**

According to Jewish writers since the Early Modern period, their faith deals with existence on Earth. As Pearl and Brookes tell us, "The Jewish faith teaches us to concentrate all our efforts and energy in conducting ourselves as Children of God in this world here and now."

Even though the official view seems to be at the time that this life is far more important than the next life—if there is such a thing—nevertheless, we do see some sixteenth- and seventeenth-century Kabbalistic thinkers who wrote about survival, including Rabbi Hayyam Vital (1542–1620), the foremost disciple of Rabbi Isaac Luria of Tzfat whose teachings Rabbi Vital recorded and edited.

Rabbi Luria's texts were later reedited by Rabbi Vital's son, Rabbi Shmuel Vital, in an eight-volume collection, the *Shemonah She'arim*. The younger Rabbi Vital also completed many of his own works, including Bible commentaries, responsa, as well as works of practical Kabbalah.

His father's *Shaar HaGilgulim*, or "The Gate of Reincarnation," is a work in which Rabbi Hayyam Vital wrote extensively about the idea of *Gilgul*, or reincarnation. Like his other work, Rabbi Vital borrows heavily from his teacher Isaac Luria.

Indeed, Rabbi Vital clearly believed in the idea of reincarnation as we can see in the following passage from his "The Gate of Reincarnation:"

> **Behold, after a person's death, he is repaid for his sins before he is entered into Purgatory, through many kinds of punishment, all termed reincarnation. This means that he can be reincarnated as a mineral, a vegetable an animal, or a person. Almost all people have to reincarnate in these ways. The reason being that a person is unable to receive his punishment until he is an embodied soul**

at which time he can suffer and feel this pain, and thereby be atoned for his sins. But the extent of his sinning determines the kind of reincarnation he will have, whether it be as a mineral, a vegetable, an animal, etc.

Another Early Modern Jewish mystic, Moses Hayyim Luzzato (1707–1746), in his work, the *Ramchal* explains that,

Reincarnation maximizes our chances of becoming virtuous. A soul could enter this world at different times in different bodies, and in this way would be able to rectify at one time that which was ruined by sinning at another time, or to perfect that which was not yet perfect."[220]

In the tradition of the Kabbalists, *Gilgul*, or reincarnation, then, was to be included alongside any other Jewish understandings of the afterlife. Though not as well-known as immortality of the soul or resurrection of the body, *Gilgul* was a central theological category among the followers of the Kabbalah.

Early on in another of Moses Hayyim Lazzato's works called *The Path of the Just*, he speaks of the *Olam Ha Ba* and how this world "is like an anteroom to the World to Come," though it is not clear whether he again refers to *Gilgul*, or Reincarnation, or to some version of immortality of the soul.[221]

Another Early Modern Jewish thinker who commented on the *Olam ha Ba*, or "World to Come," is Yom Tov Lipman-Heller (1579–1654), a Bohemian Rabbi and Talmudist best known for his commentary on the *Mishnah*.

In his *Midrash Shmuel*, or "Midrash on Samuel," Lipman-Heller speaks of the *Olam Ha Ba*. He observes:

We have to precisely examine this Mishnah as it appears that the first clause contradicts with the last clause. For in the first clause, it teaches that "One hour of repentance and good deeds in this world is greater than the whole World in the life to come."

Rabbi Lipman-Heller continues his analysis:

Obviously, this means "the whole World of the life to come, a life of spiritual pleasure in the World to Come." But in the last clause

it teaches that, "One hour of spiritual pleasure in the World to Come is greater than the whole life of this World." Again, this obviously means by "the whole life of this World" a life in this World of repentance and good deeds.[222]

Several conclusions can be made about this passage on the Mishnah. First, Rabbi Lipman-Heller appears to believe in a Life to Come. Secondly, it is not clear what form of survival after death he believes in. It could be Immortality, or it could be Resurrection, or even Reincarnation for that matter.

A third conclusion that we can make about Rabbi Lipman-Heller's observation about the *Olam Ha Ba* is that the quality of this Life to Come is of a far greater kind than the life that Jews have on Earth.

Thus, we may make the conclusion that theological Jewish thinkers in the Early Modern period sometimes endorsed the idea of *Gilgul*, or Reincarnation, like Isaac Luria and Hiyyam Vital, and sometimes assented to other forms of survival, such as the wok of Rabbi Yom Tov Lipman-Heller.

A final Jewish thinker from the Early Modern period who made many observations about the soul and survival after death is Moses Mendelssohn (1729–1786), German Jewish philosopher who was one of the chief proponents of the Jewish Enlightenment.[223]

Mendelssohn completed a work that he entitled *The Phaedo: Or Immortality of the Soul*. In this tract, the German Jewish philosopher makes several cogent arguments for the simplicity and the immortality of the soul mostly based on the arguments to be found in Plato's *Phaedo*. In the second edition of his *Critique of Pure Reason*, Immanuel Kant takes Mendelssohn's arguments to be insufficient for proving that the soul survives death. Kant argues instead that belief in Immortality is a postulate of what he calls "Practical Reason."

This brings us to the second section of Chapter Ten in which we will speak of the phenomena of hell and after death in Christian thinkers in the Early Modern period, from the sixteenth to the eighteenth century, beginning with the Protestant Reformation as well as the Counter-Reformation.

Hell and After Death in the Christian Early Modern Period

The Protestant Reformation and the Counter-Reformation in Christian history provide a variety of views about hell and after death in the sixteenth and seventeenth centuries. The two principal reformers, for example, Martin Luther and John Calvin, have very different points of view about these two theological issues. Both agree that hell is the final destination for human beings of those who are not saved.

Since both Luther and Calvin eschew Purgatory, as well as Limbo, Heaven and Hell are the only two possibilities for the German Luther and Swiss Calvin. Both men also believed that at the Final Judgment, those who are not saved will be consigned to the confines of hell.

Luther and Calvin differ, however, when it comes to the nature of the survival in each man's thought. Calvin believed in a conscious existence after death, while Luther had a very different understanding of Hades and *Gehenna*. In fact, Luther thought that death was a kind of sleep, as we shall see later in this chapter.

Several historic Protestant Confessions also contain various beliefs about hell and after death like the *Westminster Confession*, for example, that was written in 1646 and promulgated in 1647. It relates:

> **But the wicked who know not God, and obey not the Gospels of Jesus Christ, shall be cast into eternal torments and punished with everlasting destruction from the presence of the Lord, and from the glory of His power and Judgment.**

Many other confessions of the Protestant churches also indicate a belief in the torments of hell, as well as direct reference to the harrowing of hell in some denominations such as the Church of England or Anglicans, as well as the Episcopal Church in America.

The Eastern Orthodox Church celebrates the harrowing of hell annually on Easter Saturday during the liturgy of Saint Basil. During the service, the vestments worn by the celebrants and the hangings on the walls of the church are somber Lenten colors, usually purple or black. Just before the reading of the Gospel, however, the liturgical colors are changed to white and the deacon performs a censing and the priest stews laurel leaves around the church, symbolizing the opening or the broken gates of hell.

Martin Luther delivered a sermon at Torgau in 1533 in which he explicitly mentioned the fact that "Christ descended into hell." *Formula of Concord*, a Lutheran confession written in 1533, in its Article IX states,

> **We believe simply that the entire person, God and human, descended to hell after his burial, conquered the Devil, destroyed the power of hell and took from the Devil his power.**

In Book II, Chapter 16, sections eight to ten of his *Institutes of the Christian Religion*, John Calvin indicates that Christ "descended into hell."

The Catechism of the Roman Catholic Church calls the descent into hell by Jesus, "The last phase of Jesus' messianic mission," during which he "opened Heaven's gates for the just who have gone before him." One ancient homily included in the Roman readings for Holy Saturday calls the period where Christ descended into hell was a period of "silence in which the Earth was stilled while Jesus searched for Adam, our first father, as if looking for a lost sheep."

Even though the harrowing of hell is taught by the Lutheran, Catholic, Reformed and Orthodox churches there are other Christian denominations who reject the idea. Most of these say there is no scriptural evidence for it.

Both Martin Luther and John Calvin made several general comments about hell in their written works as well as their unofficial ones like Luther's *Table Talks*, for example. In one of these the German explains:

> **I admit that I deserve death and hell, what of it? For I know One who suffered and made satisfaction on my behalf. His name is Jesus Christ, the Son of God, and where he is, there I shall be also.[224]**

In another of his *Table Talks*, Luther tells us, "Many pass for saints on Earth whose souls will actually be found in hell." Or the *Table Talk* comment about education and the universities,

> **I am afraid that the schools will prove to be the very Gates of hell unless they diligently labor in explaining the Holy Scriptures and engraving them in the hearts of its youth.**

Luther, of course, threw out the ideas of Limbo and Purgatory and all that went with these ideas, including the notion that the Virgin Mary could be an intercessor between humans and God. Luther's hell was Augustine's view, dire and eternal. A place constructed by an Omnipotent God to punish the wicked.

For Luther, the devil was God's servant, created by Him and in His Divine plan destined by God to fall. Like some of the Desert Fathers, Luther believed himself to be plagued by demons and like many medievalists, he associated them with his bowels. Luther also believed in witches and their pacts with the devil.

On another occasion, Luther comments again about the universities,

> **I greatly fear that the universities, unless they teach the Holy Scriptures diligently and impress them on the youthful students, the wide Gates of hell will be waiting for them.**

In several places in his *Table Talks*, the German theologian and exegete concentrated on his overall understanding of hell such as in this comment that, "I would rather be in hell with Christ than be in Heaven without him." Or this comment about the relation of his teaching to religious truth,

> **Whoever teaches differently from what I have taught or whomever condemns me therein, he also condemns God and thereby remains a child of hell.**

Similarly, Luther remarked,

> **I have before me God's word which cannot fail, nor can the Gates of hell prevail against it; and thereby will I remain, though the whole world shall be against me.**

Needless to say, many of the remarks that Luther made about hell were directly related to his criticisms of the Roman Church like the following remark in one of his letters,

> **And I myself, in Rome, heard it said openly in the streets, "If there is a hell, then Rome is built on it."**

In another comment about the Roman Church and its tendency to execute heretics, Luther remarked:

World, death, the Devil, hell, away with you and leave me in peace. You have no hold on me. If you will not let me live, then I will die. But you won't even succeed in that. Chop off my head and even that will not harm me. I have a God who will give me a new one.

John Calvin (1509–1564), the second great leader of the Reformation, was born in France but is associated with Geneva. He came into contact with Luther's ideas while still a student. He agreed with many of his principles but in a lot of ways he went much farther than Luther, particularly regarding predestination. "From the beginning of time," Calvin taught, "God's plan had been in effect."

Calvin makes several comments in his *Institutes of the Christian Religion* about hell, the harrowing of hell, and the idea of punishment after death. About the harrowing of hell, Calvin related,

But we ought not to omit his descent into hell, a matter of no small moment in bringing about redemption.[225]

Calvin also employs Psalm 107:16 and Zechariah 9:11 to establish the truth of Christ's time in the Netherworld. He also observes in the *Institute* that,

Because language cannot describe the severity of the Divine vengeance on the reprobate, their pains and torments are figured to us by way of corporeal punishment.

Calvin speaks of the metaphorical nature of the worm that "dieth not," at the Gospel of Mark's 9:46, that he believes signifies the "human conscience." A view that was usually accepted by those in the Roman and Reformed Churches.

In addition to his *Institutes of the Christian Religion*, John Calvin also made a number of general remarks in many of his letters and other works. "The torture of a bad conscience," he once observed, "is the hell of a living soul." When asked what God was doing before creation, Calvin answered by saying, "He was preparing hell for the curious."

In his exegetical works, as well, Calvin frequently referred to the fires of hell such as in this comment on the Gospel of Matthew 5:22:

Those again who break out into reproaches are adjudged to the hell fire which implies that hatred, and everything that is contrary to love, is enough to expose them to eternal death though they may not have committed any acts of violence. hell is beyond all question a foreign word.

About Second Chronicles 33:6, Calvin relates about the Valley of Hinnom, "It was infamous for its detestable superstition that was committed in it because they sacrificed their children to idols."

At volume II, chapter sixteen, sections eight to twelve of his *Institutes*, Calvin discusses at some length the line in the Apostle's Creed that, "He descended into hell." In his analysis, Calvin goes so far as to say that Jesus, in order to truly become our substitute and to pay our penalty, had to fear for his soul and his eternal safety. This is how severe a loss of the Father's favor and love the Son experienced.

In many places in his *Institutes*, John Calvin speaks of hell as *Gehenna,* and he often refers to the context in ancient Hebrew literature of the place of human sacrifice associated with the site of *Gehinnom*, near Jerusalem.

In addition to Luther and Calvin, many other major and minor Protestant reformers made many observations about hell, the harrowing of hell, and the idea of punishment after death in the Reformation Christian Church.

Francis Turretin (1623–1687), a Geneva-Italian Reformer, was a firm defender of the Calvinist orthodoxy. He complains that in England and America, "Many Christians are turning back to the Puritans to walk in the old path." In one of his essays, Turretin asks, "Is there a hell and what are its punishments there? To answer this question, he makes twelve conclusions. These are:

1. That hell is real.
2. It is called Sheol and Hades.
3. It is not a mere figment of the imagination.
4. There is infernal punishment there.
5. The fire there torments the soul.
6. Descriptions of hell should not be understood allegorically.
7. Heavenly states should be understood mystically, not

figuratively.

8. The torture in hell is not material Fire.
9. Punishments in hell are related to moral guilt.
10. These punishments are so great they cannot be conceived by men.,
11. Duration and extension belong to the punishments.
12. There will be no respite of the punishment and torture of hell.[226]

The most famous sermon in American history by Jonathan Edwards, entitled "Sinners in the Hands of an Angry God," also speaks at length about the punishments of hell. In that sermon, Edwards relates:

> **God holds you over the pit of hell, much as one holds a spider or some loathsome insect over the fire, abhors you and is dreadfully provoked. His wrath towards you burns like a great Fire. He looks upon you as being worthy of nothing else but to be cast into the Fire.[227]**

Edwards ends the sermon this way:

> **Oh sinner, consider the fearful danger you are in. It is a great furnace of wrath, a wide and bottomless pit, full of fire and wrath that you are held over by the hand of wrath provoked and increased against you as against many of the damned who are already in hell.**

This brings us to the third section of this tenth chapter of this history of perspectives on hell in which we will analyze and discuss the views of Early Modern Islamic philosophers on the ideas of *Jahannam* and punishment after death, beginning with Egyptian scholar, al-Suyuti (1445–1505).

Hell in Early Modern Islamic Philosophy

The Egyptian scholar al-Suyuti is credited with nearly five hundred works, including his *Tafsir Al-Jalalayn*, or his "Commentary on the Two Jalals," a word-by-word commentary on the Muslim Holy Book, Al-Qur'an.

Al-Suyuti points out that the main questions about *Jahannam*, at least regarding evildoers, is why punishment should endure long and hard with respect to its strength and eternality. Suyuti argues that the longevity and intensity in hell have been brought on by the sinner's own action. Suyuti calls this the "Embodiment of Actions," but philosophers more readily refer to it as Retributive Justice Theory.[228]

Al-Suyuti also was firmly against the view of Ibn Tamiyyah that suggests that the punishment in *Jahannam* will only last as long as the sins of the nonbeliever will be satisfied. That is, that hell in Islam is not a permanent condition. Al-Suyuti suggests that Tamiyyah's view is not in the mainstream of Islamic thought.

For many Early Modern Islamic thinkers, Ibn Tamiyyah's views on *Jahannam* were a central focal point for discussions of the Islamic views on hell. Among the Islamic philosophers who criticized the position of Ibn Tamiyyah on hell were fourteenth century thinkers, al-Baydawi and Abu Adud al-Din.[229]

Both al-Baydawi and Adud al-Din found Ibn Tamiyyah's view that hell is temporary to be a position that appears to go against the views of the Muslim Holy Book, Al-Qur'an, as well as the mentions in traditional hadith literature about the matter.

Modern Islamic philosopher, Yasir Qadhi, point out that the view of Ibn Tamiyyah on the temporary nature of *Jahannam* has been revived by some members of what is known as the "Salafi Movement," a Sunni Islam philosophical movement developed at the end of the Early Modern period in the late eighteenth century. There are many Salafists to be found in the Gulf states, some advocating the temporary status of *Jahannam* much like Ibn Tamiyyah.

Another late fourteenth-century treatment of the Islamic hell is Ibn Rajab al-Hanbali's 1393 work, *Al-Takhwif min al-Naar*, or "Fleeing from the Fire," an analysis of what life in *Jahannam* is like for Ibn Rajab. Ibn Rajab also contradicts the view of Ibn Tamiyyah that hell is a temporary abode. Most of Ibn Rajab's arguments against Ibn Tamiyyah are strictly on the bases of Al-Qur'an and traditional hadith literature.[230]

Sheikh Yasir Qadhi, mentioned earlier in this section, in his article entitled, "The Descriptions of *Jannah* and *Jahannam*," tells us three other things about the Ibn Tamiyyah points of view on hell. First, it should not be considered heretical. Secondly, it is important to call to mind the many passages in Al-Qur'an that speak of the mercy and forgiveness of

Allah. And finally, it is much easier to demonstrate the eternal existence of *Jannah* than it is to demonstrate the eternal nature of *Jahnnam*.[231]

This brings us to the final section of Chapter Ten in which we will explore the phenomena of hell and after death to be found in the popular culture of the Early Modern period from the sixteenth to the eighteenth century.

Hell in Early Modern Popular Culture

The two places in Early Modern culture where views on hell and after death can be seen were in painting and in literature. Among the paintings from the period that would have been known to people living in Europe from the sixteenth to the eighteenth centuries included works by:

1. Fra Angelico, *The Last Judgment*, 1425–1421
2. Jan van Eyck, *The Last Judgment*, 1430–1440
3. Hieronymus Bosch, *The Garden of Earthly Delights*, 1490–1500
4. Pieter Bruegel the Elder, *Dulle Griet: Mad Meg*, 1561
5. Lutheran woodcuts, sixteenth and seventeenth centuries
6. Counter-Reformation art, sixteenth and seventeenth centuries

Many Renaissance painters such as Fra Angelico, for example, depicted scenes of hell and the Last Judgment in their works. Angelico's *Last Judgment* was commissioned by a newly appointed abbot named Traversari and the painting is dated from 1425 to 1421. It was originally placed in the church of Santa Maria degli Angeli but is now owned by the Museum of San Marco in Florence.

In the painting, Christ sits in judgment on a white throne surrounded by angels, Mary, John, and other saints. Jesus is shown as a judge of the living and the dead. His left hand points down to hell, his right, up to Heaven. Christ's right hand leads to a Paradise with angels who lead the saved through beautiful gardens into a shining city.

In the middle of the painting are the broken tombs of the risen dead who have come out of their graves to be judged. On Christ's left are the damned where the wicked are tormented. At the very bottom of the painting, on Christ's left, Satan chews on three of the damned, while grasping two others in his hands.

Jan van Eyck also completed the *Last Judgment* in 1426. It is an oil on woodwork now owned by the Metropolitan Museum of Art in New York City. Van Eyck's painting is a diptych of Calvary on one panel and the Last Judgment on the other. This creation is one of the earliest Northern Renaissance paintings, renowned for its complex and highly detailed iconography and for the technical skill that went into its making.

Van Eyck is well known for several of his more visceral hell scenes, but the best known for his *Last Judgment*, which takes its inspiration from Dante's "Inferno." Hell is shown as a series of compartments in which the damned are grouped according to their sins. Each compartment has its own form of torture. Those who are guilty of greed, for example, have melted gold coins poured down their throats. Those guilty of wrath are forced incessantly to fight each other.

At the base of the painting and the fiery pit of hell, Lucifer chomps on human bodies of the damned, while he simultaneously bathes in a soup of melting souls as he is dutifully urged on by his cohort of demons.

The Dutch painter Hieronymus Bosch completed *Garden of Earthly Delights* between 1490 and 1500. Bosch shows hell not as fiery pit but rather as a raucous battlefield teeming with horrifying, and perhaps surrealistic creatures who take pleasure in torturing the humans.

The fame of the Bosch painting is perhaps due to the proliferation of mesmerizing details. A dismembered foot, for example, hangs from the helmet of a spiny bird-monster. Others of the damned are stretched taut across giant contraptions, or perhaps musical instruments played by beady-eyed demons, who appear to have been eaten and are now defecated by their aggressors.

Peter Bruegel the Elder is best known for his homely peasant scenes, but he also at times had a knack for shocking his audience. This is nowhere more apparent in Bruegel's work than his 1561 canvas *Dulle Griet*, also called "Mad Meg." The painting is indebted to Bosch and explores hell through the lens of Bruegel's contemporary Flemish culture.

Bruegel's painting shows the folkloric character of Dulle Griet, the leader of an all-female army on a quest to pillage hell. Griet's strength is the product of her massive size, as she dwarfs both her opponents and her female soldiers. The painting is an early combination of fantasy and reality. It also features a gaping hellmouth whose scaly bricks resemble the bricks in the surrounding architecture.

There are no demons in Peter Bruegel's painting. Instead of devouring the dead, the monsters of his hell battle flesh and blood warriors. Interestingly enough, in Bruegel's painting, the devil had no weapons.

Another way to judge Reformation views about hell is the sixteenth and seventeenth centuries is to examine the many Lutheran artists who were at work on classic woodcuts from the Period. *The Book of the Courtier*, for example, published anonymously in 1588, featured many views of the Roman Church as the Antichrist as well as hell itself.

Perhaps the most famous of these Lutheran artists was Lucas Cranach the Elder. His 1529 work *Law and Gospel*, in which Cranach intended to illustrate Lutheran ideas about salvation. Among the several versions of this work are scenes of hell, including manuscripts owned by the Gotha Museum in Germany and another by the National Gallery in Prague.

In one image of Cranach's *Law and Gospel*, from the Gotha manuscript, Saint John the Baptist directs a naked man—most likely a Roman Catholic—while in hell.

In another image from the same Cranach's manuscript a skeleton and a demon pursue a desperate, naked man in hell, while a gaggle of four Lutheran scholars can be seen reading the Gospel on the lower right. The image was meant to contrast the fate of the naked Roman man with that of the Lutheran scholars.

What Cranach's illustrations of hell have in common is that they all placed in the confines of hell many of the contemporary popes and prominent clergymen of the Roman Catholic Church of the period.

The Church originally ignored Luther and Cranach, but later the great Reformer was asked to recant and when he refused one response was the Roman Church's Council of Trent in which Luther and his followers were declared to be heretical.

Counter-Reformation painting and wood cuts at the time often feature depictions of both Luther and Calvin being shown as residents of hell fire. The State University Library at Dresden, for example, has a collection of engravings with this theme that include unflattering depictions of Wittenberg, Luther, Cranach, and other reformers. One collection is dated 1725.

This brings us to the other place in Early Modern culture where images of hell and after death can be seen from the sixteenth to the eighteenth centuries. That is, in the literature of the period.

Among the literary depictions of hell from the period are the following:

1. William Dawes's sermon, "The True Meaning of the Eternity of Hell-torments"
2. Giovanna Pietro Pinamonti, "Hell Opened to Christians to Caution Them from Entering It"
3. John Bunyan, *Journey to Hell*
4. John Milton, *Paradise Lost*
5. Christopher Marlowe, *Doctor Faustus*

Although there were many literary views in the Early Modern Period on hell and after death, we have chosen these five mentioned above as a representational sample of the Period. Of these Christopher Marlowe's 1589 to 1592 *Doctor Faustus* is the earliest. In his work, Mephistopheles warns Faustus about the horrors of hell. The demonic figure also raises the question about why any human being would ever make a pact with the devil, particularly since Mephistopheles believes that Heaven will simply be an extension of life on Earth.

The secondary literary work about hell and after death is that of John Bunyan's *Journey to Hell*. Bunyon supplies an allegory of the depravity, wickedness, and carnal nature of life in hell through his character named Mister Badman who ultimately learns that if one can lead a successful life now, he can also be ready to enter the Eternal City of God.[232]

John Bunyan also discusses hell and after death in his *Doctrinal Discourses*, including his observation that, "There is enough sin in my best prayer to send the whole world to hell," as well as his view that, "It is impossible to save even one soul from the fire of hell."

John Milton in his 1667 *Paradise Lost* makes many comments about the ideas of hell and after death, including the features of the Lake of Fire, volcanoes, and mountains in hell. In Milton's cosmology, hell is the netherworld located at the end of a bottomless pit, as far removed from Heaven as possible. Milton describes hell in a doleful shade of horror, gloom, and desolation, including a fiery deluge with ever-burning sulfur.[233]

In 1693, Counter-Reformation thinker Giovanni Pietro Pinamonti wrote a sermon on the gory details of hell to caution his followers from entering it. Pinamonti's hell is graphic, as well as quite foreboding.

Finally, in 1701, the Rev. William Dawes produced a sermon while preaching before King William and Queen Anne. Dawes was Bishop of Chester and later Archbishop of York. His sermon was entitled, "The True Meaning of the Eternity of Hell-torments." Dawes argues in the sermon for the idea of deterrence regarding hellfire, and without that deterrence, society itself could not function properly.

In this famous sermon, Bishop Dawes suggests that the torments of hell consist of what he calls "five particulars." First, is the wicked being banished from the enjoyment of God. Second are the lashes of the sinner's own guilty minds and of all their "vexations and passions."

Third, Dawes tells us, "Are the loathsomeness and discomfort of the place of hell," and the "troublesome conversion of the devil and wicked spirits which they shall be confined in." Fourth, there are the many "pains occasioned by the fire of hell, or whatever is meant under that name."

The Rev. Dawes also points out in his sermon that no society from the ancient world until the present had been able to survive without the idea of eternal punishment. He also points out that the absence of God in modern society, and though he includes the more diabolical features of hell, like the pains of fire, eternal duration and the torments that vex the soul, in Enlightenment spirit he more emphasized the interior nature of hell and its relation to the conscience.

And finally, "In the uninterrupted continuance and eternal duration of every one of these," as mentioned earlier, Bishop Dawes gave an account of hell that married medieval views of the fires of hell with an Enlightenment spirit that also saw punishment after death as more about a human being's interior life.

This brings us to the major conclusions we have made in this tenth chapter. This will be followed by Chapter Eleven in which we shall explore the phenomena of hell and after death in the Late Modern period in the nineteenth and early twentieth centuries.

Conclusions

We began Chapter Ten by suggesting that the chapter will have four major sections. In the first of these sections, we introduced several Early Modern Jewish perspectives on the questions of hell and after death.

Among these Jewish thinkers were the perspectives of Kabbalist thinkers Isaac Luria and Rabbi Hiyyam Vital, who both suggest a brand of what they called *Gigul* in Hebrew, or Reincarnation.

A third Jewish thinker whose views on survival after death we have introduced and discussed is that of Moses Hayyim Lazzato and his perspective that "Life on Earth is nothing more than an Anteroom of the *Olam Ha Ba*, or the 'World to Come.'" We also indicated, however, that the form of survival after death that this world to come shall take in Rabbi Lazzato's view is not terribly clear.

A fourth Early Modern Jewish scholar whose perspectives on the afterlife we have examined was Rabbi Yom Tov Lipman-Heller, Bohemian Rabbi, editor of the Mishnah and Biblical exegete.

In our analysis of the views of Rabbi Lipman-Heller, we have made three major conclusions about his views on the afterlife. First, that Lipman-Heller appears to believe in some form of a *Olam Ha Ba*. Second, it is not at all clear what form of survival after death he has in mind. And finally, the quality of the life to come is of a far greater, spiritual kind that what the Jews now have on Earth.

The views of Moses Mendelssohn on death and the afterlife is the final Jewish thinker we have examined in this chapter. In our remarks on the German Mendelssohn, we have shown that he wrote a separate book on immortality of the soul modeled after Plato's dialogues called the *Phaedo*. In fact, Rabbi Mendelssohn calls his book the *Phaedo*, as well. Along with the substile, "Or Immortality of the Soul."

In this book, Rabbi Mendelssohn proposes early on to want to "demonstrate the view that the immortality of the soul is a belief that can be philosophically established." He goes on to do this principally by using several arguments that Plato introduced in the *Phaedo*, though Immanuel Kant was very skeptical about those arguments.

In the second section of Chapter Ten, we introduced and discussed several Early Modern Christian thinkers on the issues of hell and survival after death. Among the thinkers we have examined were Martin Luther, John Calvin, Jonathan Edwards, Francis Turretin, and many others.

The idea of hell, or *Jahannam* in Arabic, was the central concern of the third section of Chapter Ten. We began this section by sketching out the views of several Early Modern Islamic thinkers, including al-Suyuti, al-Baydawi, and al-Tamiyyah, who held the perspective that *Jahannam* is not an eternal place.

This was followed with an analysis of some more modern views about the Islamic idea of hell, particularly as they relate to the perspective of al-Tamiyyah on the matter. Among these more modern thinkers were the Salafi Movement and Sheikh Yasir Qadhi.

In the fourth and final section of Chapter Ten, we have analyzed and discussed many of the places and works in Early Modern history where perspectives and views on hell and survival after death can be found in the popular cultures of the sixteenth to the eighteenth centuries.

More specifically, we have shown in the final section where many understandings of hell and after death could be found—particularly in painting and drawing from the period, as well as several places in Early Modern literature where hell and after death were the subject matter.

Among the artists whose works we have examined were Fra Angelico, Jan van Eyck, Hieronymus Bosch, Peter Bruegel, and Lucas Cranach and his critics. As we have seen, each of these artists provided detailed description of what time in hell appears to have consisted of. And each of these artists provides a unique perspective on the issues.

At the very end of Chapter Ten, we pointed out the great amount of literary works in the Early Modern period where the ideas of hells after death are at the center of sixteenth to eighteenth-century literary works.

Because of the voluminous amount of this material, we have chosen instead to concentrate on five separate literary works from the period. These writers were Christopher Marlowe; John Bunyan; John Milton; Counter-Reformation writer, Giovanni Pietro Pinamonti; and Bishop William Dawes of the Church of England.

With these five representative thinkers we were able to show the range of Early Modern literary perspectives to be found on the issues of hell and the question of punishment after death in the period.

The remarks of Marlowe on hell were principally the dialogue between Dr. Faustus and Mephistopheles, the devil character in *Doctor Faustus*. John Bunyan's views on hell, as we have seen, come from two of his works, *Journey to Hell* and his *Doctrinal Discourses*.

John Milton, of course, in his *Paradise Lost*, created one of the best-known accounts of hell and after death in Western society, and we have sketched out some of the peculiar features of those views.

The perspectives of Giovanni Pietro Pinamonti were mostly a Counter-Reformation response to the views on hell on Martin Luther and Lucas Cranach the Elder. Pinamonti's hell is graphic, gloomy, and very foreboding.

Finally, in the final section of Chapter Ten, we introduced and discussed a 1701 sermon delivered before the king and queen in which Bishop William Dawes made five principal points of his views on hell and after death.

In Chapter Eleven to follow, our main purpose will be to examine the Late Modern views on hell and survival after death in the nineteenth and the early twentieth centuries, a period rife with perspectives on the issues at hand.

Queen Mary Apocalypse (early 14th C). Location: British Library, London.

Chapter Eleven
Hell in the Modern Period
Nineteenth and Early Twentieth Centuries

The definition of hell is a place where
nothing connects with nothing else.
—T. S. Eliot

After all, is not a real hell better than a manufactured Heaven?
—E. M. Forster

Introduction

The main purpose of this eleventh chapter is to identify and discuss views and perspectives on the ideas of hell and after death among scholars, artists, poets, and other thinkers who lived in the nineteenth and the early twentieth centuries. To that end, this chapter will only have two, separate sections, one on the nineteenth century and one on the early twentieth century. We also will provide some preliminary remarks on both centuries, followed by views on hell and after death.

This chapter will be followed, as we shall see later, by Chapter Twelve—the final chapter—in which we will discuss the phenomena of hell and after death in the contemporary period, from the late twentieth century until the present-time. But first we move to perspectives on hell from the nineteenth century.

Nineteenth-Century Perspectives on Hell and After Death

In the nineteenth century, there are many places to find views about hell and after death, including one French nobleman, the Marquis de

Sade, several Romantic poets, other kinds of writers, like John Furniss, Austin Holyoake, and Christina Rosetti, as well as a few artists like William Blake and Auguste Rodin and his *Gates of Hell*. Before we get to these remarks, however, we will first make some preliminary comments on the nineteenth century.

Preliminary Remarks on the Nineteenth Century

One might well argue that the nineteenth century began in 1799 after the French Revolution when Napoleon seized power of France. By 1804, he had crowned himself Emperor, after victories over the Austrian-Russian Army. In 1812, after the French invasion of Russia, the French had enormous casualties, and that was the beginning of the end of Napoleon's empire.

Meanwhile, in Latin America, many nations declared their independence from colonial powers. In 1804, for example, Haiti gained independence from France. Mexico established its independence in 1821 and many other Latin American nations followed suit, including Guatemala, Nicaragua, Costa Rica, and many other countries.

In 1848, there was a series of political upheavals throughout Europe. These revolutions were mostly democratic and liberal in nature, often in consort with the removal of monarchs creating independent nations. The first of these 1848 revolutions was in January in the Kingdom of Sicily. Another revolution began in France the next month. Over fifty countries were involved in these revolutions.

The nineteenth century also saw the abolition of slavery in many places throughout the world. The Atlantic slave trade was abolished by Britain in 1808. The Slavery Abolition Act of 1833 followed that banned slavery throughout the British Empire. Abolition movements in the United States also began, for the most part, in the nineteenth century. Slavery was abolished in America by the Thirteenth Amendment to the U.S. Constitution in 1865.

The American Civil War was fought in the nineteenth century, as was the Taiping Rebellion from 1851 to 1853. Britain annexed Burma from 1823 to 1887; The United States purchased Alaska from Russia in

1867; and the U.S. nearly doubled its size with the Louisiana Purchase from France.

The mid-nineteenth century also saw the first use of the English word "scientist." Before then, these people were called "natural philosophers." Many scientific discoveries are attributed to the nineteenth century. Potassium and sodium were isolated in 1807, Darwin published the *Origin of Species* in 1859, Gregor Mendel's laws of inheritance followed in 1856, Maxwell's treatise on electricity came in 1873, Louis Pasteur created the first vaccine in 1885, and the aspirin was patented in 1889.

The first steam engine appeared in 1804, aluminum was isolated in 1825, the first electric motor was built in 1829, the telegraph was patented in 1837, the first transcontinental railroad was completed in 1869, and Thomas Edison invented the phonograph in 1877 and the light bulb two years later.

The Church of Jesus Christ of Latter-day Saints, the Mormons, was established in 1830. Mary Baker Eddy founded the Christian Scientists in 1879. And the Persian prophet, Bab, announced to the world that he is the younger brother of Jesus Christ.

Beethoven composed his Fifth Symphony in 1808 and his Ninth in 1824. Franz Schubert, Frederick Chopin, Johan Strauss, Gustav Mahler, Richard Strauss, Carl Maria von Weber, Modest Mussorgsky, Johannes Brahms, Stephen Foster, Robert Schumann, and Pyotr Ilyich Tchaikovsky, all composed their music in the nineteenth century.

The nineteenth century was also a great period for literature around the world, including in Britain, France, Russia, and the United States. Jane Austen's *Pride and Prejudice* was published in 1813, Mary Shelly's *Frankenstein* five years later, Goethe's *Faust* came out in 1829, Melville's *Moby Dick* in 1851, Walt Whitman's *Leaves of Grass* in 1855, and Leo Tolstoy's *War and Peace* in 1869.

In the visual arts, the nineteenth century saw the works of William Blake, Mary Cassatt, Camille Claudel, Edgar Degas, Thomas Eakins, Paul Gaugin, Claude Monet, Edvard Munch, James Tissot, Ilya Repin, Francisco Goya, William Morris, Vincent Van Gogh, John Singer Sargent, Valentin Serov, to name only a few.

Thus, in the nineteenth century, we see important developments in politics, science, technology, religion, in the visual arts, in medicine, music, literature, in biology and chemistry and in scientific and technological discoveries. This brings us to perspectives on hell and after death in the nineteenth century, the subject matter of the second section of Chapter Eleven.

Hell and After Death in the Nineteenth Century

One aspect regarding views about hell in the nineteenth century is that for the first time in many Christian churches we begin to see many denominations who claimed that hell was no longer a valid belief of the Christian faith. In 1839, the great Unitarian minister Henry Giles, for example, wrote, "There is no room in the same universe for a Good God and an eternal hell."[234]

Thomas Erskine (1788–1870), a Presbyterian Scot, related that,

> **If anyone is in hell it is because he put himself there by refusing to enter Heaven. So long, therefore, as a man refuses to allow the forgiving love of God to enter his heart—if he continues in this state through eternity, he will through eternity be a child of wrath.**

Elsewhere, however, the Rev. Erskine more directly raised doubts about the existence of an eternal hell.

Frederick Denison Maurice (1805–1872) of King's College, London, in 1853, after the publication of his *On Eternal Life and Eternal Death*, was discharged from his teaching post for several reasons, including the claim that he did not believe in the eternality of hell.[235]

English philosopher John Stuart Mill (1806–1873) made the claim that, "There is a moral contradiction between belief in a loving God who could also make a place like hell." Mill adds:

> **I will call no being good who is not what I mean when I apply that epithet to my fellow creatures; and if such a being can sentence me to hell for not so calling Him, then to hell I will go.[236]**

Evangelical and English moderate Calvinist, Thomas Rawson Birks (1810–1883) suggested that,

Those in hell, while cut off directly from the presence of God, would still have the opportunity to passively observe and to enjoy God's goodness.

In addition to hell, Birks also rejected the Calvinist doctrine of limited atonement, and he had a wider view of the scope of salvation when it came to non-Christians.

In regard to the idea of an ever-lasting hell, the famous Christian missionary J. W. Colenso (1814–1883) said he had an "inner hope that there is a remedial process by which all may come to the grace of God."[237]

Finally, F. W. Robertson, minister at Trinity Chapel in Brighton, saw eternal life and death "In terms of the quality of existence and not in its temporal duration." The Rev. Robertson spoke of hell as a place that is "mostly known for its absence of God.[238]

In addition, in the 1870s and early 1880s, there was a well-known debate over the traditional doctrine of hell between F. W. Farrar, the Canon of Westminster and E. B. Pusey, who was the leader of the Oxford Movement of the Church of England. Farrar had preached a series of sermons that he later published in his volume, *Eternal Hope.* In this book, Farrar clearly asserts his belief in the "terrible retribution upon the impenitent sinner, both here and hereafter."[239]

Farrar also rejected the idea that hell is a physical place of "eternal, physical torment." He also believed that "The majority of human beings will wind up there." And Farrar left open the possibility of repentance after death. Many interpreted Farrar's book as his being arguing for Universal Salvation. But Farrar said, "I was rejecting conditionalism and Universalism."[240]

In rebuttal, Pusey published a scholarly defense of the Church of England's traditional teaching about hell. His essay was called, "What Is Our Faith as to Everlasting Punishment?" Pusey argued that the tradition Anglican doctrine on hell does not require one to believe that punishment will be physical, nor does it predict how many will be lost and saved. Against Farrar, Pusey affirmed that hell is eternal and that "the fate of each person is determined at death."

The Seventh-Day Adventist Church was formally established in 1863. It grew out of the Millerite Movement, a sect led by William

Miller who had predicted the Second Coming of Christ would occur in 1843 or 1844. They became another Christian movement, however, that rejected the idea of an everlasting hell and after death.

Nevertheless, there are several nineteenth-century figures who firmly believed in the eternal nature of hell. One of them was the Marquis de Sade (1740–1814), who in his written works was decidedly against the idea of an All-Good and All-Powerful God, while at the same time believing that "The Devil, for the most part, controls the world."[241]

His comments in another essay that de Sade wrote about hell said as much about human nature and his beliefs about his fellow humans than about hell itself. He observes,

> **To judge from notions expounded by theologians, we must conclude that God created most men simply with a view in mind of crowding hell.[242]**

In the same essay, "Thoughts on Hell," he also remarked, "For mortal men there is about one hell and that is the folly and the wickedness of other men." De Sade decidedly did not believe in God, but he did appear to believe in hell, as well as the devil.

Another way that de Sade's view of hell can most clearly be seen is his admiration for the novel of Matthew Gregory Lewis, called *The Monk*, published in 1796. In the book, Lewis recounts the diabolical decline of Ambrosio, a Capuchin superior who succumbs to sexual temptation much like the Marquis de Sade did throughout his adult life.

Another place in the nineteenth century where views on hell and after death can be seen is in the Romantic poets, particularly Lord Byron and John Keats. In two of his poems, called "Manfred" and "Cain," Lord Byron alludes to hell.[243]

Jean Jacques-Rousseau, thought by many to be the first of the Romantics, wrote an essay on the punishments of hell in which he takes a fairly traditional view. When the encyclopedist Denis Diderot read the essay, he called Rousseau,

> **A madman and a damned soul. He is right, however, to imply that there is an immense gap between Heaven and Hell.[244]**

John Keats (1795–1821) was widely regarded as the most talented of the English Romantic poets. His work was poorly received in his own lifetime, and he could not imagine the success he had after his death. Ironically, he wrote the poetic words for his own epitaph that say:

Here lies one whose name was writ in water,
Why did I laugh tonight?
No voice will tell.[245]

The epitaph is part of a larger poem called "Why Did I Laugh Tonight," in which Heaven and Hell are mentioned twice in the poem's fourteen lines. The first comes at line three, "Deigns to reply from Heaven or from Hell." The second reference comes in line eight, "To question Heaven and Hell and Heart in vain." The poem implies that Keats believes in survival after death, but he is not entirely sure where he is going after death.

The "Fall of Hyperion," is another of Keats poems that includes a vision of the underworld in which the hero of the poem is actually reading Dante. The hero also finds himself before what appears to be the steps to Purgatory which he is ordered to climb. Hyperion dutifully obeys, followed by his arrival at Tartarus itself.[246]

In several of his letters, John Keats also mentions hell and gives us some understanding of what he thinks about the realm of the Christian underworld. In one letter he says, "there is no fiercer hell than the failure in a great object." In another letter Keats proclaimed, "I would rather go to hell with my brothers and sisters than to Heaven without them."[247]

It is clear that Keats had a traditional Anglican view of Heaven and Hell, but his romantic spirit appears to give him some doubts about where he himself would wind up, as well as how and why he would get there. It could be that Keats comment is nothing more than being part of the nineteenth-century doubt about the truth of eternal punishment.

Lord Byron, another of the English Romantics, while on his honeymoon, in fact on his wedding night, was startled out of his sleep when a taper burning in the room was casting a ruddy glare through the crimson curtains of the bed and he could not help exclaiming in a voice so loud that he woke up his wife, "Good God, I am surely in hell." Before that evening, all of Byron's sexual experiences had been homosexual ones.[248]

Lord Byron also wrote about hell in his 1822 "The Vision of Judgment," a satirical poem that disputes whether King George III's soul is in Heaven. The poem was written in response to poet laureate Robert Southey's "A Vision of Judgment," which had imagined the soul of George III triumphantly entering the Gates of Heaven. Byron was provoked by Southey's Tory point of view, and he took Southey's reference to "young men of diseased hearts and depraved imaginations" who had "set up a School of Satanic Poetry" to be a reference to himself and others of the Romantics.[249]

Byron also begins his poem written in 1812 called "The Devil's Drive" with the words:

> The Devil returned to hell by two,
> And stay'd at home till five,
> When he dined on some homicides done in *ragout*
> With a rebel or so in an *Irish* stew—
> And sausages made of a selfslain Jew.

The same poem goes on for another twenty-five stanzas speaking of Lucifer or the devil and his activities in hell. Like Keats, Lord Byron also appears to have had a fairly traditional Anglican view of the demonic and their home, the fires of hell.

Another English Romantic poet, Percy Shelly (1792–1822), in his *Prometheus Unbound*, a four-act lyrical drama published in 1820, is concerned with the torments of the Greek mythological figure Prometheus, who defies the gods and brings fire to human beings. After Jupiter has been overthrown, he falls into something that looks very much like the Christian hell of Shelly's day. The text tells us:

> **Let hell unlock Its moulded Oceans of tempestuous fire,**
> **And when on them into the bottomless void.**[250]

In *A Defence of Poetry*, Shelly also discusses hell in relation to what he sees as the contours of hell in Milton's *Paradise Lost*. Shelly also takes up the same theme in another essay he calls, "On the Devil and Devils," in which the nineteenth-century Romantic poet defends the traditional Anglican views on the devil and hell as well.

Shelly's essay, "On the Devil and Devils," was prepared for publication in 1839 along with the rest of Shelly's prose works, but it was withdrawn from publication shortly before going to the press, presumably for theological reasons though we cannot be sure about the reason for its withdraw from publication.

In another of Percy Shelly's poems entitled, "Peter Bell, the Third," Shelly again speaks about hell:

Hell is much like the city of London, A populated city and smoky life. There many sorts of people are undone. And there is little or no fun done.

One conclusion, however, that can be made about Shelly's views on Satan and on hell is that, like Keats and Lord Byron, Shelly held a traditional, nineteenth-century Anglican view on the nature and extent of hell. The same cannot be said about the views on hell of a fourth English Romantic poet, William Blake (1757–1827), as we shall see next.

Blake spoke of hell in several places of his works but no more centrally than in *The Marriage of Heaven and Hell*, a series of texts written in imitation of Biblical prophecy, while still expressing Blake's intensely unique individual Romantic and revolutionary beliefs.

Like some of the other Romantics, William Blake admired John Milton as being a "true poet," but he claimed that his epic *Paradise Lost* was "of the Devil's party without knowing it." *The Marriage of Heaven and Hell* was composed between 1790 and 1793 in the radical period of the French Revolution.[251]

In Blake's work *Marriage*, observations can be seen of the philosophy of Emanuel Swedenborg's theological tract, *Heaven and Hell*, which took a mystical and a Manichean view of Good and Evil. This allowed Blake to take a unified vision of the cosmos in which the material world and physical desires are equal parts of the Cosmos. Hence a marriage of Heaven and Hell.

Blake's book describes a visit of the poet to hell, a device, of course, borrowed from Milton. For Blake, however, hell is not a place of punishment, but rather it is a source of unrepressed, somewhat Dionysian energy, opposed to the authoritarian and regulated of God and Heaven. Blake's "purpose" was to create what he called a "memorable fancy" in order to reveal the repressed nature of conventional morality, as well as organized religion.

Unlike the other Romantic poets, then, William Blake does not have a conventional and traditional view of the ideas of hell and after death. In fact, in one section from *The Marriage of Heaven and Hell* called the "Proverbs of Hell," Blake tells us simply:

> **From these contraries spring what the religious call Good and Evil. Good is the passive that obeys Reason. Evil is the active springing from Energy. Good is Heaven. Evil is hell.**

We will explore four other nineteenth-century writers and their views on hell and after death. These are John Furniss and his essay *The Sight of Hell*, Austin Holyoake's work *Heaven and Hell*, Charles Robert Maturin's 1820 story *Melmoth the Wanderer*, and Christine Rosetti's 1862 work *Goblin Market*.

John Furniss (1809–1865) was a Catholic priest and is important in terms of cataloguing the history of views on hell because his essay *The Sight of Hell* was written specifically for children. The essay was originally published as a pamphlet.[252]

Father Furniss' essay is divided into thirty-three sections in which he asks a theological question at the head of each section such as "Where is hell?" "How Far is it to hell?" "What are the gates of hell like?" ending in "What is eternity like in hell?" "What are the occupants in hell doing?" And "How is time kept in hell?"

There was much controversy about Father Furniss' essay after its publication. One response came from Austin Holyoake and his essay entitled, *Heaven and Hell, Where Situated?*[253]

Austin Holyoake (1826–1874) was an American nineteenth–century painter, publisher, and freethinker. He was born in Birmingham, Alabama, and he was the publisher of various journals such as the *National Reformer* and the *Reasoner.* Unlike many of his other writings, in *Heaven and Hell*, Holyoake took a very conservative view of the issue at hand, beginning with this opening:

> **Heaven is the hope of the Christian—hell is its dread, his fear, his abiding terror. What would Christianity be—that is, the modern faith of Europe—without these two ideas, or sentiments, or**

beliefs, or whatever they may be called.

After describing the bliss to be expected in Heaven, Holyoake turns his attention to hell. He asks:

What shall we say about the other place the abode for departed spirits, the climate of which is so warm that the natives of Central Africa will find it uncomfortable? Where is it situated? Oh, down below, of course, all Christians say so, and they alone know. Did not Christ descend into hell. And yet it cannot be far from Heaven, for did not Dives and Lazarus hold a conversation together from their respective abodes?

So far Holyoake's comments appear to be from a very conventional views of hell and after death. But by the time we get to the end of his essay, the publisher reverses positions when he tells us:

The Bible, or any other book, which teaches the doctrine of hell torments, is not, cannot be, a revelation from a God of love and mercy. It is the crude production of an ignorant, a superstitious, a priest-ridden people... This doctrine, so far from keeping men good makes good men bad and brutalize all who believe in it. It distracts men's minds from the duties of life and deludes them into a belief of another which, when looked at calmly and with reason. Will be seen to contain no worthy of their acceptance, or capable of promoting permanent happiness.

Ultimately, then, Austin Holyoake's remark about hell appears to be little more than an example of the late nineteenth century, burgeoning doubt that human beings will be punished for all eternity in hell.

Charles Robert Maturin (1780–1824) was an Irish Protestant clergyman ordained in the Church of Ireland. He was also a writer of Gothic plays and novels. His best-known novel is his work *Melmoth the Wanderer* published in 1820. The novel's titular character is a scholar who sold his soul to the devil in exchange for 150 extra years of life.[254]

Melmouth is composed of a series of nested stories gradually revealing the nature of Melmouth's narrative. The book makes social commentaries on early nineteenth century social mores and denounces Roman Catholicism in favor of what Maturin sees as "Protestant Virtues."

Maturin's novel is filled with increasing decadence, despair, and corruption, but what it lacks is a denouement with a final hell scene in which everything turns out for the good, or for evil for that matter. Maturin simply used the Wandering Jew and Faust motifs, but he adds very little improvement to those tales.

One final nineteenth–century writer on hell is Christina Rossetti and her 1862 work *Goblin Market*. Rossetti (1830–1894) was an English poet who wrote Romantic, devotional literature, as well as children's poems. For our purposes, her *Goblin Market*, written in 1859 and published in 1862, is her most important work.[255]

The poem tells the story of two sisters, Laura and Lizzie, and their adventures with some river goblins. Among these goblins are some that are "cat-faced" and others who are "rat-faced," who tempt the sisters with strange fruit. Laura becomes an instant addict to the fruit. Her virtuous sister, Lizzie, cannot bear her sister's misery and dependence on the fruit.

Eventually, Laura is taken to hell, the punishment for her addiction. She is accosted there by more goblins who show the young captive her true nature. Brave Lizzie who goes to save her sister, refuses to taste the goblin juices, and she runs home to Laura and cries, followed by finding an antidote.

This brings us to the final section of this eleventh chapter on the ideas of hell and after death in the Late Modern period, from the early twentieth century, the subject matter of the next section of this history of attitudes towards hell and after death.

Hell in the Early Twentieth Century

The early decades of the twentieth century saw many amazing scientific and technological feats. The first flight of the Wright brothers, Henry Ford's first Model-T, and Albert Einstein's Theory of Relativity. The time also included, however, hardships such as the Boxer Rebellion and the San Francisco Earthquake.

The early 1900s also saw the growth of the burgeoning film industry, first in silent films and later what were called "Talkies." The 1910s were dominated by the first "Total War," World War I. It also showed huge changes after the Russian Revolution and the beginning of Prohibition in the United States.

The Roaring Twenties was a time of a booming stock market, speakeasies, short skirts, the Charleston, and the beginning of Jazz. The 1920s also showed great strides in women's suffrage, and the discovery of King Tut's tomb. Babe Ruth hit sixty homeruns in 1927, and the first Mickey Mouse cartoon appeared in the 1920s.

The 1930s was the decade of the Depression in American beginning with the stock market crash of October 29, 1929. Franklin Delano Roosevelt proposed his "New Deal" for the American people. Germany invaded Poland in 1939, starting the Second World War that would last until 1945. The Tennessee Valley Authority was enacted into law in the 1930s.

The world was at war in the beginning of the 1940s. Pearl Harbor was attacked, bringing the United States into the war. Adolf Hitler and the Nazis were defeated, and the American economy, at the end of the decade, was again burgeoning.

The amount of material in the period from 1900 to 1950 about the phenomena of hell and after death is incredibly voluminous. Consequently, we have chosen five representative examples to give the flavor of the age. These representative examples are:

1. August Rodin (1814–1910), *The Gates of Hell*
2. Vasily Grossman (1906–1964), *The Hell of Treblinka*
3. Yoshitaka Kawamoto (1932–), *Fire in the Sky*
4. Wallace Stevens (1879–1955), "The Comedian as the Letter C"
5. Charles Demuth (1883–1935), *The Golden Swan*, also called *Hell Hole*

French artist Auguste Rodin worked on his monumental sculpture piece *The Gates of Hell* from 1880 until his death in 1917, at the time of his death. Rodin tells us that the piece is a depiction of the first section of Dante's "Inferno." It was put together and finished under the direction of Leonce Benedite with Rodin's permission. While alive, in his studio, the only version was plaster cast. After his death, however, bronze casts were created.

Rodin's initial inspiration came from Dante. The Rodin Museum in Philadelphia owns the first bronze cast of *The Gates*. The artwork consists of two separate "doors," on the right and the left. Images of demons can be seen through the grates of the doors. The gates are evocative about what appears to lie behind them.

Vasily Grossman's *The Hell of Treblinka* was published in a Soviet literary journal called *Znamya*, or "The Banner," in November of 1944. Grossman, a Ukrainian journalist, was among the first writers to visit the remains of the killing center at Treblinka. Among Grossman's many conclusions are that Treblinka is evidence that sometimes "hell can be found right on Earth."[256]

The end of Grossman's account is compelling. He speaks of walking around the grounds of Treblinka after it had been bulldozed into oblivion. He remarks:

> **We walk on over the swaying, the bottomless earth of Treblinka and suddenly I come to a stop. Thick wavy hair, gleaming like burnished copper, the delicate lovely hair of a young woman trampled into the ground and beside it some equally fine blonde hair; and then some heavy black plaits on the bright sand; and then more and more... Evidently, these are the contents of a sack, just a single sack that somehow got left behind.**

Another account of the liberated death camps of the Nazis survives in a poem from Shmuel Marvil entitled "The Street." The poem originally had thirty-seven stanzas, but now from the final line of stanza 34, it appears to have been torn away until the very last stanza that is intact.

In Yiddish, Marvil tells of his time in the camp:

> **And I did curse. Believe me I cursed myself and even the people in the streets. And my aching heart growled like a lion. A broken prayer to the sky, the sky. A crow wandered in lost, black as time, and walks with a strut of a demon no less walks over the corpses and looks them over. And who can disturb her in this, oh Who?**[257]

This poem was composed in 1943 in the middle of the life of the Jews in the Nazi concentration and death camps. Shmuel Marvil (1906–1943) was one of the victims of the Nazis. He died in their hands in 1943.

Yoshitaka Kawamoto's essay *Fire in the Sky* was written in 1945 when he was only thirteen years old. He had been in his classroom at

Zakobo-cho, less than a mile from the epicenter of the atomic bomb dropped on Hiroshima in August of 1945. In his account, Kawamoto describes his school being leveled by the blast and the injuries sustained by some of his fellow students and faculty members. The testimony of Yoshitaka Kawamoto, like Grossman's account, is another fine example of the phenomenon that sometimes hell can be found right here on Earth.

At the end of Kawamoto's account, he speaks of his later life:

> **Today, I am still working as you can see. As the director of the Hiroshima Peace Memorial, today I am handing out messages over to the children who visit here. I want them to learn about Hiroshima, and when they grow up, I want them to hand down the message to the next generation with accurate information. I would like to se them conveying the right sense of judgment so that we will not lead mankind to annihilation. That is our responsibility.**

Another first-person account of the dropping of the bomb on the city of Hiroshima can be seen in a junior high school student named Akihiro Takahasi, who was lined up for the beginning of school on the morning of August 6, 1945. He relates:

> **We saw a B-29 approaching. All of us were looking up at the sky. Then the teachers came out from the school and the class leaders gave the command to fall in. That was the moment when the blast came. I was blown about ten meters. My friends were all knocked to the ground. Everything collapsed for as far as I could see. I felt that the city of Hiroshima had disappeared all of a sudden. Then I looked at myself and found my clothes had turned into rags because of the heat. I was burned at the back of my head, on both arms and legs. My skin was peeling and hanging off.[258]**

These accounts from Treblinka, where Shmuel Marvil was imprisoned and where he was executed, as well as the narrative of Yoshitaka Kawamoto and the account of Akihiro Takahashi, all have one fundamental thing in common. To wit, that in human history, particularly in the twentieth century, it has often been the case that hell is nothing more than life on Earth.

The "Comedian as the Letter C," is a poem by Wallace Stevens from his first book of poetry called *Harmonium* published in 1923. The poem is a fine expression of Stevens' dictum that, "The artist can do nothing else but select out of life the elements for his fictive, or fictitious reality."[259]

In the poem, Stevens attempts to transcend his locality and replace it with something more foreign, starker, and more barren. What he chooses is the "green barbarism" of Yucatan, a crusty town that has characteristics that can only be described as hell-like.

The final piece of early-twentieth-century views on hell is American painter Charles Demuth's watercolor entitled *The Golden Swan*, sometimes also called the *Hell Hole* because the 1919 painting, which does contain a golden swan, also looks surprisingly like what some early twentieth-century people may have described as hell.[260]

The scene takes place in a restaurant. A waiter carries drinks on a tray. The people at the various tables have faces of gloom and discontent. In the upper right of the image is a foreboding, dark figure with a hat that some critics have suggested is the devil himself. If this is Demuth's idea of hell, then it is a very gloomy place indeed.

This brings us to the major conclusions we have made in this eleventh chapter on hell in the nineteenth and the early twentieth centuries. The conclusion to Chapter Eleven will be followed by the twelfth and final chapter of this history of views on the ideas of hell and after death in the contemporary period, from the late twentieth century to the present.

Conclusions

The main purpose of Chapter Eleven has been to identify and to discuss views and perspectives on the ideas of hell and after death among scholars, artists, poets, writers, and other thinkers who lived and worked in the nineteenth and the early twentieth centuries.

We began the chapter by making some very general observations about the nineteenth century, pointing out the most important and significant events of the century. In these preliminary remarks about the nineteenth century, we have spoken of events in Europe after the French Revolution, independence in Latin America, the abolition of slavery around the world, various scientific and technological discoveries, as well as outstanding contributions to society's music and the arts.

In the second section of Chapter Eleven, we discussed the phenomena of hell and after death in the nineteenth century. We began this section by pointing out that many Christian churches in the period had begun to say that the idea of hell and eternal punishment were no longer valid views.

Among these Christian denominations and figures we have discussed included the Unitarian Church, the Seventh-Day Adventists, Evangelical Calvinists, missionary J. W. Colenso, philosopher John Stuart Mill, Presbyterian Thomas Erskine, Anglican Frederick Denison Maurice, Calvinist Thomas Rawson Birks, and Minister of Trinity Chapel in Brighton, F. W. Robertson.

We also indicated F. W. Farrar, the Canon at Westminster, and E. B. Pusey who was the leader of the Oxford Movement in the 1870s and 1880s. As we have shown, Farrar was willing to give up the idea of eternal punishment in the Church of England, while Dr. Pusey vigorously defended the idea.

In the next portion of the second section, we have explored many nineteenth-century perspectives about hell and after death including the views of the Marquis de Sade, a few of the English Romantic poets—Keats, Lord Byron, Percy Shelly and his essay *On the Devil and Devils*, as well as William Blake and his *Marriage of Heaven and Hell.*

Following this discussion of the Romantic poet on hell, we turned our attention, still in section two of Chapter Eleven, to a series of other nineteenth-century thinkers who had some views on hell and after death. Among these thinkers were Father John Furniss whose *Sight of Hell* was written for school children; American painter and publisher, Austin Holyoake, who wrote an important essay about hell; Protestant clergyman, Charles Robert Maturin whose Gothic novel *Melmoth the Wanderer* contains a bargain that the titular character made with the devil; and Christina Rossetti's *Goblin Market*, one of the most creative plots about hell in the nineteenth century.

In the third section of Chapter Eleven, we turned our attention to several thinkers who have spoken about hell and after death in the first half of the twentieth century. Among the writers and artists we discussed in this period were French artist August Rodin and his creation known as *The Gates of Hell* and Vasily Grossman's account of entering the Nazi concentration camps with the Russian Army in November of 1944.

Other early twentieth-century writers, poets, and artists we have introduced and discussed in the third section of Chapter Eleven have included Jewish poet Shmuel Marvil and selections from his poem "The Street" written in 1943. Two first-person accounts by Japanese school children of the dropping of the atomic bomb on the city of Hiroshima in August of 1945.

The first of these was by thirteen-year-old Yoshitaka Kawamoto, who had been in his classroom when the blast struck, and a fourteen-year-old high school student named Akihiro Takahashi whose account of his survival from the bombing of Hiroshima is nothing short of being truly amazing.

Two other final pieces on hell in the first half of the twentieth century were a poem by American Wallace Stevens and a painting by American painter Charles Demuth. Stevens' poem is entitled the "Comedian as the Letter C," which was published in his first collection of poetry in 1923 known as the *Harmonium*. In the poem, Stevens transcends his time and place and replaces them with the "green Barbarism of Yucatan," a crusty town that has many hell-like characteristics.

As we have shown at the end of the third section of Chapter Eleven, American painter Charles Demuth created a work entitled *The Golden Swan* in 1919. This work is also sometimes called *Hell Hole* because, although the watercolor does contain a golden swan, it resembles what many critics in the early twentieth century believed looked more like hell itself

As we have shown, the scene of the painting is a restaurant. A waiter carries drinks on a tray. The people at the various tables of the restaurant have gloomy faces and countenances of discontent. In the upper right portion of the Demuth's watercolor is a foreboding-looking, dark figure with a dark hat that many critics have suggested is the devil himself. If this is so, then Charles Demuth's hell is a very gloomy, dark, and foreboding place indeed, much like most of the history we have described throughout this study.

This brings us to the twelfth and final chapter of this history of attitudes and perspectives on the issues of hell and after death, from ancient times until the present. In Chapter Twelve, our major interests shall be to explore the phenomena of hell and after death in the Contemporary Period, from the second half of the twentieth century until contemporary times.

As a separate feature of Chapter Twelve, we will also give a general summary of the major conclusions about hell and after death that we have set forth in this study of these two phenomena. We move next, then, to Chapter Twelve, hell and after death in the contemporary period.

William-Adolphe Bouguereau, *Dante and Virgil in Hell*, 1850.
Oil on canvas, 110.4 x 88.7 in. Musée D'Orsay, Paris, France.

Chapter Twelve
Hell in the Contemporary Period
Late Twentieth Century to the Present

You think you frightened me with your hell, don't you?
You think your hell is worse than mine.
—Dorothy Parker

There is one serious defect to my mind in Christ's moral character, and that is that he believed in hell. I do not myself believe that any person who is really profoundly humane can believe in everlasting punishment.
—Bertrand Russell

Socialism only works in two places: Heaven where they don't need it and hell where they already have it.
—Ronald Reagan

Introduction

The purpose of this twelfth and final chapter is to discuss the phenomena of hell and after death in the contemporary world, that it from 1950 until the present age in the twenty-first century.

We will accomplish this task by looking at four separate areas in this chapter. These areas will correspond to the four sections of the chapter. The first of these is general comments about hell made by thinkers in the contemporary world. In the second section, we shall examine and discuss films, books, and television shows where hell has been depicted from 1950 to the present time.

In the third section of Chapter Twelve, we shall discuss at some length the current attitudes of Americans about Heaven and Hell, at least according to two studies by the Pew Research Center from 1999 and 2014, as well as several other studies by the University of Chicago, the University of Connecticut, and several polls conducted by news organizations such as CNN, Fox News, NBC, ABC, CBS, *USA Today*, and many others.

In the fourth and final section, we shall examine and discuss some of the most recent observations about hell and after death in the twenty-first century. These points of view, as we shall see at the close of the chapter, as well as the end of this study in general, are of different kinds, including political, as well as artistic, historical, literary, and political perspectives.

This brings us to the first section of Chapter Twelve in which we will examine several comments about hell made by contemporary scholars, writers, politicians, and celebrities from the current age, that is, 1950 to the present time.

General Comments about Hell in the Contemporary Period

In the period from 1950 until the present age, there has been a large variety of comments made about the nature and extent of hell and after death. In this first section, we will examine the thoughts and words of the following people, some of whom have been used as epigrams for this final chapter:

1. Albert Camus
2. Nikos Kazantzakis
3. John F. Kennedy
4. Bertrand Russell
5. E.M. Forster
6. Dorothy Parker
7. Sylvia Plath
8. Ronald Reagan
9. Butch Hancock
10. Jim Carrey

In this section, we will show the range of comments about hell and after death among contemporary thinkers, beginning with existentialist Albert Camus and his comment in his novel, *La Peste*, or *The Plague*, in which Dr. Rieux, the narrator of the novel, tells us this:

> **We are all in the same game, just different levels, dealing with the same hell, we just have different Devils.[261]**

The novel is set in the North African city of Oran, where the bubonic plague has inundated the city and now the residents are trapped there in their own kind of hell. Each central character's views become clear as they individually and collectively deal with the terrible disease.

The Greek novelist Nikos Kazantzakis (1883–1957), in his novel, *The Last Temptation of Christ*, offers a theological reflection about Heaven and Hell when he observes,

> **The Devil can and does enter only hell, an angel can and does enter only Paradise. The man, wherever he wants.[262]**

In a speech from 1961, President John F. Kennedy quoted Dante about hell, but in actuality it was something that Dante did not say or write. The line in question is this,

> **Dante once said that the hottest places in hell are reserved for those who in a period of moral crisis maintain their neutrality.[263]**

In point of fact, the residents of Circle Nine of Dante's hell are actually frozen in ice accompanied by the devil himself, who is stuck up to his chest in the ice, an obvious contrast to the fire and brimstone found in most accounts of hell in the West.

In a comment from English philosopher Bertrand Russell (1872–1970), a comment used as an epigram for this chapter, the Cambridge Don made this remark about Jesus and hell,

> **There is one serious defect to my mind in Christ's moral character, and that is that he believes in hell. I do not myself feel that any person who is really profoundly humane can believe in everlasting punishment.[264]**

Professor Russell made this comment in his book *Why I am Not a Christian*. It is one of the many arguments to be found in that book on why the great philosopher had given up the faith on which he was raised—the Church of England. Russell's comments are also part of a movement beginning in the late 1960s, when many mainline Christians had begun to give up the ideas of hell and eternal punishment.

In an essay written in 1965, English essayist, critic, and writer of libretto E. M. Forster (1879–1970) asked the following question about Heaven and Hell:

After all, is not a real hell better than a manufactured heaven?

Forster's comment again came at a time when traditional views of Heaven and Hell in Britain were on the wane.[265]

American writer, poet, satirist, and political critic Dorothy Parker (1893–1967), again around the same time as Professor Russell and Mr. Forster, this time in 1963, made the following comment that we have employed as another epigram for this twelfth chapter. Parker says this about the burgeoning "Born-Again Christians" of her day,

**You think you are frightening me with your hell, don't you?
You think your hell is worse than mine.**[266]

American poet, novelist, and short-story writer Sylvia Plath (1932–1963), who was diagnosed with clinical depression early in her adult life, talks about the nature of her neurosis and hell in an interview on November 19, 1960. She observes in an essay about psychology and religion in 1960:

If neurosis is wanting two mutually exclusive things at one and the same time, then I am as neurotic as hell. I'll be flying back and forth between one mutually exclusive thing and another for the rest of my life.

Another comment made by American President Ronald Reagan (1911–2004), one also employed as an epigram for this chapter, in the context of a speech about socialism on October 11, 1982, he said,

Socialism only works in two places: Heaven where they don't need it and hell where they already have it.

Country music singer and musician Butch Hancock, who was born in 1945 in Lubbock, Texas, made this observation in an interview on October 6, 2006, about growing up in his Texas hometown.

> **Life in Lubbock, Texas, taught me two things. One is that God loves you and you are going to burn in hell. And the other is that sex is the most awful and filthy thing on Earth.**

Finally, Canadian-born comedian Jim Carrey (1962–) made the funniest and most recent contemporary comment about hell in an interview on June 18, 1996. He tells us,

> **Maybe there is no actual place called hell. Maybe hell is just having to listen to our grandparents breathe through their noses while they are eating sandwiches.**

Again, Mr. Carrey's comments are related to two themes we have seen before in this study. First, in the contemporary world the traditional beliefs in hell and eternal punishment are on the wane. And secondly, there are many things in contemporary times that remind us that many times we believe that hell is right here on Earth.

This brings us to the second section of Chapter Twelve in which we will analyze and discuss films, television shows and books that have depicted hell in the contemporary period from 1950 until the present time.

Hell in Film, Television, and Books in the Contemporary Period

In the contemporary period, there have been many films devoted to the hell motif. Among other films, these include:

1. *Black Orpheus* (1959)
2. *The Devil's Messengers* (1961)
3. *Drag Me to Hell* (1972)
4. *The Devil and Miss Jones* (1973)
5. *Aliens* (1986)
6. *Hellbound* (1988)
7. *Deconstructing Harry* (1997)
8. *Hell* (1999)
9. *Fucking Hell* (2008)
10. *Tales From the Script* (2009)
11. *To Hell and Back* (2015)
12. *Chilling Adventures of Sabrina* (2018)

The 1959 film, *Black Orpheus*, is a romantic-tragic film that was shot in Brazil by French director Marcel Camus. It tells the story of Orpheus and Eurydice, in the underworld of Hades. Camus' hell includes many traditional elements of hell, including the three-headed hound, Cerberus who guides the Gates of Hades.

The Devil's Messenger directed by Herbert L. Strock is a 1961 feature film cobbled together from three episodes of a failed Swedish television series called *13 Demon Street*. Lon Chaney stars in the role of Satan. Much of the film is purportedly taking place in hell. Chaney is a very convincing devil, but the scenes in hell are mostly overdone and very artificial.

Drag Me to Hell written by Ivan Raimi was originally a 1972 film, that was re-issued in 2009 and directed by his brother, Sam Raimi. The plot involves a young loan officer who decides not to extend the mortgage of an elderly woman who later puts a curse on the loan officer. Eventually, the loan officer is sent to hell, where she receives a sentence of three days.

The Devil and Miss Jones is a 1973 movie that is a remake of a 1941 film of the same name that starred Jean Arthur, Robert Cummings, and Charles Coburn. The 1973 version is directed by Gerald Damiano and stars Georgina Spelvin, Harry Reems, and John Clemons. Miss Jones commits suicide and then comes to a place where it is decided whether she goes to heaven or to hell. Because of her suicide, she should go to hell, but she is given the option of returning to Earth, which she eventually takes.

The 1986 film *Aliens* directed by James Cameron and starring Sigourney Weaver as a space-age Inanna who descends into a fearful hell-like place to rescue a child from a monstrous demon named Errisjkegal. This is a comic hell full of imps both real and cartoon.

Woody Allen's *Deconstructing Harry* is a 1997 film in which the protagonist, played by Allen, descends to hell where he has a chance to learn from the devil himself, played by Billy Crystal. Allen stars in the movie as a character named Harry Block. Block is a writer who has been accused by the people in his life of using them in his work.

Hellbound is a 2012 movie directed by Aaron Norris that stars Chuck Norris, Calvin Levels, and Christopher Neame. Two Chicago homicide cops investigate a murder only to come in contact with an ancient demon who most likely is Satan himself. Several scenes in the film are shot in a hell-like atmosphere.

Brothers Jake and Dinos Chapman in 1999 and 2008 made two films entitled *Hell* and *Fucking Hell*. The latter is an extraordinary 3D interpretation of a Hieronymus Bosch-like, post-apocalyptic world, otherwise known as Fucking Hell. The Chapman's hell is filled with over six thousand toy soldiers, all arranged in various ways.

Tales From the Script is a 2009 movie directed by Peter Hanson and written by him and Paul Robert Herman. It features Allison Anders, Jane Anderson, and Doug Atchison. Dozens of screenwriters share hilarious anecdotes and penetrating insights about the craft of writing and making a film. The "Crypt," or "Script," turns out to be the films both successes and failures of the many screenwriters.

To Hell and Back was originally the title of a 1955 film directed by Jesse Hibbs and starring Audie Murphy who plays himself. It is a film about war and the old adage that "War is hell on Earth."

In 2015, *To Hell and Back* was remade as an American stop motion adult animated fantasy-comedy directed by Tom Gianas and Ross Shuman. The film features the voices of Nick Swardson, T. J. Miller, Rob Riggle, and Susan Sarandon. The plot involves a carnival barker (Nick Swardson) who is desperate to bring his business into better financial shape. Among the rides at the carnival is called "The Gates of Hell" attraction.

The chief character, Augie, sees strange weather approaching and he is mysteriously sucked into a portal within the ride. Others take a car from the ride to rescue Audie and his wife who are discovered to be among demons who have taken the couple to hell.

At this point the plot begins to take up the theme of Orpheus and Eurydice, where Audie's wife goes missing deep in hell and in order to get her back Audie makes a bargain with one of the demons who turns out to be Satan who has the final line of the movie, "Welcome to hell."

Finally, the *Chilling Adventures of Sabrina* directed by Kiernan Shipka is a 2018 film that was made as a spin-off of Netflix television series called *Sabrina*. In the movie, Sabrina spends a lot of time in hell. At first, the underworld is depicted as a demented version of *The*

Wizard of Oz and a road where a straying off path leads to the axe-murdering Tin Man and an Edward Scissorhands-like schoolteacher.

In Sabrina's hell there are forests and fiery lakes, with many twists, as well as political intrigue. Sabrina battles for supremacy of hell with an overly ambitious Prince who also desires the throne of hell. There is also much demonic in-fighting between the characters.

Various contemporary-era writers have used hell themes in their work. Hannah Greenberg, for example, uses luminous Miltonic imagery in her *I Never Promised You a Rose Garden*, published in 1964. So does Doris Lessing in her *Briefing for a Descent into Hell* from 1969. Stanley Elkin's *The Living End*, a dark-comic book published in 1979, is set entirely in hell, but it is a hell of the Middle Ages and not of modern times.

Inferno is a fantasy novel written by Larry Niven and Jerry Pournelle published in 1976. The book was nominated for the 1976 Hugo Awards as well as the Nebula Award given for an outstanding first novel. *Inferno* is loosely based on Dante's "Inferno," but the story is told in a first-person narrative of an agnostic, science fiction writer who died while entertaining his fans at a science fiction convention.

In his novel, *City Infernal* (2021), Edward Lee created a hell that is a modern metropolis where bones are the currency and electricity is provided by tapping into the kinetic energy of tortured souls in hell.

Limbo's Inferno is a 2006 graphic novel created by Gary Panter and published by Fantagraphics Books. Panter's Inferno is a Los Angeles mall named Focky Bocky. The content and plot of the novel are from *Jimbo* #7 from Zongo Comics from 1997. The story is loosely based on the first two books of Dante's *Divine Comedy*.

Hell has also been used as a theme in many television shows over the years, including a 1960 episode of *The Twilight Zone* called "A Nice Place to Visit." The television show, *The Simpsons*, has used the theme of hell in numerous episodes such as one called "Bart Gets Hit by a Car" from 1991, in which Bart enters hell due to a car accident and hell looks like a Hieronymus Bosch painting *The Garden of Earthly Delights*, and Satan has a MacIntosh computer to keep track of his affairs.

In the television show *Bleach* from 2021, hell is the destination of those who commit unforgivable sins during their lives in the human world. The character named Hollow, whose mortal soul is too wicked to enter what is called "Soul Society," is slain by a Zanpakuto. The "Gates of Hell" are giant doors decorated with long skeletons open and a giant, laughing, demonic spirit with a long spear drags Hollow down to hell.

In the satirical, television puppet show called *Spitting Image*, hell is depicted as a fiery inferno containing people like Hitler, Adolf Eichmann, Joseph Stalin, and several other Nazi and Russian leaders.

And in many episodes of the television series *South Park* directed by Trey Parker, like "Do the Handicapped Go to hell? Probably" from 2000, the hell motif is employed and Satan appears in many episodes accompanied by his homosexual lover, Saddam Hussein, who seems ever more sadistic that his partner, the devil.

The fantasy comedy *The Good Place* is a television series created by Michael Schur. The show began on NBC on September 19, 2016, and in four seasons it aired fifty-three episodes. The series revolves around a woman named Eleanor Shellstrop played by Kristen Bell, whom after her death, is transported to the "Good Place," a highly selective version of Heaven. However, Eleanor must hide some aspects of her past that if known might transfer her to the "Bad Place."

Hazbin Hotel is an American adult animated musical comedy television series written and produced by Vivienne Medrano. This television series was released on *YouTube* on October 28, 2019. Its final episode was in August of 2020. A spin-off of *Hazbin Hotel* was called *Helluva Boss* that was also written, directed, and produced by Ms. Medrano.

Helluva Boss follows characters and societies that already exist in hell with the main focus of the series on the interpersonal relationships between the characters. The first episode of this show was aired on October 31, 2020.The second episode did not appear, however, until December 9, 2020.

Helluva Boss follows the employees of a company known as IMP, or "Immediate Murder Professionals," a murder for hire company. The members of IMP include Blitzo (the "O" is silent), who is the boss of the company, as well as Moxxie, a weapons expert, a character known only as "Powerhouse Willie," and a receptionist named Hellhound

Loona, who runs the office. IMP has an ancient book that was obtained from a demon of hell known as Stolas who helps to make IMP's work possible.

This brings us to the third section of Chapter Twelve on views about hell in the contemporary period, in which we will speak of three studies done by the Pew Research Center. In 1999, 2007, and 2014 about American attitudes toward Heaven and Hell, as well as other data that comes from the Roper Center at the University of Connecticut, from a study by the University of Chicago and several news organizations who have done polls of Americans' attitudes and beliefs about religion. Among these news organizations, as we shall see, who have conducted studies are NBC, CBS, Fox News, *USA Today*, CNN, ABC, as well as many other news agencies.

Views of Heaven and Hell in Contemporary Research

Since 1999, a variety of research has been conducted in the United States about the attitudes of Americans about various aspects of their religious lives. In 1999, 2007, and 2014, for example, the Pew Research Center interviewed Americans about their religious beliefs about the afterlife. The researchers of the Pew Center have found that over the period from 1999 to 2014, the number of Americans who believe in Heaven and Hell has been quite constant in that time. The Pew results indicate that roughly seven out of every ten Americans, or 72 percent, say that they believe in Heaven, defined as "a place where people who have led good lives are eternally rewarded."[267]

At the same time, the Pew research also indicates that only 58 percent of American adults believe in hell, defined as a place "where people who have lived bad lives and die without being sorry are eternally rewarded."

There are also some distinctions to be seen in various religions and even among different denominations of the same religion, as we shall see next. More than 95 percent of all Mormons have a deep belief in the idea of Heaven. This is also true of historically Black Protestant denominations where 94 percent believe in Heaven. More than 80 percent of Christians who identify themselves as "Evangelicals" also indicate their belief in Heaven.

Members of the Roman Catholic faith, who are convinced there is a Heaven, is at 85 percent, according to the Pew Research Center, and 81percent of Orthodox Christians, as well as 88 percent of mainline Protestant denominations also believe in Heaven.

On the other hand, only 50 percent of Jehovah's Witnesses believe in Heaven, 40 percent of Jews, only 47 percent of Buddhists, and 48 percent of Hindus in America. Among the followers of the Muslim faith, 89 percent of all members express a belief in *Jannah*, or "Heaven," in Arabic.

Among Americans who classified themselves as "Unaffiliated" were those who call themselves atheists, agnostics, and "nothing in particular," only 37 percent of the Unaffiliated believe in Heaven.

The Pew Research Center's figures on belief in hell are also quite consistent from their polling of Americans. In 1999, 2007, and 2014, only 58 percent expressed a belief in hell, 82 percent of Catholics; 75 percent of Evangelicals; only 60 percent of mainline Protestant denominations; 62 percent of Mormons; and 60 percent of historically Black churches.

On the other hand, belief in hell among non-Christian faiths has figures that are much lower in America. Only 22 percent of Jews believe in hell; while 76 percent of Muslims believe in *Jahannam*, the Arabic word for "hell;" 32 percent of Buddhists; 28 percent of Hindus; and only seven percent of Jehovah's Witnesses express a belief in hell.

Among the unaffiliated, only 3 percent of atheists, nine percent of agnostics, and 36 percent describe themselves as "nothing in particular" indicate a belief in hell and an eternal punishment.

Research conducted at the Roper Center for Public Opinion and Research at the University of Connecticut since the 1990s found that 80 percent of Americans believe that "God performs miracles in the world." About 36 percent of the people the Roper Center interviewed have said that they have personally "experienced or witnessed" what they considered to be a miracle.

Other research on religious matters has been conducted by Princeton University Survey Research associates, by CBS News, as well as by Fox News.[268] These sources of research confirm that 88 percent of all Americans believe in Heaven, while 71 percent of Americans express belief in hell.

ABC News poll takers, CNN, and *USA Today*, along with the Gallup Company, in December of 2000, also conducted a study of the religious beliefs of Americans. These researchers found that 86 percent believe in God and at the same time and in the same polling, only 63 percent of Americans said they believe in the devil.

There is also some research to say that belief in the afterlife is growing among American Jews. In research done by the University of Chicago's National Opinion Research Center in the 1970s reported that only 19 percent of American Jews believed in survival after death. Twenty years later, in 1995, the same researchers indicated that 56 percent of all Jews believed in the afterlife.

Similarly, the percentage of Roman Catholics who said they believed in Heaven and Hell rose from 74 percent in 1975 to 84 percent in 1995, according to the researchers at the University of Chicago. From these various research sources, we may make the following conclusions.

First, the overwhelming number of Americans believe in the existence of Heaven. Second, just slightly more than half of Americans surveyed believe in hell only 58 percent. Third, American Jews have tended not to believe in either Heaven or hell. Fourth, the great majority of Muslims in America are firm believers in both Heaven and Hell. Fifth, neither American Hindus nor American Buddhists express beliefs in either Heaven or in hell.

Sixth, a small number of unaffiliated Americans—atheists, agnostics, and nothing in particular—believe in Heaven (32 percent), or hell (22 percent) in the American polled about religion in the studies mentioned.

This brings us to the fourth and final section of Chapter Twelve, in which we will discuss some of the most recent sources from the contemporary period, where hell and after death is discussed in the twenty-first century.

Hell in the Twenty-First Century

By the term "twenty-first century," we refer to the present time in history from September 11, 2001, and the attacks on the World Trade Center and the Pentagon to the present age. In that time, we have seen a burgeoning of perspectives and responses to the ideas of hell and after death. Because of the voluminous amount of these views, we will only mention a few of them to give us a flavor of the age.

Among the responses and views on hell we will examine in this section, as well as this study on the history of hell, are the following:

1. Harry and the Howlers' song, "Hell in High Heels"
2. The views on hell of Christian Universalists.
3. David J. Powys, *Hell: A Hard Look at a Hard Question* (2007)
4. David Bateman, "The Eighth Circle of Hell in the 21st Century" (2014)
5. Guantanamo music tapes from American detention camps in Cuba. (2018)

Each of these five examples, a different contemporary view on hell and after death, will collectively give us a good flavor of the age's views on hell and eternal punishment after death.

The lyrics of the Harry and the Howlers song, "Hell in High Heels," in the opening two stanzas tells us this:

> They say that my soul is red
> but they don't mean my shoes.
> I try to pray before the lord
> but my knees keep getting bruised.
> I try to be a good woman
> but I keep getting accused.
> So I walked into the grass roads
> And I learned to play the blues.
>
> We walked through hell in a pair of high heels.
> Had to find the Devil and make a deal.
> Walked through hell in a pair of high heels
> Had to find a devil to make a deal.

Harry Jordan, the leader of the band, also employs the hell theme in many of his other songs, including, "Devil in a Push Up Bra" and "Bad Woman," both on the same album, *Hell in High Heels.*

In his lyrics to these songs, Jordan combines some traditional ideas about hell, like the use of the color red and the identification of the devil with hell, along with a kind of post-modern flare that the "old truths" no longer hold sway in the contemporary world.

The ideas of "Christian Universalism" grew out of the eighteenth-century Unitarian-Universalist Movement. In his *Plain Guide to Universalism*, Thomas Wittemore tells us about the identity of the movement.

> **The sentiment by which Universalists are distinguished is this that at the last every individual of the human race shall become holy and happy, or, in other words, everyone will be saved.**[269]

Although Christian Universalists agree on the idea that all are saved, they often disagree on whether or not hell exists. They do agree, however, that if hell does exist, the punishment that goes on there is corrective and remedial and does not last forever.

As we have shown in the previous section of this chapter, the Christian Universalists are not alone in making their claims about hell and eternal punishment. As indicated in the research, only slightly more than half of the Americans surveyed admit to a belief in hell, or about fifty-eight percent.

David J. Powys' 2007 book *Hell: A Hard Look at a Hard Question, The Fate of the Unrighteous in New Testament Thought*, published by Paternoster books, is a rigorous examination of some of the many questions that are raised by the doctrine of hell, at a time when it is even rare to hear of Heaven spoken in our churches.

In his book, Dr. Powys examines the Christian Universalist's views, argues against them primarily on a scriptural basis, and his conclusion is that "The unrighteous will forfeit resurrection life in the Kingdom of God to come." Dr. Powys examines the Biblical evidence carefully, arguing that the Christian Universalists have often misrepresented scripture or have simply employed it selectively for their own purposes.[270]

One of the most interesting views on hell and after death in the twenty-first century comes from attorney David Bateman and his essay entitled, "The Eighth Circe of Hell in the 21st Century." Bateman begins his essay by describing the nine circles of hell in Milton's *Divine Comedy* that we have examined in an earlier chapter of this history.[271]

Then Mr. Bateman goes on to concentrate on the eighth circle of Dante's hell, a place reserved for people who have committed fraud. Bateman goes on to employ the Italian word *Bolgia*, which is most often in modern Italian translated as "Ditch."

This is followed in the Bateman essay with ten Bolgias that may be applied to ten different versions of fraud to be found in the twenty-first century. The following is a summary of Mr. Bateman's "Eighth Circle of Hell."

Bolgia 1. Financial Frauds.
Bolgia 2. Seducers and Flatterers Who Defraud the Elderly.
Bolgia 3. Accountants Who Conjure Up Fraudulent Financial Statements.
Bolgia 4. Occupational Fraud and Abuse.
Bolgia 5. Unscrupulous Politicians.
Bolgia 6. Hypocrites.
Bolgia 7. Theft of Intellectual Property.
Bolgia 8. Those Who Commit Ponzi Schemes.
Bolgia 9. Affinity Fraud.
Bolgia 10. The Fraud of Family and Friends.

Mr. Bateman ends his essay with the remark,

> **Had Dante lived today, he certainly would have found a need to expand his Eighth Circle of hell to encompass the creativity of today's fraudsters.**

And we heartily agree with his judgment.

Our fifth and final item to give a flavor of twenty-first-century perspectives on hell is the loud music that often was played in the cells of U.S. detainees while interrogators were attempting to break their wills. Often, the music that blared into the cells at the Guantanamo Bay Detention Center was most often loud rap music or heavy metal music.

It goes without saying that songs like Deicide's "Fuck Your God" or Queen's "We are the Champions," a peon to American values, must have seemed like hell on Earth to the Muslim detainees at places like Guantanamo Bay, Abu Ghraib, Bagram, and Mosul.

This brings us to the major conclusions we have made in Chapter Twelve, as well as to the close of this history of attitudes on, and beliefs about, hell and the idea of punishment after death.

Conclusions

We began this twelfth chapter of views on hell and after death by suggesting that the chapter will be divided into four essential parts or sections. In the first of these sections, we provided a catalogue of ten contemporary American, British, and French perspectives of observations about hell and after death.

In this catalogue in section one, we provided the remarks of two U.S. presidents (Kennedy and Reagan), five writers (Camus, Kazantzakis, Forster, Parker and Plath), one country singer (Hancock), one celebrity (Carrey), as well as one philosopher (Russell).

In the second section of Chapter Twelve, we have identified, analyzed, and discussed twelve contemporary period films that all employ hell as a theme. In this section, we have discussed two films from the 1950s and 60s, two from the 1970s, two from the 1980s, two from the 1990s, and three movies from the 2000s.

Following our discussion of these twelve films, we turned our attention to several novels that also have used a hell motif. These novels included two from the 1960s (Greenberg and Lessing), two from the 1970s (Elkin and Niven), as well as two novels from the early twenty-first century (Edwards and Panter).

At the end of section two of Chapter Twelve, we have identified and discussed several television shows and television series in which hell and after death has been depicted in television in the contemporary era. Indeed, altogether we have named and discussed eight separate television programs that have employed the hell motif, from a 1960 episode of *The Twilight Zone* called "A Nice Place to Visit," to more current times and shows like "Bleach," "Spitting Image," "South Park," "The Simpsons," the fantasy-comedy "The Good Place," as well as Vivienne Medran's two hell series called the "Hazbin Hotel" and its sequel, "Helluva Boss."

What we have seen in most of these television programs on hell in the contemporary period is that they often have employed traditional elements of hell taken from history, like the devil resides there with the morally inferior who also can be found there.

In these eight television shows on hell, we have also seen some creativity on the part of their creators, both in terms of plot, as well as the idea of character development, and even what residents are to be found in the various depictions of hell.

The third section of Chapter Twelve has been taken up with the idea of scientific research that has been conducted since the early 1990s having to do with the religious opinions and theological beliefs of the American people. In this section, we introduced the research conducted by the Pew Research Center in 1999, 2007, and 2014, which interviewed cross-sections of American society about their religious beliefs.

Among the findings of the Pew Research was the fact that 72 percent of all Americans, from various religious perspectives, believe in the existence of Heaven, while only 58 percent assent to the idea of the eternal punishment of hell. We have also shown in the Pew findings that the different world religions, like Hinduism, Buddhism, and Islam in America have their own peculiar beliefs about Heaven and Hell. For the most part, Moslems in the U.S. believe in the existence of hell, while Hindus and Buddhists in America do not.

We also have shown that in the Pew findings, Mormons, historically Black Protestant churches, and Roman Catholics have a far greater percentage of their members who believe in hell than in other Christian denominations. We also have mentioned the Pew findings that the number of Americans who believe in hell is on the rise, among Catholics, as well as among Jews, for example.

In addition to the findings of the Pew Center's three studies in 1999, 2007, and 2014, we have also introduced in the third section, research done by other organizations on the beliefs and opinions of religious questions among Americans.

Among these other pieces of research, we have mentioned polls done by the University of Chicago, by the Roper Center at the University of Connecticut, as well as polling completed about American attitudes toward religion by various news organizations and periodicals like *USA*

Today, *New York Times*, CBS, NBC, Fox News, CNN, ABC, as well as the Gallup Company.

From these various news agencies, we have made six conclusions about America's views on religion. First, the overwhelming number of people believe in the existence of Heaven, somewhere around 70 to 75 percent, consistently over time. Second, just slightly more than half of Americans express a belief in hell and eternal punishment.

Third, we have shown that American Jews have tended to neither believe in Heaven, nor in hell. Fourth, the great majority of Muslims in America are firm assenters to the existence of both Heaven and Hell, or *Jannah* and *Jahannam*, in classical Arabic.

Fifth, the research from these universities and news organizations has shown that neither Hindus nor American Buddhists have tended to assent to a belief in either Heaven or in hell.

And sixth, and finally, the number of unaffiliated Americans, that is atheists, agnostics, and those who say they believe in "nothing in particular," we have seen in the research that only thirty-two percent of them believe in the existence of Heaven, while only twenty-two percent of unaffiliated Americans polled said they are confident that there exists a hell.

In the fourth and final section of Chapter Twelve, we have identified, analyzed, and discussed five separate manifestations of beliefs about hell and after death to be found in the twenty-first century.

In this final section of Chapter Twelve, as well as this history of views about hell and after death, we have discussed the thoughts and beliefs about hell from the rock band Harry and the Howlers and their song "Hell in High Heels."

Second, we also discussed the Contemporary Christian Universalist Movement that essentially argues that all human beings will eventually reach salvation, though members of the movement disagree about whether there is a hell, as well as whether punishment goes on there.

In the fourth section of Chapter Twelve, we spoke of scholar David J. Powys and his book entitled *Hell: A Hard Look at a Hard Question*, published in 2007, in which Dr. Powys responds to the views of the Christian Universalists and concludes that their fundamental belief about universal salvation is not scripturally sound.

Perhaps the most interesting item in the fourth section of the twelfth chapter is the views about hell and after death we have introduced in an article written by attorney David Bateman entitled, "The Eighth Circle of Hell in the 21st Century."

In his essay, Mr. Bateman suggests that if Dante was alive in the twenty-first century, he would have to extend the eighth circle of hell reserved for those who commit fraud. Using the Italian word *Bolgia*, or "Ditch," Bateman suggests ten separate categories of fraud that Dante would find in contemporary society in America.

Finally, in our fifth and final twenty-first-century perspective about hell, we have spoken of the tactics that the U.S. Government used in their detainment camps in the contemporary period in places like Guantanamo Bay, Cuba, the Abu Ghraib Prison, as well as facilities at Bagram and Mosul.

Among these tactics, we have mentioned the practice of playing very loud rap and heavy metal music to the detainees for the purposes of getting them to cooperate with their interrogators, or to give up their dedicated world views. If nothing else, one conclusion we can make about these practices is that for the detainees, it must have certainly seemed to them to have been hell on Earth.

Postscript

The doors to hell are locked from the inside.
—C. S. Lewis

I have been planning to write this book since my first days as a graduate student at Yale in the early 1970s. Over the course of my academic career since that time, I have been gathering information for when this project would eventually come to fruition. Among the material I collected in those years were the following:

1. Biblical Sources on Sheol, Gehenna, etc.
2. Hell in Other Semitic Languages
3. Egyptian Understandings of the Afterlife
4. Greek Mythology and Philosophy
5. Hell in Comparative Religions
6. Data on Historical Events
7. Literary Themes and Images
8. Artistic and Musical Sources
9. Popular Culture
10. Information From Sabbaticals

I will end this work by making some comments on each of these items. When I first met Professor William F. Albright of Johns Hopkins University when I was in high school in the mid-1960s, I became interested in Semitic languages, and particularly Classical Hebrew, Syriac, Aramaic, and finally Arabic in the 2000s. All of this study greatly increased my understanding of the Hebrew Bible, and particularly the Book of Job and the problem of evil. Through Professor Albright, I also was able to gain some knowledge of the ideas of hell, the underworld, and punishment in other Semitic languages and cultures such as the Egyptians, Babylonians, Persians, and Canaanites.

Beginning in the early 1970s, I began teaching a course at Johns Hopkins University entitled Death: The Individual and Society, which concentrated on the definition of death, funeral rites and practices, concepts of the afterlife, and moral issues like abortion, suicide, and the question of euthanasia.

While teaching at the University of Maryland in the late 1970s, I began teaching several courses that greatly increased my knowledge of funeral rites and practices in the ancient world, as well as another course on comparative religions. While teaching at Maryland, I also taught a third course whose material centered on the relation of religion to Greek mythology.

More specifically, I was interested in certain aspects of Greek mythology, including the Orpheus and Eurydice narrative, the idea of the River Styx, the gods Demeter, Hades, the Furies, Hecate, Charon, Nyx, Cronos, and the personification of death in ancient Greece, Thanatos, as well as Socrates, Plato and Aristotle's view on the soul and survival after death, as well as other Greek thinkers on the material of the study, such as Homer, Hesiod, and many other ancient thinkers and scholars.

Hesiod, for example, in his *Theogony*, suggested that Thanatos has no father, but is the son of Nyx, or Night and the brother of Hypnos, or Sleep. Homer, in his *Iliad*, described Hypnos and Thanatos as twin brothers.

In ancient Greek art, Thanatos was often depicted as a winged and sword-bearing woman, such as in the sculpted marble column drum from the Temple of Artemis at Ephesus around 325 to 300 BCE. Other negative images were counted among the siblings of Thanatos, such as *Geras*, or "Old Age;" *Oizys* (Suffering); M*oros*, or "Doom;" *Momus* (Blame); and *Nemesis*, or Retribution.

Over my forty-three years of college and university teaching, I also collected information on certain historical events such as the emergence of the bubonic plague in Europe in the fourteenth and fifteenth centuries, the Lisbon earthquake in 1755, the Holocaust in the mid-twentieth century, and most recently, the Covid-19 virus from 2020. Each of these events, and my study of them, helped to make this book possible. As we have shown, the issues of hell have frequently arisen in the West with certain historical events where it was asked, "How could God allow such a thing to happen?" And I have spent my career trying to give sufficient answers to just that question.

I also have collected over the years information related to certain literary texts and literary images related to the content of this study. Including works by Homer, Hesiod, Augustine of Hippo, Thomas Aquinas, Dante, Christopher Marlowe, Albert Camus, and many others.

Among the literary themes and scenarios that have been prevalent regarding hell and after death were the use of certain names such as Nick—a version of "Ole Nick," a name of the Devil—Satanya, a derivation of Satan, and Shaytan, a Semitic cognate to Satan, as well as cognates in other languages to the Latin *Diablos* and the Persian *Devi*.

Over the years, I also have collected many images of the ways that the demonic have been shown mostly in Western culture, such as the devil having horns, a long tail, often shown in the colors red and black, the idea of a wager between Satan and humans to save their souls, and the idea of hell having gates through which humans must enter.

In fact, in this study I have shown how many of these themes and literary images and motifs have shown up in both artistic and musical works in which they have appeared over the centuries in the West, and, to some extent, in the East as well, and we have shown that in the four appendices of this work.

I also have shown that many of these same literary images and motifs, like the uses of the colors red and black, and the devil with horns carrying a trident or pitchfork, and a long, curly tail, for example, have also been shown in popular culture, as well., particularly in comics and cartoons, as we have shown earlier in this study.

Finally, much of the material I have collected in the writing of this project, I acquired during the many sabbaticals I have had in my academic career. At the American University in Cairo, I studied and collected material on ancient Egypt and their funerary and burial customs.

In Damascus, Syria, I extensively studied the Muslim Holy Book, Al-Qur'an, and gained much information on the figure of *Shaytan* and the realm of *Jahannam*, or "hell" in Classical Arabic.

In my sabbatical at the National University in Lagos, Nigeria, I studied the religions of Africa, mostly in the northwest and east of the continent, as well as the views of the soul, hell, and survival after death in many African tribes over the centuries, including the Igbo, Ibibio, Hadzabe, Yoruba, in Nigeria, the Swahili people of East Africa, the LoDabaa in Ghana, and the Agikuyu in Kenya. At the time, I took extensive notes in my stay at the National University in Lagos and have incorporated some of that material in this study, as well.

Among the many myths and rituals among Arican people in regard to the ideas of the demonic, hell, and punishment after death, I found many that seemed to be peculiar to the Western English mind. Among these were the following: that ancestor worship is a common belief in Africa; that the ghosts of the dead are believed to be reincarnated in many African cultures; that if a person lived a life in "dishonor," after death he may wander around the living and cause harm.

In addition, the undeserving may be denied a "proper burial." Death rituals for removing the body from the house to take to the morgue or the burial site are often meant to confuse the dead so he or she cannot find their way easily back to the living. Some customs involve taking the dead body out of the house through a hole in the wall, for example; the taking a zigzag path to the burial site to confuse the dead if he attempts to go back home; and to throw such obstacles as thorns, branches, or other barriers on the path, again to make it difficult for him to find his way back to the land of the living.

I also learned in my time in Africa that the deceased may be wrapped in his or her clothes for burial and often covered with the skin of a slaughtered animal. In some places in Africa, the body is wrapped in a linen shroud. Personal items are often buried with the deceased to help him or her in the afterlife. The Yoruba tribe of Nigeria, for example, includes food, clothes, fowl and other animals as accoutrements to the dead. Other tribes even include spears, shields, bow and arrows, as well as pots and pans, so the dead have all they need in the afterlife. And all of this I learned while on sabbatical in northwest Africa.

In a real way this "hell postscript" has been a way of describing the many ways, places where I have acquired the content of this study on the ideas of hell, the demonic, and punishment after death. I hope you have enjoyed these remarks.

SJV
September 2023

Acknowledgments

I have been aided by many individuals in the construction of this work, including my main intellectual companion these days, my son John "Jack" Vicchio, as well as my cousins, Peter Celli Sr., Nick Caprio, and John Appel. I also wish to thank my friend Irene Burrell who helps to keep my life going forward. And finally, I am indebted to friends Linda Canestraro, Mario Villa Santa, and Tina Gioioso, for their support in the writing of this project.

Part IV
Appendices

Gustave Doré, illustration to Dante's "Inferno," 1857.

Appendix A
Foreign Words and Phrases

The definition of hell is a place where
nothing connects with nothing and nothing else.
—T. S. Eliot

In this first appendix of this study on the history of hell and after death, we will list foreign words and phrases from thirty-six different languages employed in this study. Among those languages, we have used:

1. Seven ancient languages: Hebrew, Mesopotamian, Greek, Latin, Koine, Greek, Chinese, and Sanskrit.
2. Sixteen European languages: Finnish, Hungarian, Italian, Norwegian, Albanian, Gaelic, Old English, Welsch, Anglo-Saxon, Frisian, German, Proto-German, Old Slavic, Russian, French, and Estonian.
3. Seven Asian languages: Chinese, Japanese, Punjabi, Tamil, Tagalog, Marwari, and Fiji.
4. Three Native-American languages: Aztec, Sioux, and Seminole.
5. One African religion: Swahili.
6. Three Semitic or ancient Near-Eastern Languages: Old Babylonian, Hebrew, and Arabic.

We have provided transliterations of all thirty-six languages into English, along with the sources of a particular foreign word or phrase employed in this study on the history of hell and after death.

The most foreign words and expressions in this study come from:

1. Hebrew (41)
2. Arabic (30)
3. Chinese (20)
4. Latin (17)
5. Sanskrit (16)
6. Greek (12)
7. Ancient Egyptian

Altogether we have employed the use of thirty-four languages in this study of the history of hell. These include:

Four Semitic tongues: CHb, MedHeb, ModHeb, and Arb.

Seven Asian languages: AC, AE, Jap., Sankt, Fign, PF, and HND.

Two Greek tongues: CGK and KGR.

Two Latin languages: Lat and M.Lat.

Three Native American tongues: SEML, SuX, and AZT.

And fourteen European languages: Fr, SWD, STENG, GAE, OE, ME, ICE, Germ, Frs, Fin, Alb, Hung, Latv, and ONor.

This study also contains references to seventeen languages whereby there is only a single item. These are: Latvian, Hungarian, Italia, Gaelic, Albanian, Frisian, Swahili, Tagalog, French, Tamil, Aztec, ancient Slavic, Seminole, Finnish, Estonian, Welsch, and the language of the Sioux.

Alphabetical Listing:

Word	Meaning	Language
Abaddon	synonym for "hell"	Classical Hebrew
Abaq	dust	Classical Hebrew
Acaph	to gather	Classical Heb

Adein	to see	Classical Greek
Adhab	punishment	Arabic
ahadith	plural of hadith	Arabic
Aizshule	hell	Latvian
Angrboda	goddess	Finland
Aphar	dust	Classical Hebrew
Apollyon	god of destruction	Greek
Arbuda	blister	Sanskrit
Atata	shivering	Sanskrit
Atman	soul	Sanskrit
atsam	bones	Classical Hebrew
Avici	uninterrupted	Sanskrit
Avilag	hell	Hungarian
Ayat	verse of the Qur'an	
Bab	founder of Bahá'í faith	
Baghi	rebellion	Arabic
Bahá'u'lláh	foretold prophet among Bahá'í	
Baldur	Norsegod	
Bao	fifth Chinese court in afterlife	Chinese
Bar Kochba	second-century Jewish rebellion	
Bawabah	gate	Arabic
Bhur	Earth	Sanskrit
Bhuvas	middle region	Sanskrit
Bi	sixth Chinese court in afterlife	Chinese
Biancheng	judge of sixth Chinese court in afterlife	Chinese
biqah	valley or plain	Classical Hebrew
Bohr	pit	Classical Hebrew
Bolgia	ditch	Italian
Ceilid	hell	Gaelic

Celare	to hide	Latin
Chickee	corpse	Seminole
Chitragupta	record keeper in Indian afterlife	Sanskrit
Chujiang	judge in second Chinese court of afterlife	Chinese
Confessio	confession	Latin
Daemon	devil or demon	Classical Greek
Deutero Thanatos	second death in New Testament	
Dhuma Probha	fifth level of hell in Jain-ism—means smoke	
Diyu	Chinese realm of the dead	Chinese
Dong	seventh Chinese court in afterlife	
Duat	underworld in ancient Egypt	Egyptian
Dushi	eighth judge of Chinese court in afterlife	Chinese
Duzakh	underworld	Zoroastrianism
Eclesiastica gentis Anglorum	history of the English people	
Elibanus gehennae	furnace of hell	Latin
Fahashaba	sufficient	Arabic
Fenrir	wolf god	Norse mythology
Ferri	hell	Albanian
Gan	garden	Hebrew
Gan Eden	Garden of Eden	Hebrew

Gaon	master teacher	Hebrew
Gathas	ancient Persian scripture	Persian
Gay	valley	Classical Hebrew
Ge bene Hinnom	Hebrew valley of Hinnom	CH
Gehenna	hell in New Testament	
Gehinnom	Talmud's spelling of Ge Hinnom	
Gilgul	reincarnation	Hebrew
Gimie Hel	hell	Norse mythology
Goel	redeemer	Classical Hebrew
Great Baal	Canaanite god	
Ha Neser ha Godol	The Great Eagle	Hebrew
Hades	Greek god and hell	Greek
Hahava	lamentation	Sanskrit
Halachot	oral law	Hebrew
Haljo	hell	Proto-German
Hameen	boiling water, hell punishment	Islam
Hawiyah	a deep abyss	Arabic
Hel or helle	hell	Old English
Helan	hell	Anglo-Saxon
Helle	hell	Frisian
Helle-Rune	hell	Old English
Helli-witti	hell	Old Saxon
Herod	Nordic god	
Hirabah	crucifixion	Arabic
Historia Abbatum	history of the abbots	
Holie	hell	German
Huang	eighth court in Chinese afterlife	Chinese
Hudud	punishment	Arabic

Hujjat	Prove	Arabic
Hutama	broken into pieces	Arabic
Hydra	ancient Greek god	Greek
Inferno	hell and Dante's word for hell	medieval Latin
Infurnus	Vulgate translation of Hades	
Jaaniw	place of ancestors	Swahili
Jahannam	hell	Classical Arabic
Jahannam	hell	Classical Arabic
Jahim	blazing fire	Arabic
Jahm	darkest part of hell	Arabic
Jannah	heaven	Arabic
Jiang	first Chinese court in afterlife	Chinese
Jiva	soul	Jainism (Marwari)
Jormungand	Norse serpent god	
Kabalah	Jewish form of mysticism	
Kaddish	Jewish prayer for the dead	
Kafir	non-believer in Islam	
Kalam	Jewish term for philoso-phy of religion	Classical Hebrew
Kalasutra	level of hell in ancient India	Sanskrit
Kalyotein	to hide	Classical Greek
Kel	to hide	Sanskrit
Kherty	ferryman in Egypt across the River Styx	
Kirtan	prayer	Punjabi
Kisanaan	underworld	Phillppines (Tagalop)
Kthon	Earth	Classical Greek
Kuzima	hell	Swahili

Lay	ninth Chinese court in afterlife	Chinese
Laza	blazing fire	Arabic
Lex talionis	the law of retribution	Latin
Li	name of Chinese court in afterlife	Chinese
Limbus Patrum	compartment in hell for fathers who did not know Jesus	Latin
Limbus Pavulorum	compartment in hell for fallen angels	Latin
Limnu puro	lake of fire	New Testament
Loki	god in Norse mythology	
Lu	fourth level of Chinese courts of afterlife	Chinese
Lucifer	demonic figure who appears at Isa. 14:12	
Mahapadma	region of Indian afterlife	
Maharaurav	hurt others	Sanskrit
Meivazhi	the true path	Tamil
Mequbbal	Hebrew name for mysticism	
Michtlan	Aztec hell	
Midgard	dragon god	Norse mythology
Midrash Shmuel	midrash on the Book of Samuel	Hebrew
Minila	hell	Finnish
Mishpetsi ha-Mazzelot	judgment of the Zodiac	Hebrew
Moloch	Canaanite god of sacrifice	They spoke a version of Phoenician.
Muramoria	underworld	Fiji
Muratorian fragment	early New Testament fragment	Latin
Naar	the fire	Arabic
Nafs	soul	Classical Arabic
Nak and Peklo	hell	Slavic mythology

Naraka	Chinese beliefs about afterlife	Chinese
Navagotio	navigation	Latin
Nefesh, plural is *nefishim*	soul	Classical Hebrew
Neshamah	breathe or spirit	Classical Hebrew
Nirabuda	region of Indian afterlife	Sanskrit
Occulere	to hide	Latin
Olam ha ba	the world to come	Hebrew
Padma	blizzard	Sanskrit
Panka Probha	fourth level of hell in Jainism—means mud	Marwari
Phaedo	dialogue on Plato	Classical Greek
Phlegethon	river	ancient Greece
Pingdeng	ninth judge of Chinese court	Chinese
Pratapana	great heating	Sanskrit
Pseudo	false	Classical Greek
Puranas	genre of Indian literature	Sanskrit
Purgatorio	purgatory	
Qeber	grave	Classical Hebrew
Qingusmy	judge in first Chinese court of afterlife	Chinese
Ragot	French dish, pig's ears	
Ramadan	Islamic month of fasting	
Ramchal	Eighteenth-century Jewish philosopher	Hebrew
Raphael	name of an angel	Hebrew
Ratna Probha	first level of hell in Jainism—means jewels	Marwari

Raurava	screaming	Sanskrit
Rephaim	spirits or shades	Classical Hebrew
Riddah	apostasy	Arabic
Ruah.	spirit	Classical Hebrew
Sa'er	to eat up the flesh	Arabic
Saba	seven	Arabic
Sala ni Yalo	path of souls	Fiji
Samghata	level of hell in ancient India	Sanskrit
Sanjiva	level of hell in ancient India	Sanskrit
Saqar	intensely hot	Arabic
Sariqa	amputation	Arabic
Sarkats Probha	second level of hell in Jainism—means gravel	Marwari
Sefer ha mo'adim	Book of Festivals	Hebrew
Sefirtot	inner life	Hebrew
Shaar Ha Gilgulim	Gate of Reincarnation	Hebrew
Shabat	the Sabbath	Hebrew
Shahat	pit	Classical Hebrew
Shariah	name for Muslim Law	
Shemonah She'arim	Gates of Righteousness	Hebrew
Sheol	Jewish underworld	
Sheol Gehinnom	medieval Jewish expression for hell	
Shub al-Khamir	provision against alcohol	Islam
Simran	meditation on God	Punjabi
Sita	six	Arabic
Sitra Achra	the "other side"	Hebrew
Songdi	judge in third Chinese court of afterlife	
Suala	place beneath the Earth	Old Babylonian
Summa Theologica	major work on theology	Latin
Surah	chapter of the Qur'an	

Svar	sky	Sanskrit
Swahil	coast	Arabic
Tafsir Al-Jalalayn	commentary on the two Jalals	Arabic
Taichan	judge of seventh court of Chinese afterlife	
Tajhwif min al-Noor	fleeing from the fire	Arabic
Tama Probha	sixth level of hell in Jainism—means darkness	Marwari
Tamatama Probha	seventh level of hell in Jainism—means extreme darkness	Marwari
Tapana	impaled with swords	Sanskrit
Targum	Jewish commentary of Scripture	
Tartarus	New Testament name for hell	
Tataroo	ancient Greek underworld	
Temelecus	leader of devils in vision of Paul	Latin
Temporibus	time	Latin
Tisa	nine	Arabic
Toonili	hell	Estonian
Tophet or Toppheth	location in the Valley of Hinnom	
Torah	first five books of the Hebrew Bible	
Torah ha Adam	the Laws of Adam	Hebrew
Tuonili	hell	Welsch
Tzorh Rotachat	boiling excrement	Classical Hebrew
Uffern	Hell among Celts	
Uptala	blue lotus	Sanskrit
Vahala	Nordic paradise	

Valuha probha	third level of hell in Jainism—means sand	Marwari
Visio	vision	Latin
Visio Pauli	vision of Paul	Latin
Visio Tundale	vision of Tundae, 12th century figure	Latin
Wanagi Yato	place of spirits among Sioux	
Wuguang	judge of fourth Chinese court in afterlife	
Xalji-witjan	hell	Proto-German
Xue	tenth Chinese court in afterlife	
yabesh	died	Classical Hebrew
Yahweh	God of ancient Israel	
Yama	court	ancient Chinese
Yanluo	judge of fifth court in Chinese afterlife	
Yawm al-Qiyamah	Judgment Day	Arabic
Zakobo-cho	fire in the sky	Japanese
Zaqqum	tree in Muslim hell	
Zhuluan	judge of tenth court of Chinese afterlife	
Zina	illicit sexual behavior	Arabic
Zion	Hebrew synonym for Jerusalem	Classical Hebrew
Znamya	banner	Russian
Zuhr	One of the required daily prayers of Islam	

William Blake, *Dante and Virgil Gazing into the Bolgia Ditch of Flatterers (from Dante's "Divine Comedy")*, 1824–1827. Watercolor, black ink, graphite, and black chalk on off-white antique laid paper, 14 9/16 × 20 9/16 in. Harvard Art Museums/Fogg Museum, Bequest of Grenville L. Winthrop. Photo Credit: © President and Fellows of Harvard College, 1943.435.

Appendix B
Hell in Art

Man would indeed be in a poor way if he had to be
restrained by fear of punishment and hope of reward after death.
—Albert Einstein

Introduction

We will divide this second appendix into two parts, hell in medieval and Renaissance art and hell in modern art. In the first part, we will examine twenty pieces of hell art. In the second part, we will provide ten examples and comments on each. We will begin with the fourteenth and fifteenth centuries where we will discuss four different pieces of art in the West. And several not from the West.

Art of Hell in the Medieval and Renaissance Periods: Fourteenth and Fifteenth Centuries

The number of artistic creations on hell in these periods is staggering. We will mention five examples to give a sense of the wide range of these images. Our first example is by Italian painter Giotto di Bondone, who in 1306 painted a series of what are known as *The Last Judgment* frescoes. They are located in the Scrovegni Chapel, Padua, Italy. Giotto was born in the town of Vicchio in Calabria in 1267 and died in 1337.

Giotto's *The Last Judgment* is part of a cycle of frescoes that show the life of the Virgin Mary and Jesus Christ. *The Last Judgment* is the largest of these works. The top show Jesus seated on his throne in Heaven, surrounded by his twelve apostles. Jesus is in the act of casting the Final Judgment. The lower part of the image shows the elect—those who will be saved—and will be escorted by angels to Heaven.

On this lower level, the archangels Michael and Raphael are holding up the cross in the middle. One curious feature of this image is that at the bottom of the fresco, the Commissioner of the Arena Chapel—a man named Enrico Scrovegni—is shown as presenting a model of the chapel to the Virgin Mary. We know that Giotto was familiar with Dante, and it is possible that this painting was one of the sources for the "Inferno."

Fra Angelico's *The Last Judgment*, completed in 1431, is our second depiction of hell. It is a tempera on panel painting that was commissioned by the Camaldolese Order for the newly elected abbot, Ambrogio Travarsari, and located in the Museum di San Marco in Florence. In the upper register of the painting, Jesus is seated in the Heavens, surrounded by saints on the left and the twelve apostles on the right. Human beings are on a lower register. Those on the left are standing and appear to await salvation, while those on the right—most likely the damned—are arguing with each other.

The *Crucifixion and Last Judgment* diptych by Jan van Eyck, completed in 1440 to 1441, located at the Metropolitan Museum of Art, New York City, is our third image of hell. The work consists of two panels. The one on the left shows the Crucifixion of Christ and the two thieves on either side. The panel on the right depicts the resurrected Jesus with light shining on him. Jesus is surrounded by orderly rows of saints and apostles and hovering angels. These two panels are sometimes known as the "New York Diptych."

In the lower register of the right panel, the Archangel Michael, in a dashing garment that has rainbow wings stands astride the Earthly realm, where some of the desperate cry out to be saved. The angel prepares to strike down a personification of Death—a winged and grinning skeleton that roosts over the mouth of hell. Devils sport with the damned, splitting them at the seams and swallowing them whole.

The work was completed at the end of van Eyck's life. It is likely that the craftsmen in his workshop helped the painting of the panel on the right, with its lavish use of gold and precious pigments like lapis lazuli. There are many Biblical quotations in multiple languages on both the frame and the painting of the right panel. Whoever commissioned this work must have been very wealthy and educationally sophisticated, for the work certainly is.

Our fourth image of hell is Sandro Botticelli's *Map of Hell*, created between 1480 and 1490 and located at the Vatican Library. The painting features a detailed outward depiction of the nine circles of hell as outlined in Dante's "Inferno." It took more than a decade to complete the map. It consists of a huge vortex, wide at the top and narrow at the bottom that contains the nine cycles or circles of hell built into the vortex.

Many figures in each of the nine circles have been painted into the creation. There are 102 figures provided into the painting, some easily identified as Florentine figures of the day, and others not so much.

Our final fourteenth- and fifteenth-century depiction of hell is a work in the public domain attributed to a man named Dionisius. The painting shows a glorified Jesus "descending into hell," as the Apostles Creed tells us, a depiction of First Peter 4:6. Jesus stands at the heavenly realm, while in the lower register, two angels have descended into the underworld, preparing the way for the Savior. On either side of the angels are condemned souls who seem to be wary of the angels.

Images of Hell: Sixteenth and Seventeenth Centuries

The penchant for depicting hell in Western art continued into the sixteenth and seventeenth centuries, primarily in two separate ways. First, the continuation of earlier themes in the late Middle Ages, and second in representations of what has been called the "Hell Mouth."

Perhaps the best known of the first type is the work entitled *The Garden of Earthly Delights* by Hieronymus Bosch. This artwork is a spellbinding triptych whose nightmarish details remind us of the modern Surrealist movement. The work consists of three panels of oil on wood. It was completed between 1490 and 1500. The original is owned by the Museo Nacional del Prado, in Madrid, Spain This has been its home since 1933.

The work consists of a large center panel, flanked by two hinged smaller panels that, when closed display the formation of the Earth on the third day of creation in the Book of Genesis. When opened, the left panel depicts God presenting Eve to Adam in a very simplified Garden of Eden, filled with a menagerie of animals.

A second image from the sixteenth century is entitled, *Lazarus's Soul Carried to Abraham*. The Flemish work was completed between 1510 and 1520 by the Master of King James IV of Scotland. It is likely that the work is a depiction of the Gospel of Luke 16:22 that tells us in English translation:

The time came when the beggar died and the angels came and carried him to Abraham's side; and the rich man also died and was buried.

In the painting, the soul of Lazarus is being carried by a pair of elegant angels. Abraham looks down at Lazarus, while the angels look up to Abraham. Lazarus is on his knees and his hands are together as if praying. Meanwhile, the poor man is being tortured in hell by demons in many different ways.

Pieter Bruegel's *Dulle Griet* or *Mad Meg* is a third sixteenth-century depiction of hell and is located at the Museum of Ghent University. This work was completed in 1561 to 1564. Dulle Griet is a figure of Flemish folklore. She forms an army and goes to pillage hell. In Flemish culture, Dulle Griet is a disparaging name given to any bad-tempered shrew. Griet's mission in hell, depicted in the painting, is also sometimes related to a Flemish proverb that tells us:

She could plunder in front of hell and then returned to Earth unscathed.

The painting depicts the battle of Dulle Griet's army with many and varied demon warriors in the scene. The painting employs many of the traditional Medieval themes of hell.

This leads us to three seventeenth-century artistic creations of hell, one by Peter Paul Rubens, one by Filippo di Liagno, and the third an etching by Jacques Callot that illustrates Dante's "Inferno" and was completed in 1612. We will discuss these three works in reverse order, beginning with French illustrator Callot (1592–1635). The etching *Dante's Hell* by Callot is after another by Bernardino Poccetti, and the scene is a depiction of the inferno that shows a hell of nine concentric circles, each reserved for a particular sin.

The Callot etching in question also shows many acts of torture. For example, the dead are shown enduring the prodding of pitchforks, savage beatings and other brutalities at the hands of very evocative demons.

Peter Paul Rubens' *The Fall of the Damned* located at the British Museum, London, is a monochromatic painting enlivened by shades of reddish brown, ochre and greyish blue. The work shows the entanglement of many twisted bodies and devils precipitating into darkness. Above, an armed archangel—perhaps Michael—holding a round shield and sword emerges from a halo of light in the top, left corner. The scene is the Final Judgment at the end of time as outlined, for example, at the Gospel of Matthew 13:40–43.

By using this monochromatic technique, Rubens reinterprets some of the earlier, great models of the Final Judgment like that of Michelangelo's *The Last Judgment* from 1546, or Fra Angelico's *The Last Judgment* discussed in the previous section of this appendix.

Another seventeenth-century artistic rendering of hell is Filippo di Liagno's 1622 painting *Dante and Virgil in Hell* located at the Museum d'Orsay, Paris. Like Rubens, Liagno's rendering of Dante is exceptionally dark and terrifying. Liagno shows a fiery scene of damned souls clamoring to escape the torments that brought them to hell, while various demons roam the underworld torturing the human souls.

The other aspect of depictions of hell from the twelfth through the seventeenth centuries is the many examples of the "Hell Mouth" that appeared in the period. This is the topic of the next section of this appendix.

Depictions of the Mouth of Hell: Eight Hundred to the Seventeenth Century

There was another artistic theme on hell that, for the most part, can be seen in Britain in the beginning and later throughout Europe. That is, artistic depictions of the mouth of hell, most often shown as the mouth of some great animal or demon. Many of the depictions of the creature called Leviathan in the Biblical Book of Job, for example, show the monster with a gaping mouth as the entrance to hell. One fine example of this phenomenon can be found in the manuscript known as the *Exeter*

Book in which the mouth of hell is compared to the mouth of a whale, an animal often identified with Leviathan in the Book of Job.[272]

The oldest of these hell mouths, at least according to scholar Meyer Schapiro, is an ivory carving from around 800 CE that is owned by the Victoria and Albert Museum, but most of the examples of the motif came after the twelfth century. In this analysis we will provide several examples of the hell mouth motif, four of these are medieval and the fifth is a more contemporary example of the phenomenon.

The *Winchester Psalter* at the British Library was created around 1150 and has a version of the hell mouth out of character with most of the other examples because the hell mouth in this Psalter is the jaws of an archangel.

The *Psalter of Blanche of Castile* contains an image of the hell mouth. It is a fantastic, early Gothic manuscript created by a team of skilled masters in Paris around 1230. The supposed patron was the Queen of France who was a famous patron of all the arts. Before the rise of printing and the book, the Psalter was the most richly illuminated genre of manuscripts.

There is also a fourteenth-century Book of Hours with a hell mouth. It is English, possibly from Yorkshire. It shows a standing Christ with staff in his right hand. With his right hand he grasps the right hand of Adam followed by Eve, both with their left hands raised. The first human couple is accompanied by fourteen men and women. All are nude and stand in the hell mouth, which appears to be a medieval city gate manned by three demons with spears and pitchforks, including one devil who blows a horn. The scene has a gold, punched background within a decorated frame with foliate terminals at the corners.[273]

Another example of the same theme of Jesus leading souls out of the mouth of hell can be seen in the Saint Mary's Church of Pickering in Yorkshire. The hell mouth is a feature of the church and the mouth is that of a huge demon.

From the first quarter of the fourteenth century, the *Queen Mary Apocalypse* at the British Museum London, contains a hell mouth in which an angel holds a key in the upper left. Below him is a dragon who is chained to the key. Both figures are inside the hell mouth, the jaws of a much larger dragon, perhaps a Leviathan whose lower teeth are visible.

One of the latest hell mouths was created by El Greco in a painting called *Adoration of the Holy Name of Jesus* from 1557 and is located at the Monastery of Escorial, Madrid, Spain. Jesus is glorified in a middle register, Heaven above him and hell below. The residents of hell are standing in a large hell mouth, with their arms raised in protest and supplication to no avail. The hell mouth is that of a great monster but cannot easily be identified.

Finally, artist Bijan Samerel of Los Angeles has constructed several hell mouths for his business and home. Perhaps the most useful of these is the fireplace in his Los Angeles office and a similar one at his home used for the same purpose. This brings us to the two final sections of Appendix B in which we will discuss depictions of hell in East Asian art, as well as images in contemporary Western art.

Hell in East Asian Art: Twelfth to the Nineteenth Century

Between the twelfth and the nineteenth centuries, several examples of the depictions of hell can be seen in China, Japan, and Korea. More of these can be found in Japanese art in comparison to the other two cultures. In our analysis, we will begin with nine examples from Japan, followed by artist depictions in China and Korea. Most of these East-Asian examples can be found on what are called "hanging scrolls," which are mostly owned by museums in the three cultures.

One theme on hell that can be seen in the art of all three cultures is the belief in the Ten Kings (or gods) of hell. The notion of these deities originated in China were said to judge the soul after death and to determine the punishment that soul was to be. Visual representations—usually paintings—were often produced at places like the port of Ningbo in South China in the twelfth and thirteenth centuries.[274]

In most of these Chinese paintings beginning in the twelfth century there are lists of the Ten Kings or gods, the domain of sin that each control and how long it takes for a soul to be sent to each of the Ten Kings after death. According to Chinese records, in a text called *A Chinese Traveler in Medieval Korea*, completed in 1123, the diplomat

Xu Jing (1091–1153) gives a clear account of the names, functions and punishments for various offenses.[275]

There is evidence that the practice of worshipping the Ten Kings of hell and their specific infernos first developed in Chia during the Tang dynasty that lasted from 618 to 907 CE. The surviving works from this period are mostly found in hand scrolls in murals excavated from ancient sites in the Dunhuang Region of Northwest China.[276]

Many of these images of the Ten Kings of hell are now owned by universities and libraries around the world. Harvard University Library, for example, owns three images of the Ten Kings. One of these is from the Ming dynasty in the fifteenth and sixteenth centuries. It was donated by Clifford A. Kaye in 1966 and is now designated as Object Number 1966.89.1. Two other Chinese images of the Ten Kings are part of a collection known as "Reigning Over a Hellish Bureaucracy," located at the Harvard University Museum.

The most substantial collection of depictions of hell in East Asia is to be found in Japan. The Japanese government owns dozens of Japanese paintings that represent hell from the twelfth to the nineteenth century. We will speak of nine of these to show the variety of the collection.

The earliest of these paintings from the Heian to Kamakura periods is called *The Extermination of Hell*, or *Five Hanging Scrolls* and is located at the Japanese National Museum, Tokyo. It shows the fate of the soul in the domain of one of the Ten Kings. Another early Japanese manuscript is one that depicts the fate of "wayward priests." This twelfth or thirteenth century work shows a demon jailer leading the souls of evil Buddhist priests to a river of excrement, their final resting place. Another Japanese hanging scroll comes from the thirteenth-century Kamakura period. It is entitled *The Hell of Endless Rebirth*, a reference to the Buddhist belief in reincarnation.[277]

A fourth Japanese collection of nine scrolls called the *Illustrated Legends of the Kitano Tenjin Shrine in the City of Kyoto*, Kyoto, Japan, also depicts hell in the hanging scroll tradition, as does the thirteenth-century Japanese *Hanging Scroll Depiction of King Enma* and his court. Enma is one of the Ten Kings.

The Nara National Museum of Japan owns a painting entitled the *Illustrated Legends of the Jizo Statue of Yatadera Temple*. It is a sixteenth-century hand scroll that shows a figure rescuing the dead from various of the ten hells.

The Japanese government also owns three other eighteenth and nineteenth century depictions of hell. The first of these is entitled, *Hell and Pure Land Painting*. It is an illustration that can be found in the text *Hell in Japanese Art*. It is owned by the Kumamoto Prefectural Museum of Art in Japan. Another modern text from 1885 is written by Kawanabe Kyosi entitled, *Yamato Anthology of the Eighth Aspects of Shaka*. It is now housed at the Kanawabe Kyosi Memorial Museum in Fukushima.

Finally, several Japanese depictions of the ten hells are contained in a collection called *Five Hundred Arhats*, a set of one hundred hanging scrolls from the Zojoji Temple in the city of Tokyo. The collection is the most substantial set of Japanese art on the depictions of hell.

In Korea, the practice of worshipping the Ten Kings of hell also can be seen going back to the tenth century, during the Goryeo period (918–1392). In the Korean tradition, throughout a forty-nine-day mourning period, family members and friends of the deceased made offerings and supplications to the Ten Kings at proper intervals to ensure that the newly deceased person could escape severe judicial torture and earn a pardon from the Ten Kings of hell.

Those souls whose families failed to make proper supplications were left to endure the worst kinds of punishments for their past sins. These will be enacted the Koreans believed in the subsequent lives of those souls.

This brings us to the final section of Appendix B on depictions of hell in art in which we will explore pieces of art from the nineteenth century until the present in the twenty-first century.

Depictions of Hell in the Modern Period: Nineteenth to the Twenty-First Century

Some of the most important depictions of hell in the nineteenth century were completed by English artist William Blake. Among his many examples of this phenomena are three that stand out. The first of these is entitled *The Punishment of Thieves*, completed between 1824 and 1827. This artwork is located at the Tate Museum, London, England.

The Punishment of Thieves is a piece of ambiguously gendered figures. The title suggests these figures are thieves. Snakes are biting at some. Others appear to be dead. Ostensibly, the illustration is a depiction of Dante's circle of thieves, as most of the images from this collection tend to be.

Another illustration from the same set is entitled *Dante and Virgil Gazing into the Bolgia Ditch of Flatterers*. It is described in Canto XVIII of the "Inferno." In Dante's work, the flatterers are designated to exist in a great ditch. Dante relates through his character Beatrice: "These wretched souls are stewed in human filth and suffer for the sin of flattery."

In Blake's illustration, Dante and Virgil are gazing into the ditch of flatterers. Four of those flatterers can be seen below. Two are below a body of water. Two others are in supplication, a female figure with outstretched arms and a male with both hands atop his head.

A third image from the same set of illustrations is entitled, *Ciampolo the Barrator Tormented by the Devils*, located at the Tate Museum, London, England. The figure Ciampolo appears in Canto XXII of the "Inferno." Ciampolo is hooked by a devil who patrols that ditch. Ciampolo tells Dante of some of the other grafters punished there. In the Dante text, Ciampolo eventually tricks the devils and then makes his escape back to the boiling pitch. In Blake's illustration of the scene, Ciampolo is escaping back into the pitch.

A fourth nineteenth-century image of hell is John Martin's work entitled *Pandemonium*, completed in 1841 and located at the Louvre, Paris, France. Pandemonium is the capital of hell in John Milton's *Paradise Lost* at the end of Book I of the work. John Martin imagines Pandemonium as being comparable to his contemporary London. Martin, one of the English Romantic painters, pictures Pandemonium as a large, white marble building with numerous columns surrounded by a body of very murky water.

The French painter William-Adolph Bouguereau (1825–1905) also completed a series of Dante and Virgil in 1850 located at the Museum d'Orsay, Paris. In one painting, Dante and his guide Virgil are taken into the underworld, as they see a pair of damned souls in the midst of engaging in a bitter struggle.

One of the only early twentieth-century depictions of hell is August Rodin's *The Gates of Hell*, which he worked on from 1880 until 1917. The work was commissioned by the director of fine arts and was meant to be completed by 1885, but Rodin worked on the piece until his death. *The Gates of Hell* is now owned by the Museum Soumaya in Mexico City. Mexico.

The chief aspect of the Rodin "gates" is his deviation from the medieval tradition of compartmentalized scenes on church portals, specifically the doors to the baptistry in Florence (1425–1452) by Italian artist, Lorenzo Ghiberti. Rodin abandoned the formal structure for his doors and created instead an environment of tormented souls in which figures float in a surging sea of fire, representing the agony and suffering of human beings.

Another early twentieth-century depiction of hell is the 1903 Edvard Munch painting entitled *Selvportrett I helvete*, in Norwegian or in English, *Self-Portrait in Hell*, located at the Metropolitan Museum of Art in New York. In some versions of the same work, it is sometimes referred to as "Self-Portrait in Hell." The painting features a naked man in hues of yellow who clearly is in great pain. It is nearly as evocative a painting as Munch's more famous *The Scream*.

Another early twentieth-century painting is Franz von Stuck's *Inferno*, also located at the Metropolitan Museum of Art. It is a 1908 rendition of Dante. The painting consists of five figures who are seated in the depths of hell, all with looks of torture on their faces, symbolizing their shared fate.

In the second half of the twentieth century, in 1963, Rico Lebrun completed three drawings of the Inferno. One of these is a twisted figure with thick legs and one arm with giant eye sockets and a gaping mouth. Lebrun was an Italian-born painter who died shortly after the three representations of the Inferno. These drawings can be found at the Worcester Art Museum, Worcester, Massachusetts.

English painter Francis Bacon completed *Study for a Nude* in 1949, located at the Sainsbury Centre for Visual Arts, Norwich, England. It is another depiction of Dante's "Inferno," this time of the eighth circle of hell, "the pit of thieves and poets," as Bacon called it. The painting consists of a murky figure, standing and male from the back view.

Bacon reports that Dante tells us it is the place "where everything is changed into everything else." He adds:

> **Later in the 8th Circle you will meet fraudulent counsellors and all kinds of falsifiers (generally speaking) the Post-Modernists.**

Finally, the most recent piece of art that depicts hell is a work by Jake and Dinos Chapman entitled *Fucking Hell*, constructed in 2008. The piece consists of 60,000 toy soldiers built by the Chapman brothers to symbolize many of the ways that human beings have created evil against other human beings. The artwork is a 2008 installation piece of art ostensibly depicting a monumental battle of miniature skeletons, Nazi soldiers, and other evil figures. It is also related to the Chapman brother's earlier 1999 work called *Hell*, which was lost in a fire. Thus, all that remains of it are photographs.[278]

This brings us to the conclusions of this appendix on hell in art.

Conclusions

We have divided our analyses of Appendix B on hell in art into five parts. The first of these was "Art of Hell in the Medieval and Renaissance Periods." In the first section, we examined five separate paintings by Giotto, Fran Angelico, Van Eyck, Sandro Botticelli, and Dionisius.

In the second section of Appendix B, we identified and discussed ten different illustrations and paintings of hell by Hieronymus Bosch, the Master of King James IV, Pieter Bruegel, Paul Rubens, two by Filippo di Liagno, and several illustrations by Jacques Callot.

In section three, we concentrated our attention on what has come to be known as the "hellmouth" motif, a tendency to show the mouth of hell as a giant animal, a demon, or some other creature, including, as we have seen, an angel. All told, we have examined seven different versions of the hellmouth theme, including one artist who is very contemporary, Bijan Samerel, who made a fireplace in his office a hellmouth.

In the fourth section of Appendix B on hell in art, we turned our attention to the East Asian artistic motif known as *The Ten Kings of Hell*. It that section, we examined and spoke of two dozen artistic depictions, between the twelfth and nineteenth centuries, of the theme in China, Japan, and the history of Korea.

Finally, in the fifth section, we examined and discussed three creations related to our themes by William Blake, Joh Martin's painting *Pandemonium*, a sculpted piece by August Rodin called *The Gates of Hell*, and a painting by Frenchman William Bouguereau entitled *Dante and Virgil in Hell*.

We also have examined artistic creations of hell by Norway's Edvard Munch, German painter Franz Von Stuck, Rico Lebrun, Englishman Francis Bacon, and the extraordinary creation and depiction of hell made and installed by Jake and Dinos Chapman entitled *Fucking Hell*.

In all, we have identified and then discussed over fifty different artistic creations that have illustrated the motifs of hell from the twelfth to the twenty-first centuries. In our discussion, we introduced many theological and artistic themes found in these paintings, sketches, and prints, and even a major sculpted piece that Rodin labored on for many years until 1917, the year he died.

In our analyses in Appendix B, we have identified and discussed artistic creations by people from Italy, France, Germany, Norway, Britain, Holland, Flanders, China, Japan, Korea, and the United States.

This brings us to Appendix C in which we will examine many of the places in music where the motifs of hell may be seen. As we shall see, there is also a plethora of musical creations of the motifs of hell, as well.

John Martin, *Pandemonium* – One out of a set of mezzotints with the same title, 1823–1827. Louvre, Paris, France.

Appendix C
Hell in Music

The safest road to hell is the gradual one—the gentle slope, soft underfoot, without sudden turnings, without milestones, without signposts.
—C. S. Lewis

Introduction

There are two main places where music related to hell may be found. The first of these is in classical music, and the second is in the late-twentieth and early twenty-first-century rock music. Another place to find music related to hell is in the world of opera. To that end, this appendix consists of three separate sections: classical music, opera, and rock music.

Hell in Classical Music

There are dozens of pieces of classical music in which the themes of hell can be seen. In our analysis we will discuss ten of these works. The first is J. S. Bach's the Toccata and Fugue in D minor, BWV 565.[279] It is a two-part musical composition for organ written around 1708. The piece is known for its majestic sound, dramatic authority, and driving rhythm. It is best known for its use in the opening minutes of the Disney film *Fantasia*, which also has a hell scene. Bach's Toccata and Fugue also has been employed in many Western horror films from the 1930s to the present.[280]

The 1931 film *Dr. Jekyll and Mr. Hyde* features an orchestral arrangement of Bach's Toccata and Fugue. It was also used in the 1934 film *The Black Cat*, directed by Edgar G. Ulmer and starring Boris

Karloff. Finally, the 1996 film *Dr. Who*, as well as a television movie at the same time. The television film was a joint effort of Universal Studios and BBC Worldwide. Both the film and the TV movie employed J. S. Bach's Toccata and Fugue.

Giovanni Pacini (1796–1867) wrote a piece entitled *Sinfonia Dante*, which was produced in 1865. The piece is for four voices, and piano and harp. It has four movements, the first of which is the Inferno, followed by Purgatorio, Paradiso, and *Ilritorno triofale di Dante sulla terra*. Pacini was one of the many Italian composers who honored Dante's *Divine Comedy*.

Hector Berlioz (1803–1869) wrote of a "Dream of a Witches' Sabbath" in his *Symphonie Fantastique* in a French Romantic spirit.[281] Berlioz also completed a musical composition on the "Damnation of Faust" in 1845. It is Opus no. 24 of his body of work. Hungarian composer Franz Liszt was another European composer who wrote a "Dante Symphony."[282] Liszt wished to combine music, poetry, and the visual arts in his reading of the *Divine Comedy*. In fact, he immersed himself in a close reading of the Dante text.

Originally, Liszt thought of projecting lantern slides on the stage and using an experimental wind machine. In fact, at the close of the first movement, the music was meant to evoke "the winds of hell," according to Liszt's notes on the work.

Italian composer Giuseppe Verdi (1831–1901) declined to compose a piece of music to celebrate the birth of Dante. Verdi said at the time, "Yes, Dante is the greatest of all. Homer and Shakespeare are great, even sublime, but neither is universal like Dante." Verdi must have changed his mind about writing Dante music because he later wrote *Il Credi di Dante*, or *The Belief of Dante*, which the Italian composer says are "texts of faith and prayers." This piece is filled with characters such as Cleopatra and Judas Iscariot.

French composer Camille Saint-Saens (1835–1921), wrote a *Danse Macabre*. It is a tone poem for orchestra. It had its premiere on January 24, 1875. Saint-Saens was aware of the tradition that Dante appears at the stroke of midnight every Halloween. Supposedly, Death calls forth the dead from their graves to dance, while Death plays his fiddle, represented in Saint-Saens's piece with a solo violin.

The solo violin enters the composition playing a tritone that has come to be known as the *Diabolus in musica*, or "The Devil in Music." This piece of Saint-Saens originally was not well received. But, in 1942, Vladimir Horowitz made extensive changes to the Liszt transcription. This version is now played most often after the mid-twentieth century.

Our seventh musical composition on the themes of hell is that of Modest Mussorgsky (1839–1881) entitled "A Night on Bear Mountain."[283] This series of compositions was inspired by Russian literary works and legends. Among the pieces of "Night" are two related to our purposes. One is an opera that Mussorgsky planned to call "The Witch" and was completed in 1860. The other is also an opera project based on a Gogol short story named "St. John's Night." The Russian composer began this project in 1858 but never finished it.

Norwegian composer Edvard Grieg (1843–1907) wrote a composition he called, "In the Hall of the Mountain King." It was created to accompany the sixth scene of Act II of Henri Ibsen's 1867 drama *Peer Gynt.* This composition includes a "great crowd of troll couriers, gnomes, and goblins." King Dovregunnen sits on his throne with crown and scepter but acts like the king of hell. This piece was the origins of the 2019 film *Parasite*.

Edvard Grieg later created two suites from his *Peer Gynt* music in the early 1880s. In fact, these suites at the end of the nineteenth century received coverage in popular culture in Sweden, Finland, Norway, and Denmark. Henrik Ibsen, the author of *Peer Gynt*, was the impetus to get Grieg to write the music for his 1867 drama.

The ninth piece of classical music is by Austro-Bohemian Gustav Mahler (1860–1911). We have in mind here Mahler's Second Symphony composed in 1894. Mahler's Second is usually referred to as the "Symphony of Resurrection" because it is filled with images of death and religious imagery. The theme of death also pervades the piece, as does the hint of demons and darkness that interfere with the Resurrection of the Dead. It was first performed in 1895.

Finally, our tenth piece of classical music on the theme of hell is from Hungarian composer Gyorgy Ligeti (1923–2006). More specifically, his Etude 13, written in 1985, which he entitled "The

Devil's Staircase." It clearly was no mistake that Ligeti numbered this etude thirteen.

One aspect of this piece is that it is much more optimistic than the other nine compositions we have described here. That is principally because there is almost always an upbeat movement while trying to escape from hell on the devil's own staircase. The piece is exciting and is a very clever musical composition. Another big difference in Ligeti's piece is the many crossings over of the hands in the work on the piano, as well as large leaps and spans.

Above all, however, the "Staircase" is about the fiery escape from torture and death and ultimately a wished for a way of escaping the clutches of Satan, or the devil, himself and with success by the end of the piece.

This brings us to the second section of Appendix C on the themes of hell in the world of opera. As we shall, there are a significant number of operas in the West that employ the motifs of hell.

Hell in Western Opera

In Wendy Heller's Princeton dissertation alone, she provides an analysis of dozens of Italian operas that employed the themes of hell.[284] The eighteenth and nineteenth centuries continued this trend, many composers created operas based on the Greek myth of Orpheus and Eurydice and the Faust narrative. Even in the early twentieth to the early twenty-first centuries, a significant number of hell operas also have been created.

Because of the voluminous amount of material, we will limit our discussion on hell in opera to ten operas: one in the seventeenth century, one in the eighteenth century, three in the nineteenth century, two in the twentieth century, and three in the twenty-first century.

The earliest example on Ms. Heller's dissertation is the 1600 opera written by Italian composer Jacopo Peri, called *Euridici*. The work was commissioned by Maria de' Medici and her husband King Henry IV of France to be played at their wedding. In fact, the work was performed at their wedding in Florence and the composer Jacopo sang the lead part of Orpheus.[285]

The example we have chosen from the eighteenth century is Christoph Gluck's *Orfeo ed Euridice*, written in 1762 and first performed on October 5, 1762. The opera is based on the Homeric myth of Orpheus and Eurydice and includes scenes of an underworld or Hades that is populated by nymphs, snakes, furies, and ghosts. The Gluck opera was set to a libretto by Ranieri de Calzabigi. It belongs to the opera genre known as *Azione Teatrale*, meaning an opera based on a mythological setting with lots of singing and dancing.

The three operas that employ the motifs of hell in the nineteenth century were by Charles Francois Gounod (1818–1893), Arrigo Boito, and Jacques Offenbach. Gounod's 1859 version of *Faust* follows the main feature of Goethe's *Faust*, with one main deviation—the ultimate fate of Faust is ambiguously unknown.

Italian composer Arrigo Boito (1842–1911) was also a journalist, a poet, and a novelist. He used the Faust narrative in his opera *Mefistofele*. The opera had its premiere in the fall of 1868, but it closed after only two performances. Later, it was revised and revived at the Bologna Opera House in 1875.

German-born Jacques Offenbach's (1819–1880) *Orphee aux enfers* or *Orpheus in the Underworld* was written and first performed in 1874. Offenbach was also a cellist and impresario of the Romantic period. He wrote nearly one hundred operettas from 1850 to 1880, the year of his death. One of the finest was his *Orpheus in the Underworld*, where he treats the Homeric myth with a good bit of deviation.

The earliest twentieth-century opera on our list that employs the motifs of hell is Puccini's *Gianni Schicchi*, a work that he calls a "comic opera in one act." The opera contains the well-known soprano aria, "O Mio Babbino Caro," or in English, "Oh, My Dear Father." The Italian libretto for the Puccini opera was composed in 1917–1918 by Giovacchino Forzano. The libretto, as we have said, was based on incidents in Dante's *Divine Comedy*. The opera premiered on December 14, 1918, at the Metropolitan Opera in New York.

Our other twentieth-century opera that uses the themes of hell is a seventy-minute opera entitled *Satan's Place: A Soap Opera in Hell*, written by Melanie Johnson and Alfred Ramirez. It was written and first performed in the winter of 1988. Ms. Johnson described the opera as "A horror anthology in which the beautiful, beach-blonde Stephanie Spencer fields a series of crude remarks after she farts several times."

The opera is set in hell and takes several liberties with the traditional understanding of Hades.

The two twenty-first-century operas we have selected that employ the motifs of hell are by composers Michael Webster and Matthew Aucoin. Michael Webster's *Hell: The Opera* was written and premiered at the Performance Space 122 in New York City in 2006. It was directed by David Chambers and the music was conducted by Jonathan Yates. Webster's hell is far more like life on Earth than what would be considered as life in hell.

Another twenty-first-century employment of the motifs of hell in opera is a work written by composer Peter Josheff and librettist Jaime Robles, whom in 2009 collaborated on a work they entitled *Hell in Song*. It is described as "a piece for three voices." They use Dante's "Inferno" as their model. One of the voices is named "Hell's Wind," which blows around the other pair of main characters. This opera runs for about seventy minutes.

Finally, the most recent twenty-first-century opera that incorporates the themes of hell into the plot is composed by Matthew Aucoin, who in November of 2021, wrote and produced his version of *Eurydice*. Eric Morley sang the role of the heroine, Eurydice, while Joshua Hopkins supplied the voice of Orpheus. Composer Aucion, however, changed the Homeric myth in several ways. First, Eurydice dies because of some machinations in Hades.

Secondly, the emphasis is taken off the love between Orpheus and Eurydice and concentrates more on Eurydice's relationship with her father. And thirdly, and perhaps most importantly, the shades of Aucion's hell—the inhabitants of Hades—have no memory. The dead characters know nothing because their memories have been obliterated.

This brings us to the third and final section of Appendix C on hell in music in which we will discuss many rock songs and groups that have put an emphasis on the themes of hell.

Hell in Rock Music

Since the late 1960s, there have been more appropriations of the themes of hell, punishment, and the devil in the English-speaking world of rock music than any other genre. In the 1960s, Rolling Stones' song

"Sympathy for the Devil," written and performed first on June 4, 1968, is one of the classic rock engagements with the genre. The John Lennon song "Imagine" is another fine example of the employment of heaven and hell. The song was released in May of 1971. There is evidence of the existence of some of the lyrics going back to 1966.

The first stanza of "Imagine" speaks of the afterlife both in terms of heaven and hell. Lennon wrote:

> Imagine there's no Heaven.
> It's easy if you try.
> No hell below us,
> Above us only sky.
> Imagine all the people
> Living for the day…

In the 1970s, we see dozens of rock songs with hell, punishment, and the devil in their lyrics. We will point to seven in our analysis to give a flavor of the variety of the genre. The Grateful Dead song "Friend of the Devil" was written and first performed in 1970. AC-DC's "Hell Ain't a Bad Place to Be" was produced in 1977, as was Meat Loaf's "Bat Out of Hell."

Over the next two years, the band Judas Priest had a song in 1978 called "Saints in Hell" and another in 1979 with the title "Hell Bent for Leather." To round out the 1970s, AC-DC produced another song in 1979 called "Highway to Hell." In fact, it was the name of the entire album and the sixth studio album by the Australian hard rock band. The same year, the group called Pink Floyd also featured a tract they called "Run Like Hell."

English-speaking rock bands of the 1980s continued the trend of using motifs of hell, punishment and the devil in their songs and albums. We will point to eight examples from the decade.

The Black Sabbath heavy metal song "Heaven and Hell" was performed and released in 1980. AC-DC's tune "Hell's Bells" followed a few months later in 1980. It was the first track of the Australian band's first album without singer Bon Scott. The song is on the album entitled *Back in Black.*

The heavy-metal group Venom produced an album in 1981 entitled *Welcome to Hell*. The lyrics include the line "Burning lives burning, asking me for the mercy of God." In fact, on the back cover of the original album, the band related, "We serve at Lucifer's right hand," along with the obedience to the genre.

In 1984, the rock band Twisted Sister performed a song called "Burn in Hell." It was a track from their breakout album *Stay Hungry*. The song is written from the perspective of Satan, warning that "some of you will join me down below." In 1985, Twisted Sister made an appearance in the movie *Pee Wee's Big Adventure*. One interesting turn of events was when the band was recording the basic tracks for "Burn in Hell," the studio they were working in New York City caught fire. So, the album was completed in Los Angeles.

The heavy-metal group Slayer released their second studio album in 1985. There is a track called "Hell Awaits." The lyrics contain the line:

> Priests of Hades seek the sacred star and Satan sees the answer lies not too far.

Our final example from the 1980s is the band GWAR. This heavy-metal band, which formed in Richmond, Virginia, in 1984, often uses the word "hell" and related concepts in its albums. Two good examples are the 1988 tunes "Beyond Hell" and "Hell-O."

The 1990s also produced many songs with the themes of hell, punishment, and the devil. At the beginning of the decade, Guns N' Roses performed their song "Right Next Door to Hell" on September 17, 1991. The lyrics refer to a neighbor who lived next to Axl Rose with whom the singer did not get along. Thus, he sang:

> Right next door to hell, why don't you write a letter to me/
> I said I am right next door to hell, and so many eyes are on me.

This is followed by a fleet-fingered solo and a full-throated "Fuck You Bitch."

Heavy metal group Megadeath continued employing the motifs of hell, such as in their 1992 track "Go to Hell." In the same year, the group Iron Maiden also performed their song "From Here to Eternity" for the first time, the lyrics of which contain several references to hell.

Two other 1990s bands that incorporate themes of hell in their lyrics are Marilyn Manson and Ozzy Osbourne. The former wrote a song and performed it in 1997 named "Long Hard Road Out of Hell." In the same year, Osbourne's tune "Hellraiser" was also produced. In the opening lyrics of the song, Osbourne hints at the theological content:

> You make a promise of protection
> To a future afterlife
> To the final resurrection
> And to eternal Paradise.

But the second stanza is considerably less pessimistic. It tells us:

> But then I am blinded with temptation
> And to every mortal sin
> Is it God that sits there waiting?
> Or will the darkness suck me in?

A twenty-first-century rock band that incorporates themes of hell in their music is Insane Clown Posse whose 2004 album is entitled *Hell's Pit*. On many of the songs of this album, the band incorporates the motifs of hell, such as the songs "Carnival of Carnage" and "The Wrath: Hell's Pit."

There are also several more contemporary appropriations of the themes of hell in the twenty-first century. We will point to three of these. The first is Dua Lipa's song "Hotter Than Hell," released in 2017. The second is Billy Raffoul's track "Hell or High Water" written and performed first in 2019. And the third is Lorley Rodriquez's 2017 release "Good as Hell." All three of these songs are by up-and-coming artists who clearly are familiar with the hell music genre.

This brings us to the fourth and final section of this appendix on hell in the world of music. In this section, we will mostly be concerned with bands and individual performers who employ the motifs of Appendix C, but for the most part they are not traditional rock bands.

Hell in Other Modern Artists

In this final section, our goal is to identify and discuss other musical artists and groups that are not associated with hard rock or heavy metal rock but nevertheless still have engaged in the motifs of this appendix. We will explore about a dozen examples in our analyses.

One of the earliest uses of these non-rock applications of our themes is Hank Williams Jr.'s 1979 song "Whiskey Bent and Hell Bound." It is a track from the artist's thirteenth studio album and fourth on the Elektra/Curb labels. This was his second album in 1979, with *Family Tradition* being the first. "Whiskey Bent and Hell Bound" is considered in the country music genre.

Mr. Williams later claimed that the impetus for the song came while hanging out with the Allman Brothers after Dickey Betts asked him how he writes country songs. Hank reported he replied, "Well, I got a good woman at home," and the remainder of the song supposedly was written in ten minutes.

Tom Waits (1949–) wrote and performed his song "Everyone Goes to Hell" but the date of its origin is not clear. The song does appear, however, in his three-disc set entitled *Orphans*, which was produced in 2006. The song has haunting lyrics, such as this first stanza:

> There is a place I know where the trains go slow
> Where sinners can be washed in the blood of the lamb.
> There is a river by the trestle down by Sinner's Grove
> Down where the willows and the dogwood grow
> Down there by the train
> Down there where the train goes slow.

Another stanza of the song takes a decidedly pessimistic view of life, sometimes with overt sexual language:

> Why be sweet? Why be careful? Why be kind?
> A man has only one thing in mind
> Why ask politely? Why go lightly? Why say please?
> They only want to get you on your knees.

Mr. Waits is an American musician, composer, songwriter, and actor. Like the words above, his lyrics often concentrate on the underbelly of society, and he usually delivers them in his trademark deep, gravelly voice. He worked primarily in jazz in the 1970s, but since 1985 or so, he has had a greater influence from the blues, from some rock groups and artists, as well as experimenting with some new genres.

Many of the uses of the themes of hell may be seen in several early twenty-first-century musical artists and groups. We will point to five of these to bring Appendix C to a close. These are the following:

1. Pat Benatar, "Hell is For Children," 1980
2. Pistol Annies, *Hell on Heels*, 2011
3. Good Company, "In Hell I'll be in Good Company," 2014
4. Blake Shelton, "Hell Right," 2019
5. Billie Eilish, "All Good Girls Go to Hell," 2019

The first of these songs, from Pat Benatar, was written by guitarist Neil Giraldo, bass player Roger Capps, and Ms. Benatar. Ostensibly, the song is about child abuse and was recorded for her second studio album entitled *Crimes of Passion*. The Benatar song was also featured in the 1981 film *American Pop*.

Hell on Heels is the name of the first studio album of Pistol Annies. It was released in 2011. The album sold 45,000 copies in the first week, landing at number five on the Billboard chart. By June of 2013, the album had sold half a million copies. The album featured many songs by Miranda Lambert such as "Takin Pills," "Hunter's Wife," "Family Feud," and the popular "Trailer for Rent."

The group Good Company's 2014 Bluegrass tune called "In Hell I'll be in Good Company" was written by Colton Crawford. The opening stanza sets the plaintive tone:

> Dead love couldn't go no further.
> Proud of and disgusted by her.
> Push shove, a little bruised and battered
> Oh Lord, I ain't coming home with you.

The final stanza mentions the title. It tells us:

> After I count down, three rounds,
> in hell I'll be in good company.
> In hell I'll be in good company.
> In hell I'll be in good company.

The two most recent songs on our list that employ the motifs of hell are those by Blake Shelton and Billie Eilish, both released in 2019. In the former, Blake Shelton asked Trace Adkins and Michael Hardy to what he called the "Hell's Right Festival." Some critics complained the festival is part of a Satanic cult. Shelton wrote the song in question with David Garcia and Brett Tyler.

Like our next artist, Billie Eilish and Blake Shelton, some of their fans complained about the lyrics of their songs, and that they may have Satanic implications. Shelton's song in question is called "Hell Right." One stanza tells us this:

> You ain't done nothin' if you did it halfway
> If you are going to raise hell, then you better damn raise
> hell right, hell right, hell right.

Finally, Billie Eilish is a singer/songwriter who took the music industry by storm in the early years of the twenty-first century. One of her videos shows the star depicting herself as a fallen angel, which outraged many conservative Christians, making many of her fans wonder if Billie Eilish is Satanic. The skit in question, which made fun of the Christian Nativity, was first seen on an episode of *Saturday Night Live*, in which, among other things, the early Christians were taught how to "Twerk." The SNL skit was recorded and broadcast on December 12, 2021.

In interviews, however, despite Ms. Eilish's unique look and sound, the music video, she says, was a call to arms about the global environmental crisis and not a depiction of the artist's theological views. As we have seen, she is by far not the first to use images of hell, punishment, and the demonic in her music, and for certain, she will not be the last. Another problem, of course, is figuring out just what various people and groups mean by the "Satanic." But we will leave that to another day.

This brings us to the major conclusions we have made in this appendix on the motifs of hell, punishment, and the Satanic in music. The subject matter of Appendix C of this work is hell in film.

Conclusions

We began Appendix C of this study on hell by suggesting that the appendix will unfold in four sections. The first of these was ten composers who employed the themes of hell in their musical compositions. In this first section, we identified music by Bach, Pacini, Berlioz, Franz Liszt, Italian Giuseppe Verdi, French composer Saint-Saens, Modest Mussorgsky, Edvard Grieg, Gustav Mahler, and Italian composer Gyorgy Ligeti.

In the second section, we turned our attention to the phenomenon of hell in the world of opera. We began by pointing out that our main source for these operas was Wendy Heller's Princeton dissertation where she provides dozens of examples in Italian opera that have used the motifs of hell.

In our analyses, we limited our discussion to ten separate operas from the eighteenth century to the twenty-first century. Many of these operas, as we have shown, were versions of the Orpheus and Eurydice myth or Faust and one Italian composer who based his opera on the figure of Mephistopheles.

Hell in rock music was the concentration of the discussion of the third section. All told, we examined twenty separate groups and artists from the 1960s until the twenty-first century when the motifs of hell played large roles in the music of these groups and single artists. Among these were the Rolling Stones, John Lennon, AC-DC, Twisted Sister, Judas Priest, Black Sabbath, Guns N' Roses, Venom, Pistol Annies, Marilyn Manson, and many others.

In the final section of Appendix C, we examined the works of several other modern composers who have employed the themes of this study. Among these artists and groups we have examined were Hank Williams Jr., Ton Waits, Pat Benatar, the group Good Company, Blake Shelton, and single artist Billie Eilish, who played an angel in one of her music videos that outraged some conservative Christians among her followers.

The major conclusion we may make about the material and musical artists from Appendix C is that first, many of the tried-and-true theological themes we have seen in art were also employed in music. Second, some of the traditional and classic literary pieces have been used as models for hell in music, such as Orpheus and Eurydice, Dante's "Inferno," Goethe's *Faust*, and many others.

A third conclusion we may make about the music in this appendix is that it has come from many different musical styles and kinds such as classical music, hard rock, country, bluegrass, American pop music, folk music, acoustical music, as well as more contemporary music artists.

This brings us to the fourth appendix of this study in the motifs of hell in the industries of film and television. As we shall see, the number of examples that employ our themes in these venues is great, as well. It is to film and television, then, to which we turn next.

Lucas Cranach the Elder, *Law and Grace/Law and Gospel*, 1529–1530. Woodcut print.

Appendix D
Hell in Film, Television, and Radio

Cry about the simple Hell people give each other—without even thinking. Cry about the Hell that white people give to colored folks, without even stopping to think that they are human too.
—Harper Lee, *To Kill a Mockingbird*

Introduction

In this appendix, our principal aim is to explore how the motifs of hell have been incorporated into the genre of film. To that end, we will divide the appendix into five parts, which will consist of the following:

1. Films from 1911 to 1934
2. Films from 1935 to 1975
3. Films from 1976 to 1999
4. Films from 2000 to 2020
5. Hell on TV and the Radio

In this appendix, we will discuss more than fifty films, and a dozen TV shows and radio programs. Many of these are famous movies, while others are quite obscure. We will begin with an analysis of five films in the first section from 1911 to 1934.

Hell in Film: 1911 to 1934

L'Inferno is a 1911 Italian silent film directed by Giuseppe Liguoro. The film contains horned demons, headless specters, winged harpies, and a preponderance of naked flesh. It also revels in the grotesque and the macabre. Some critics say the film is "like a fairy tale gone wrong."

Like many of the pieces of art we have seen in Appendices A, B, and C, those in Appendix D, including the Liguoro film, are based on literary sources. Indeed, in this appendix, we will discuss movies that are sometimes very loosely based on great literary classics, such as:

1. The Greek Myth of Orpheus and Eurydice
2. The Greek Myth of Cerberus
3. *The Canterbury Tales*
4. Dante's "Inferno"
5. Goethe's *Faust*
6. Christopher Marlowe's *Doctor Faustus*
7. Charles Dickens's *A Christmas Carol*
8. And many other literary classics.

The 1922 Swedish silent film *Haxan, or The Witch*, also called *Heksen* or "The Witches" in Danish, was directed by Benjamin Christensen. The film combines documentary style, superstitions, and a narrative sequence that also charts the historical roots of ideas related to medieval European witchcraft. Although it is a Swedish film, it was made in Norway in 1920 and 1921. At the time, the production of *Haxan* was the most expensive Swedish film ever made, costing nearly two million dollars.

In a very real way, the director Christensen seems to suggest that the graphic depictions of torture, nudity, and sexual perversion in the film may have been the result of mental or neurological disorders, triggering forms of mass hysteria. In 1968, the Metro Picture Corporation re-edited and re-released the film under the title *Witchcraft Through the Ages.* This version is in English and is narrated by William S. Burroughs. Some say that *Haxan* is the very first example of the genre horror films.

A third 1920s film that employed the motifs of hell is the 1924 version of Dante's "Inferno." It was directed by Henry Otto and was Hollywood's answer to the very expensive Italian films of the "Inferno" in the early 1920s. The protagonist is a man named Mortimer Judd, a ruthless slum landlord who is determined to get ahead at every cost. Judd is also obsessed with Dante's "Inferno."

Some of Judd's tenants were evicted, and they pleaded with him to let them stay in their homes. One tenant warned Judd that if he continues his ways he will wind up in hell, and that is precisely what happens. In the end, the landlord is thrown into a molten pit of sinners at the hands of the devil himself, which appears to establish that the tenant was correct.

There is also an appearance of hell in the 1926 version of *Faust*, directed by F. W. Murnau. In the film, angels try to stop the devil as he races across the Earth. The devil insists that the planet belongs to him, so he strikes a bet with the angels about whether he could corrupt the soul of the aged scholar Faust. Appearing in the guise of Mephisto, the devil infects Faust's town with the plague. Faust struggles to find a cure. Mephisto tempts him with the power to control the dead. Then Mephisto promises to give Faust youth and love in exchange for being his forever.

"Hell's Bells" by James Young is a Silly Symphony that debuted on November 21, 1929. Satan and his demons gather for a wild party. After some of the demons play some somber music, Satan has others "milk" burning flames out of a dragon cow, and Satan drinks the milk. Then Satan feeds one of his smaller demons to Cerberus, the three-headed beast from Greek mythology. Eventually, Satan is forced off a cliff and is consumed by the flames. This is, undoubtedly, the first cartoon horror film.

This brings us to the second section of this appendix on hell in film, where we will identify and discuss twenty films from 1935 to 1975. The first of these may be the most famous of these movies.

Hell in Film: 1935 to 1975

In this second section, we will identify and discuss twenty separate films: seven in the 30s and 40s, eight from the 50s and 60s, and five in the 1970s, beginning with *Dante's Inferno* from 1935 and directed by Harry Lachman. It is a taut drama starring Spencer Tracy as a ruthless promoter named Jim Carter, who is determined to succeed at any cost. Eventually, he is given a glimpse of hell and suddenly sees the errors in his ways. But it is too late for him to repair the damage he has done to others. The film also stars Claire Trevor, and there is a brilliant performance by Alan Dinehart (1899–1944), one of the great supporting actors of Hollywood's golden age.

There is a segment called "Night on Bald Mountain" in the 1940 Disney movie *Fantasia*, which was produced under the supervision of Ben Sharpsteen. It is part of the final segment of the Disney concert. It was inspired by the music of Russian composer Modest Mussorgsky, which in Russian is called *Noch na lyso gore*.

The first Three Stooges movie, *I'll Never Heil Again*, from 1941, is a spoof on Hitler and Mussolini. Moe Hailstone is a Hitler-like dictator. Curly Howard plays Field Marshall Herring, who has so many medals that he wears them on the front and back of his uniform. Larry plays the Minister of Propaganda. The drama takes place in a hell-like environment.

A 1942 film on the same motif is entitled *The Devil with Hitler*. It is a forty-four-minute movie directed by Gordon Douglas and stars Alan Mowbray, Robert Watson, Joe Devlin, and Marjorie Woodworth. In the film, the board of directors of hell has put the devil on notice that they intend to replace him with Adolf Hitler unless he can convince the German leader to commit a good deed.

In Ernst Lubitsch's 1943 film *Heaven Can Wait*, Don Ameche (Henry Van Cleve) presents himself at the outer office of hades, where he asks a bemused Satan for permission to enter through the gates of hell. But the devil doubts that Henry has committed sufficient sins to earn him a spot there. So, Henry recounts his life of wooing and pursuing women long before his happy marriage to Martha, played by Gene Tierney. The film was nominated for Best Picture and for Best Director Academy Awards. The movie combines Ernst Lubitsch's talent for wit, urbanity, and grace.

Eddie Kagle, played by Paul Muni, goes to hell in Archie Mayo's 1946 movie *Angel on My Shoulder*. Gangster Eddie Kagle is murdered by his childhood friend and business partner, Smiley Williams (Hardie Albright). Kagle is sent to hell, where he meets a man named Nick, played by Claude Rains, who tries to get Eddie to return to Earth to take over the body of Judge Frederick Parker, also played by Muni.

Eddie agrees, enticed by the possibility of getting revenge on Smiley, but Kagle's attempt to tarnish the character of the judge fails and Kagle eventually confronts Smiley directly when his frustration over his murder has peaked. *Angel on My Shoulder* was director Archie Mayo's final film. It is the only film of the genre that involves a deal between the devil and a dead man. In mid-making, the name of the film was changed from *Me and Satan*. Claude Raines' performance as Nick is spectacular.

The film version of *Damn Yankees* was directed by George Abbot and Stanley Donen and was released in 1958. All the actors in the film version played the same roles in the Broadway play, except Tab Hunter, who played the role of Joe Hardy, who replaced Stephen Douglass, who played the role on stage. Later, a made-for-television version on NBC in 1967 starred Phil Silvers as Applegate, Lee Remick in the role of Lola, and Ray Middleton. The drama version won the 1956 Tony Award. Hell appears in both the play and the movie version.

Hell is also shown in the 1959 Rene Cardona film *Santa Claus* and the 1962 Herbert Strock movie *The Devil's Messenger*. Lon Chaney Jr. plays the devil, and Karen Kadler is Satanya. *The Devil's Messenger* opened in Los Angeles in October 1962. Chaney's performance is memorable. It is one of his finest horror films, shot in black and white.

Ten Seconds to Hell is another 1959 American movie that employs the motifs of hell. It is directed by Robert Aldrich and stars Jeff Chandler and a scary Jack Palance. After the end of World War II, six German soldiers return to Berlin and form a bomb disposal unit. The director pays particular attention to the details of bomb deactivation in the middle of the twentieth century. Chandler plays a man named Karl Wirtz and Palance plays Eric Kroetner. These are the only two survivors of the original band of six.

The only Japanese film on our list is Nobuo Nakagawa's 1960 movie *The Sinners of Hell*, also called *Jigoku* in Japanese. The film stars famous Japanese actors Utako Mitsuya and Shigerou Amachi. The film was remade ten years later and directed by Tatsumi Kumashiro.

A 1960 episode of the television series *The Twilight Zone*, "A Nice Place to Visit," has a plot involving a thief who ends up in the afterlife only to have his every wish granted. He never loses at the casino, and attractive women cannot get enough of him. For him, it appears to be Heaven.

After a while though, it becomes boring, and he desires a change of scenery. In typical classic tragedy he is doomed to remain where he is for all eternity and this perpetual state of dissatisfaction. Thus, of course, prompts the question, "Can people have too much of a good thing?" Rod Serling, the writer and director of "A Nice Place to Live," suggests that in hell maybe they can.

The only other television piece on our list is the 1978 movie *Devil Dog: The Hound of Hell*, starring Kim Richards and Yvette Mimieux and directed by Curtis Harrington. The plot centers on a suburban family and the harrowing experiences they endure from an apparently demon-possessed dog.

Hot Rods in Hell is a 1967 film directed by John Braham and starring Dana Andrews and Jeanne Crain. The Andrews character brings his wife and family to California to start a new life but finds a gang of juvenile delinquents who like to race their hot rods. Tom Phillips—the Andrews character—arrives in the California town to find that the inn he had purchased is in disrepair and used by the teens who do not like the plan to refurbish the facility. Phillips can tolerate a great deal, but his rage finally erupts followed by significant bloodshed.

Ebenezer Scrooge, played by Albert Finney, goes to hell in the 1970 film *Scrooge*, directed by Ronald Neame. Scrooge is the definitive miser. Although he is rich, he is completely stingy and exploits the good nature of his employee, Bob Cratchit, played by David Collings. On Christmas Eve, however, Scrooge is visited by the spirit of his old business partner, Jacob Marley, played by Alec Guinness.

Marley tells Scrooge he will be visited by three ghosts, including the Ghost of Christmas Past (Edith Evans) and the Ghost of the Present, played by Kenneth More. The film also features Laurence Naismith as Mr. Fezziwig and Michael Medwin, who plays the nephew. Needless to say, the film follows the plot closely of Charles Dickens's *A Christmas Carol*.

Hell is shown in Freddie Francis's 1972 movie *Tales from the Crypt*. Hell also makes an appearance in Pier Paolo Pasolini's 1972 version of *The Canterbury Tales*. Justine Jones is in hell after committing suicide in the film *The Devil in Miss Jones*, the 1973 Gerald Damiano film.

Finally, *The Legend of Hell House* is a 1973 horror film directed by John Hough and stars Pamela Franklin, Roddy McDowall, Clive Revill, Gayle Hunnicutt, and Ronald Culver. Scientist Lionel Barrett, played by Clive Revill, and his wife, Gayle Hunnicutt, lead a team of researchers into a famous haunted house called the Belasco House. The previous owner was a notorious serial killer. Though the rational Dr. Barrett does not believe in ghosts, the other researchers do. These include the devout spiritualist Florence Tanner, Pamela Franklin, and psychic medium Benjamin Fischer (Roddy McDowall). Fischer has been to Belasco House before and has seen the horrors of those who enter it.

This brings us to the third section of Appendix D on the motifs of hell in films from 1976 until 1999. In this period, we will identify and discuss ten separate movies.

Hell in Film: 1980 to 1999

In this section, we will identify and discuss nine different films, beginning with the 1980 movie *Motel Hell*, directed by Kevin Connor and starring Rory Calhoun, who plays the character, Vincent Smith. Smith and his wife Ida (Nancy Parsons) run a rural hotel. But they gain most of their income by operating a food stand that specializes in world-famous sausages.

Vincent's brother, Bruce, played by Paul Linke, is the sheriff of the county. Eventually, he discovers the gory details of his sibling's operation. Vincent and Isa are swindling their hotel guests, killing and dismembering them, and then grinding them into great-tasting frankfurters.

The Devil and Max Devlin is a 1981 film directed by Steven Hilliard Stern and written by Mary Rodgers. To save his soul, minor league sinner Max makes a deal with the devil's right-hand man Barney. Within three months, Max must convince three innocent people to sell their souls to the devil. Max makes the dreams of his three victims come true and then tricks them into signing a "contract."

Max realizes that Barney lied to him and risks eternal damnation and burns the contracts. Elliot Gould plays the part of Max Devlin, Bill Cosby plays Barney, and Susan Anspach is Penny. Cosby's devilish look, created by make-up artist Bob Schiffer, is very convincing.

The 1985 film *Legend* stars Tom Cruise, who descends into the domain of the Lord of Darkness ruled by Satan, played by Tim Curry. The movie is directed by Ridley Scott. Cruise's character Jack's mission is to save his lover, Lily (Mia Sara), from hell. The make-up for Curry's Satan is extraordinary. The film is creepy, elegant, and hypnotic all rolled into one.

Two 1991 movies that employ the themes of hell are *My Life in Hell* and *Bill and Ted's Bogus Journey.* The latter is directed by Peter Hewitt and the former by Josiane Balasko, who also stars in the film. In *Bill and Ted*, the amiable pair is once again roped into a fantastic adventure. Bill is played by Alex Winter, and Ted by Keanu Reeves. The villain's name is De Nomolos, played by Joss Ackland. He is a devil of the future who sends robot duplicates of Bill and Ted to replace the originals.

The robots succeed in killing the original Bill and Ted, but when the two are sent to the afterlife, they challenge the Grim Reaper, played by William Sadler, to a series of games with the ultimate prize being a return to the land of the living on Earth.

My Life in Hell is a French film produced in France. Josiane Balasko plays a middle-aged French woman who falls in love with an annoying demon. The results, needless to say, are hellish and full of punishment. The movie also stars Daniel Auteuil, Richard Berry, and Michael Lonsdale.

Another 1997 science-fiction/horror film the heavily uses the motifs of hell and punishment is called *Event Horizon*. It was directed by Paul W. S. Anderson and produced by Lawrence Gordon, with Philip Eisner writing the screenplay. Laurence Fishburne and Sam Neill star in this great science fiction movie. The special effects are truly extraordinary and were organized by Richard Yuricich. Despite a strong opening of the film, *Event Horizon* quickly devolves into an exercise of style over substance, so much so that it obscures the plot by means of what are now cliches in the horror film genre.

The *Event Horizon is* a spacecraft that vanished years earlier and now suddenly reappears. A team is dispatched to investigate, led by a scientist named William Weir, played by Sam Neill. Another ship named the *Lewis and Clark*, captained by Mr. Miller and played by

Lawrence Fishburne, begins to explore the *Event Horizon*. The ship is abandoned, but it soon becomes evident that something sinister resides in the inner parts of the ship, and the horrors that befell the original crew are still at work on the vessel.

In Woody Allen's 1997 movie *Deconstructing Harry*, the hero, played by Billy Crystal, descends into hell. It is Allen's twenty-seventh film, which was written and directed by him. He stars in the movie as a character named Harry Block. Block is a writer who has been accused by the people in his life of using them in his work. Mariel Hemmingway is also featured in the film, her second Allen movie, *Manhattan* being the first. Jennifer Garner makes her film debut.

During the film, Harry sometimes sees himself as Satan, often calling himself "Old Harry." The plot relates that Harry's sister-in-law is concerned that she and her husband are the thinly veiled characters in Harry's latest book.

What Dreams May Come is a 1998 film directed by Vincent Ward and produced by Stephen Deutsch. The movie stars Robin Williams in hell. Williams's character dies and is sent to Heaven, leaving behind his wife, played by Annabelle Sciorra. When he finds out later that she is in hell for committing suicide, he sets out to free her from the harsh punishment.

Director Ward's vision of hell is nothing short of surreal, with its share of creepiness and bleak surroundings. Roger Ebert began a review of *What Dreams May Come* with these words, "Vincent Ward's *What Dreams May Come* is so breathtaking, so beautiful, so bold in its imagination that it is a surprise at the end to find out it does not finally deliver."

This brings us to the fourth section, where we will identify and then discuss another thirteen films that appropriate the motifs of hell in the directors' artistic proclivities. All of these movies are products of the twenty-first century, beginning with the 2000 film *The Cell*.

Hell in Twenty-First Century Film

In this section, we will look at thirteen movies that incorporate the themes of hell. The first of these in the 2000 feature called *The Cell*, directed by Indian filmmaker Tarsem Singh. Singh's vision unfolds by looking into the mind of a serial killer named Carl Rudolph Stargher, played by Vincent D'Onofrio. The goal is to find the human character of hell. Singh manages to create a hell that is regal, demented, cold, lonely, and quite beautiful.

Another 2000 movie that leans on the hell motifs is *Little Nicky*, directed by Steven Brill and starring Harvey Keitel, who plays the role of Satan. Adam Sandler plays the role of the protagonist Nicky. He is a spawn of Satan, but his two brothers, Cassius and Adrian, who are played by Tommy "Tiny" Lister and Rhys Ifans, are reasonably presented characters.

Their brother Nicky, on the other hand, looks like what one critic wrote, "Looks like the star of a low-rent road company version of 'Richard III.'" *Little Nicky* also features a long list of cameo appearances, including Rodney Dangerfield, Ozzy Osbourne, Quentin Tarantino, and Reese Witherspoon, who plays an angel of confusing genetics who talks like a Valley Girl and tells us that she "knows God personally." In fact, she tells us, "He's so smart!" She adds, "like Jeopardy smart."

Crazy as Hell is a 2002 movie directed by Eriq La Salle and stars Ty Adams as a gifted psychiatrist who likes to play God. But when a new patient shakes his theological view of the world, he is subjected to hellish consequences. *Crazy as Hell* is, at the same time, a film that is ambitious and arrogant.

Freddy Versus Jason is a 2003 Ronny Yu movie featuring the character of Freddy Krueger who is rendered powerless when Springwood forgets him. Eventually, however, Freddy resurrects from his residence in Hell. Another 2003 movie that employs the themes of hell is *In Hell*, directed by Ringo Lam and stars Jean-Claude Van Damme. It is an action-packed thriller with all of Mr. Van Damme's usual bravado.

The 2005 Francis Lawrence film *Constantine* is a graphic version of the traditional Christian view of hell, except they look like the world we live in but twisted. In hell, a constant blast wave from a nuclear explosion hits the fronts of the principal characters. Similarly, the 2006 Christophe Gans movie *Silent Hell* shows a modern hell that is decayed rusted, and populated by strange and horrific characters, indeed.

Another filmic version of Dante's "Inferno," called *Dante's Inferno*, was directed by Sean Meredith in 2007. The movie traces the circles of hell. Many of them look like seamy neighborhoods in New York City. In this version, Dante is remorseful when he wakes up in a modern alley, only to find Virgil ready to take the Italian to hell.

Drag Me to Hell is a 2009 movie directed and co-written by Sam Raimi with Ivan Raimi. It is the tale of a woman cursed by a gypsy who eventually sends the woman to hell. The movie stars Alison Lohman and Justin Long. It is a sometimes funny and often startling horror film. *Drag Me to Hell* is sometimes called a "dark comedy."

Two other hell films from around the same time are also referred to as comedies. These are *I Hope They Serve Beer in Hell*, a 2009 film and Matthew Spradlin's 2012 movie *Bad Kids Go to Hell*. The former also has been called a "dark, comedy thriller," and was co-written by Barry Wernick. *I Hope They Serve Beer* is loosely based on the life of writer Tucker Max who also co-wrote the screenplay.

Camp Hope is a 2010 film directed by George Van Buskirk. At the end of every summer, the children of a Christian community in suburban New Jersey attend Camp Hope. The campers travel deep into the woods. Here the children are taught the ways of the Lord, the perils of the flesh, and the horrors of the devil. A charismatic priest leads the group. But he unknowingly brings something with him that will cause illicit horror among the children.

Another filmic version of Dante's "Inferno" was made by director Ron Howard in 2016. It is based on a novel by Dan Brown. Howard shows the themes of hell in modern popular culture terms.

The Void is a 2016 movie directed by Jeremy Gillespie and Steven Kostanski. *Inferno* stars Ellen Wong, Kathleen Munroe, and Kenneth Welsh. This film has a smart use of practical effects, as well as a hellish, cult-like plot.

This brings us to the final section of Appendix D, in which we will discuss how hell has appeared on television and the radio. There is a surprising number of examples of the latter, as opposed to the former.

Hell on Television and the Radio

Earlier in this study, we mentioned and discussed the 1960 episode of *The Twilight Zone* entitled "A Nice Place to Visit." We also discussed the television movie called *Devil Dog: The Hound of Hell*, starring Kim Richards. They have also appeared on television, where hell has been a major theme. The HellTV.Store, for example, is an ACS2 case unboxing site that allows players to offer cases, with the object of the game to win "skins."

Hell on Wheels was an American television series from November 2011 until July 2016. The plot revolved around the building of the first transcontinental railroad in the United States. It was broadcast in the U.S. and Canada on the AMC television channel. The series starred Anson Mount and Colm Meany Common, as well as Dominique McElligott. The story chronicles the Union Pacific Railroad across America. The title comes from the name of the encampment that accompanied the laborers, prostitutes, surveyors, etc., that was called Hell on Wheels.

Hazbin Hotel is an American adult animated musical comedy TV series created by Vivienne Medrano. The series revolves around Charlie Morningstar, who is the Princess of Hell. She is on a quest to find a way where demons can be rehabilitated and thus allowed into Heaven. She opens a rehabilitated hotel that she calls "Hazbin Hotel." The first episode appeared on YouTube on October 28, 2019. The success of the series allowed Medrano to bring out a spin-off called *Helluva Boss* on October 31, 2020.

Mercury Theatre on the Air shows that the motifs of hell on the radio go back at least as far as 1938 and Orson Welles' drama *Hell on Ice*. Some have called Welles's radio effort the "Devil's Symphony."

Finally, *Welcome to Hard Rock Hell Radio*, also known as *Hell Talk Radio*, attempts to marry hard rock music and the motifs of hell on the radio. This effort is a satirical talk show featuring interviews with improvisation artists, stand-up comedians, and many comedy writers.

This brings us to the major conclusions we have made in Appendix D, followed by Appendix E: Hell in Popular Culture.

Conclusions

Like Appendices B and C on art and music, Appendix D on the motifs of hell in the genres of film and television has been divided into four sections. But the organization of Appendix D on film, TV, and radio was entirely chronological, beginning in Section I with films from 1911 until 1934. We began Appendix D by pointing out that the subject matter of these films are most often based on literary classics such as:

1. The Greek Myth of Orpheus and Eurydice
2. The Greek Myth of Cerberus
3. *The Canterbury Tales*
4. Dante's "Inferno"
5. Goethe's *Faust*
6. Christopher Marlowe's Doctor Faustus
7. Charles Dickens's *A Christmas Carol*
8. And many other literary classics.

Next, in Appendix D, we identified and discussed at some length five separate films from 1911 to 1929. These five early films were Italian, Swedish, French, and one Walt Disney animated work called *Hell's Bells* from 1929.

In section two, we identified and discussed films from 1935 until 1975, beginning with the 1935 Spencer Tracy movie *Dante's Inferno*. We went on to point out that in this period, the Three Stooges, Walt Disney, and two films on hell and Adolf Hitler were also featured in this section.

The next several films we discussed were Hollywood productions like *Heaven Can Wait* (1943), *Angel on My Shoulder* (1946), *Damn Yankees* (1958), *The Devil's Messenger* (1962), and the only Japanese film on our list, *The Sinners of Hell* from 1960.

In our next task of Appendix D, we identified and then discussed one of the only television episodes on the theme of hell. It was a 1960 episode of *The Twilight Zone* called "A Nice Place to Visit." In this version of hell, the occupant receives all that he or she wishes until becoming bored.

In the third section of Appendix D, we identified films from 1980 until 1999 that employed our theme of hell. We identified and discussed ten movies directed by Steven Hilliard, Paul Anderson, Woody Allen, Vincent Ward, and many other directors.

In the fourth section, we examined another ten films where our themes have played central roles. This section was devoted to movies and television shows from the twenty-first century. The films were directed by Tarsem Singh, Eriq La Salle, Ringo Lam, Sean Meredith, Ron Howard, and many others.

Some of the stars in these twenty-first-century movies were Harvey Keitel, Tom Cruise, Ellen Wong, Kathleen Munroe, Kenneth Welsh, Robin Williams, Woody Allen, Mariel Hemmingway, Sam Neil, and Jean-Claude Van Damme, among many others.

We indicated two creations considered to be comedies. The first of these was Matthew Spradlin's *I Hope They Serve Beer in Hell*, loosely based on the life of writer Tucker Max, and the 2010 movie *Camp Hope*, which has comedy and elements of science fiction in its plot.

Finally, in the fifth and final section of this appendix, we discussed many of the uses of the motifs of hell and suffering in American television and radio. As we have seen, many of these efforts were by well-known people like Rod Sterling and Orson Welles, and others were produced by more obscure artists and writers.

This brings us to Appendix E, in which we will explore our themes in many of the aspects and venues of contemporary popular culture in the English-speaking world, in America and abroad.

Mosaic of the archangel Uriel, 1888. James Powell and Sons of the Whitefriars Foundry, St John's Church, Boreham Road, Warminster, Wiltshire, England.

Appendix E
Hell in Popular Culture

Despair is the damp of hell, as serenity is the joy of heaven.
—John Donne

Introduction

The main purpose of this appendix is to explore the theme of hell as employed in popular culture in the contemporary English-speaking world. The motif of hell may be seen in many aspects of pop culture, including an amusement park ride at Universal Studios in Hollywood, California.

Other aspects of popular culture where these may be seen at work include television, books, radio, comics and cartoons, and the world of games and gaming. In fact, this appendix will be divided into five sections, one each of the phenomena just mentioned, beginning with television.

As we shall see, we will reiterate much of what we have introduced in the final section of Appendix E on the radio and in the television industry. There are, for example, two other episodes of *The Twilight Zone* where the motifs of hell and punishment have come into play.

Hell on Television

Already in this work, we have mentioned a few examples of places where hell has appeared on television, such as the 1960 episode of *The Twilight Zone* entitled "A Nice Place to Visit." In the 1980s, the show had a bit of a revival that included another episode where hell came into play.

The episode in question is "Dealer's Choice," which portrays a game of poker in a suburban New Jersey home. One of the players, Nick, is new to the game. He is filling in as a substitute for his cousin, who could not make it. Nick is a bit mysterious and sly, and he keeps getting dealt sixes.

Eventually, Nick's true identity is revealed. Another player, played by Morgan Freeman asks Nick, "What is the devil doing here in New Jersey?" The fourth player at the table answered Freeman's character who is named Tony and said, "What are you talking about Tony? I think he lives here."

A third *Twilight Zone* episode called "The Hunt" is the eighty-fourth episode in the original series. It first aired on CBS on January 26, 1962. In the plot, Hyder Smith is an elderly mountain man who lives with his wife, Rachel, and their hound dog, Rip, in the back woods. Walking along a country road, Hyder and Rip come to an unfamiliar fence with a gate tended by a man who explains to Hyder that he may enter the Elysian Fields, while telling him that Rip could not.

Later, traveling along the same road, Hyder and Rip meet a young man who introduces himself as an angel. The angel says his mission is to bring the man and his dog to Heaven. When Hyder tells the angel about the earlier gate, the angel tells him that it was actually the entrance to hell. He explains that the fate keeper would not let Rip enter because the dog would have smelled the brimstone.

The characteristic ending narration of the episode delivered by Rod Sterling says this:

> **Travelers to unknown regions would be well advised to take along the family dog. It could just save you from entering the wrong gate. At least it happened that way once—in a mountainous area of the Twilight Zone.**

In season three (2018) of the Netflix show *The Chilling Adventures of Sabrina*, the heroine spends a good amount of time in hell. In the first appearance, the realm is portrayed as a demented version of *The Wizard of Oz*, a world where people who stray from the proper path come into contact with the axe-wielding Tin Man, along with deceased relatives, and Edward Scissorhands, who is a schoolteacher.

There are forests and lakes in Sabrina's hell but with a grim twist. Most of the season's material on hell revolves around Sabrina's battle for supremacy against an ambitious prince who wants the throne of Sabrina's realm. It is a fascinating set of plots in season three, with a considerable amount of demonic in-fighting.

In the 1997 television series *Futurama*, the main characters occasionally visit a place called "Robot Hell." The Robot Satan, as well as other evil robots, live in Robot Hell, which has a worldly entrance in New Jersey.

Two adult television-animated dark comedies are also set in hell. The first is called *Hazbin Hotel* from 2019, which is only nominally ruled by Lucifer. However, the residents there appear to live in a state of anarchy because the residents allow powerful demons and gangs to exert their influence. A spin-off series called "Helluva Boss" is also set in hell. The sequel follows the employees of the I.M.P.—the Immediate Murder Professionals—an imp-run assassination/hitman company.

The central characters travel to hell several times in the television show Dragon Ball Z. When first translated to English, hell was changed to "HFIL" to avoid offending American watchers. In fact, most of the episodes that take place in hell were not aired in the United States.

The *Disenchantment* television series created by Matt Groening had twenty episodes that were later shown on Netflix. One episode from 2019 was entitled "Stairway to Hell." In it, the lead character, Bean, wants to retrieve his friend Elfo's soul from the underworld.

The Simpsons has had references to, and action in, hell occasionally. Perhaps the best-known of these is "Homer vs. Lisa and the Eighth Commandment" from 1991. In the episode, Lisa imagines her father going to hell because of his illegal cable hookup. In the episode called, "The Treehouse of Horror IV," the devil looks exactly like Ned Flanders, who sends Homer to hell for a day, while it is determined who has the ownership of this soul.

In the 1993 episode called "Treehouse of Horror XI," Homer's soul fails to perform a good deed to gain entrance to Heaven, so he is sent to hell, where Satan promises him an eternity of torture.

In the television series *Reaper* (2007–2009), Sam, the main character, works as a bounty hunter for the devil. Entrances to hell are places considered to be hell on Earth, like the Department of Motor Vehicles. In the American supernatural TV series *Ghost Whisperer* (2010), hell is the destination for souls that fail to "cross over into the Light," so instead they "go to the Dark Side."

In many episodes of *South Park* (July 2000), the realm of hell appears, including the famous "Do the Handicapped Go to Hell?" And another episode entitled "Probably." In the former, the boys begin to attend Sunday School and learn that it is important to confess their sins. But they find the lessons on that and eating Christ's body and blood confusing. They are also horrified to discover that Timmy cannot go to Heaven because he cannot confess his sins and that Kyle cannot go there because he is Jewish.

Meanwhile, back in hell, Satan is horrified when his ex-lover Saddam Hussein returns to disrupt his relationship with his new flame, Chris. The three have an uncomfortable dinner together, after which Saddam gives Satan his hotel room key. Later, Satan stands before Saddam's hotel room, wondering if he should use the key or not.

But back on Earth, the boys rush to Sunday School to confess their sins. Kenny is run over by a bus as they cross the street, dying with his sins still on his soul. Terrified, the others hurry to the confessional only to find the priest, Father Maxi, having sex with a woman parishioner. The boys are disillusioned, but they decide from now on, "They will take on their own salvation in their own hands."

Hell on the Radio

In this section, we will examine nine separate pieces on the radio in the twentieth century that make some interesting conclusions about the nature and the purposes of hell.

Some have interpreted the 1938 radio drama "The War of the Worlds" by Orson Welles on the Mercury Theatre on the Air as a demonic plot to convince the American listening public that they were hearing a description of the contents and actions in hell after life on Earth.

In the 1940s, during World War II, radio correspondent Edward R. Murrow did a series of broadcasts he called *Orchestrated Hell*. One of the finest of the series was from December 3, 1943, an account of air raids over Berlin. Murrow's style and descriptions were clear and forceful, and they continued into late 1943. They are now available at the U.S. Library of Congress.

In 2008, BBC Radio 4 had a series of spoofs loosely based on Dante's "Inferno." The series had four episodes all together. In the second of these, hell is spoken of as "An Underworld where all souls are assigned to their respective Heaven or Hell."

In 1995, The BBC also had another radio series called "Old Harry's Game," which was written by Andy Hamilton, who also stars as the voice of Satan in the series, which is set in hell. Hell is described by Satan as, "The worst thing that possibly could ever happen to your theme park." But because of the cover, and ever-increasing population of hell, Satan desires to expand, but God refuses. In fact, he decides to make it a "half a size smaller."

Several radio Mystery Theatre episodes from the 1970s in the United States featured themes of hell and punishment. Among these are ten from January 7 to 15, 1974, including "The Bullet," "Lost Dog," "Honeymoon with Death," and "I Warned You Three Times."

Beginning late in the 1990s, radio dramas from hell made a revival. An American Radio program broadcast weekday mornings from Salt Lake City, Utah, entitled "Radio From Hell," on KXRK, 96.3 FM. *Rolling Stone* cited KXRK as one of the "top five rock and roll stations in the United States," and that "Radio From Hell" is one of the longest-running local radio programs in America.

Another program that aired on Saturdays for four hours, beginning in 1998, was called "This is Hell." The show is hosted by Chuck Mertz on WNUR-FM, from Evanston, Illinois.

Contemporary artist Lizzo has taken part in several radio broadcasts that she collectively calls "Good as Hell" since March 8, 2016. In one episode, she tones:

> I do my hair toss, check
> My nails
> Baby, how you feelin?
> Feelin good as Hell.

The Incomparable Radio Theatre is a series of original radio shows that pay homage to classical mid-twentieth-century radio while also giving a nod to modern pop culture. One show that aired on January 10, 2018, is called "A Mysterious Place Filled with Wonders." It is a techno-thriller about what has happened to an international team of undersea adventure, and the rescue team goes missing themselves, asking demonic and hellish questions about where they went.

Finally, in 1998, WBJC Radio broadcasted Stephen Vicchio's *Ivan and Adolf: The Last Man in Hell*. Mark Steiner played the voice of God, Vicchio of Fyodor Karamazov, and Christopher Dreisbach the part of Adolf Hitler. It is a stage play adapted by Vicchio and Steiner for the radio.

This brings us to books in contemporary popular culture in which the motifs of hell and punishment may be detected in twenty-first-century literature, the topic of section three of Appendix E on the theme of hell in popular culture.

Hell in Literature

In this third section of Appendix E, we will identify and then discuss ten separate novels that employ the motif of hell in their books, from lesser-known works to some better-known books by writers like Edward Lee, Flannery O'Connor, and Pulitzer-Prize winner Robert Olen Butler.

As we have indicated earlier in this work, and even in these first five appendices, certain works of Western literature have long stood as models for writing about the motifs of hell and punishment in literature and drama. Thus, Homer, Dante's "Inferno," Goethe's *Faust*, Christopher Marlowe's *Doctor Faustus*, and a host of other pieces of literature have served as a basis for writing about the afterlife.

In the popular culture literature of contemporary culture, certain writers reference the underworld or the abode of the dead. American author Stephen King, for example, uses the themes of death, hell, and punishment in his *Dark Tower* series of books.

Many of these cultural references to hell connect with the pop group *Nine Inch Nails*. For example, in Book 12 of *Animorphs*, Cassie tells Rachel that she told her mom that NIN means "Nice is Neat." In Marishka Pessl's novel *Special Topics in Calamity Physics*, one of the principal characters, a man named Milton, no less, wears a Nine Inch Nails T-shirt.

Jhonen Vasquez's graphic novel *Johnny, the Homicidal Maniac,* makes nine references to NIN. In Piers Anthony's series *Incarnations of Immortality*, Heaven, Hell, and purgatory are locations populated by the main characters and the souls of the dead. Wayne Barlowe's novel, *God's Demon,* is set in hell and follows a powerful demon named Sargatanas. Edward Lee's novel *City Infernal* and its sequel *Infernal Angel* and a second entitled *House Infernal*, hell is shown as a modern metropolis. In fact, it is called Mephistopholis.

The novel *Eric*, written by Terry Pratchett, is his version of the Faust narrative. Rincewind and Eric travel to hell, where they discover it has become steeped in bureaucracy, so much so that the Satan figure, named Demon King Astfgl, has now concluded that boredom is the greatest punishment.

The motifs of hell and punishment frequently appear in the fiction of Flannery O'Connor. In her story, *Revelation*, for example, while waiting in the doctor's office, the self-righteous Ruby Turpin tells a young girl by the name of Mary Grace to "Go back to hell where you came from, you old wart hog."

Pulitzer Prize winner Robert Olen Butler's new novel *Hell* is a clever and well-written novel of good, evil, and free will. The book is set in a hell populated by figures from history and contemporary times like William Randolph Hearst, Ann Boleyn, Humphrey Bogart, and George E. Bush, among many others. One critic says of Butler's hell, "It is crammed with random celebrities. It is plagued by modern problems like four-hour erections and crashing hard drives."

Novelist Jared Joseph has written a novel entitled *A Book About Myself Called Hell*. It is another modern retelling of Dante's "Inferno" from the vantage points of the Covid-19 pandemic, the crises of global capital and global warming, and modernity, in general. The book is a kind of tragic-comic collage of the combined fictive and historical through the lens of hell in the High Middle Ages in Dante's time.

This brings us to section four of Appendix E on hell in popular culture, in which we will examine many examples in comics and cartoons where hell can be found.

Hell in Comics and Cartoons

Earlier in this study, we suggested that the first full-length depiction of hell in the world of cartoons came from a segment of the Walt Disney movie *Fantasia* in 1929. Since that time, the underworld has been shown in a variety of other cartoons and comics, as we shall see in this section of Appendix E.

Adolf Wolf is blasted to hell at the conclusion of the 1942 MGM's *Blitz Wolf*. The American cartoon is a parody of the Three Little Pigs told from the perspective of the World War II. It was directed by Tex Avery—it was his first cartoon for MGM. *Blitz Wolf* was produced by Fred Quimby. It was nominated for an Academy Award for Best Short Subject, but it lost to another anti-Nazi World War II parody that starred Donald Duck.

In a 1949 *Tom and Jerry* cartoon, after being crushed by a piano and then denied entrance to Heaven, Tom is instead transported to hell for eternal punishment. The only proviso is that if he could get Jerry's signed confession for sins he has committed.

Warner Brothers, who own both Looney Tunes and Merrie Melodies cartoons, has appearances of hell in the 1954 "Satan's Waitin" starring Sylvester the Cat and Tweety. The "Devil's Feud Cake" is a 1964 cartoon that stars Yosemite Sam and Bugs Bunny. Yosemite Sam robs the Last National Bank and makes his getaway in an airplane piloted by Bugs Bunny. Sam falls from the plane and dies. He ends up in hell, where he makes a deal with the devil. If Sam can bring Bugs to hell, he will be set free. After three failed attempts to coax Bugs to hell, Sam tells the devil that if he really wants Bugs, he can do it himself, and he announces that he is content to stay in hell. This comes in a sequence of the cartoon where Sam wears a devil suit while wielding a pitchfork.

Over the years, cartoonist Jeff Larson has produced at least forty pieces set in hell. Some of the most prominent are ones with Satan, "who is always dressed to kill," in a carton named "Anarchy is My Business and Business is Good," and another with the devil entitled "Hot Enough for Ya?" In this comic, two figures stand beneath a hot sun. The man is perspiring profusely and has a towel on his forehead.

He is next to a trident-carrying demon with great horns, wings, and a long tail. Presumably, the figure on the left has just asked the demon, "Is it hot enough for you?" because the devil answers, "Just a few degrees more, and it will, in fact, be hot enough for me. Thanks for asking."

Cartoon artist Lev Grossman created a book series called *The Underworld*. One book in the series is called "The Magician King." The protagonist Quentin must go to hell to retrieve something from a fallen comrade. What he is faced with when he gets there is a terrifying version of hell that is simply "Very Grossman."

DC Comics has had several demonic characters who sometimes live in hell. In a comic by Jack Kirby from 1972 there is one demon named Etrigan, who is bound to a human named Jason Blood, who frequently speaks in rhymed poetry. Another DC Comics character is named Blue Devil, who originally was simply a stuntman named Daniel Patrick Cassidy, who wore an exoskeleton mask. Later, however, in another cartoon, Blue Devil dies and comes back to Earth as a real demon. He is unable to set foot on "consecrated ground" unless he is in the act of self-immolation.

Another demonic character in the DC Comics vault is Hellboy. Although his origins are murky, he is brought to Earth by Nazi scientists who are engaged in the occult. Although Hellboy looks like a devil, he is actually on the side of the United States in the Cold War. Mike Mignola created the figure of Hellboy, which Dark Horse Comics now publishes.

A fourth DC Comics demonic figure is named Ghost Rider, who has a dark leather costume with chains, a fiery motorcycle, and a flaming skull for a head. His soul has also been traded to the devil. Two other demonic characters are also featured in DC Comics. Their names are Hellstrom and Hot Stuff. The former is Damien Hellstrom, who was born in the fictional town of Greentown, Massachusetts, but his father was Satan himself. Despite his demonic pedigree and look, he chooses to use his powers for good. He even becomes a member of the superhero team, the Defenders.

Hotstuff is a little devil with white horns and large eyes. He carries a pitchfork. He stars in comic books from Harvey Comics, who are famous for their depictions of witches, ghosts, devils, and obscenely rich kids. Hotstuff is not really a superhero, but he performs good deeds that irritate his demonic brethren.

Cartoon artist Peter Kuper produced several cartoons over the years that are set in hell. In one, a demon sits in hell with a notepad and pencil in hand. He is red with white horns. The caption reads, "Be in the moment. It helps all of eternity to seem less overwhelming." In the other Kuper creation, the souls of the damned can be seen in hell guarded by demons with pitchforks. One damned soul says to another, "Dammit, I just realized now I am going to miss the appointment for my second shot." Needless to say, this cartoon from March of 2021, was created during the Covid-19 pandemic.

In 2019, Peter Kuper also published a graphic adaptation of Joseph Conrad's 1902 novel *Heart of Darkness*. The novel was based on Conrad's experiences in the Congo when a small boy of eleven.

Marvel Comics and artists Stan Lee and John Buscema have created an image of the devil that often can be seen in their comics. His costume is dark with a dark mantle over his left arm and black horns on his head. In one creation, the devil character says:

While man remains an educated savage,
my ranks of the damned are swollen to overflowing

And:

Thus I have ordained that nothing shall
change the unthinking masses of humanity.

Stan Lee, the world-famous architect of the Marvel Universe, also teamed up with *New York Times* writer Jay Bonansinga to collaborate on a new superhero series. The collection is called *The Devil's Quintet*. It is a thrilling, action-packed adventure series of novels featuring an all-new universe and cast of characters from the legendary co-creator of Spider Man, the Avengers, X-Men, and many other iconic heroes.

The "Quintet" are five extraordinary individuals who have been granted super-human power by the devil himself, but they are determined to use their hell-born gifts for the good of humanity, whether the devil approves or not.

This brings us to the final section of Appendix E on the motifs of hell on the uses of these themes in the world of games and gaming. As we shall see next, there is a plethora of images in that commercial realm.

Hell in the World of Games and Gaming

In the world of games and gaming, the theme of hell can often be seen in both role-playing games and video games. In the former, for example, in the game called *Dungeons and Dragons*, there are seven hellish levels or "Planets." The one most often referred to is the Outer Plane Baator, which contains nine different levels. In the same game, there is also a series of underground networks of caves filled with howling winds. These are referred to as Pandemonium.

In the role-playing game *Nomine*, hell is the location and home of all demons. Hell is again subdivided into what are called Principalities, each ruled by one or more demons or Princes. All of these principalities are named after a traditional name of the underworld, like Hades, Sheol, Tartarus, etc. An additional lower hell is where Lucifer is said to reside.

The theme of hell also appears in many video games. We will point to five of these to give a flavor of how ubiquitous these motifs are in the realm of video games. In the first of these, *Diablo*, hell is shown as a deep pit underground and largely characterized as a traditional place of suffering. The bodies of many tortured people reside there. The manual that comes with the game tells us that this place is "actually part of the mortal realm, where the boundaries with the metaphysical realm have been weakened."

A video game named *Fear Effect* has many affinities to the Chinese understanding of hell. This game has many levels of hell related to the Ten Kings of Hell, or *Diyu* in classical Chinese, which we have explored earlier in this study. In a third video game known as *Hellgate London*, demonic armies have emerged from hell to reduce the city of London to ruin. Their mission is to slowly convert the human inhabitants to a process known as Hellforming. The protagonist must defeat the Demonic Army to keep the conversions from taking place.

A fourth video game with hell elements is called *Minecraft*. The players attempt to create a portal to the Nether World, which is inspired by the fire and brimstone versions of suffering in the underworld.

Finally, in the video game *The Heroes of Might and Magic*, there is a place known as Sheogh. It is the home of what is called the Inferno Faction, a dark faction of demonic creatures who reside there.

This brings us to the conclusions of Appendix E on the themes of Hell in Popular Culture.

Conclusions

This appendix has been organized into five parts or sections. In the first of these, we continued our conversation about hell and television by pointing out that another episode from the show *The Twilight Zone* that was entitled "Dealer's Choice" was also set in hell in a revival of *The Twilight Zone* in the 1980s. In fact, the show stars Morgan Freeman, as we have shown.

We also identified a third episode of *The Twilight Zone* called "The Hunt" about a man and his dog who meet two strangers on a country road. The remainder of the first section of Appendix E was spent discussing several other mostly American television shows where the themes of hell appear.

Among these shows were the *Chilling Adventures of Sabrina*, a few episodes of *The Simpsons*, some episodes of the television series *Reaper*, as well as a continual appearance of the themes of hell in *South Park*, particularly the episode, "Do Handicapped People Go to Hell?"

In the second section, we turned our attention to mostly classical radio programs that have employed the themes of hell. In that Section, we spoke of two programs on *BBC Radio* during World War II, as well as radio broadcasts from Edward R. Murrow that he collectively called *Orchestrated Hell*.

We have also identified and discussed a series of radio broadcasts by the organization *Incomparable Radio*, including an episode entitled "A Mysterious Place Filled with Wonders." We have also spoken of Stephen Vicchio's drama *Ivan and Adolf: The Last Man in Hell*, which was originally written for the stage but turned into a radio drama by Vicchio and radio host Marc Steiner in Baltimore.

In the third section of Appendix E on the themes of hell in popular literature in the late twentieth and twenty-first centuries, we have identified literary works by ten popular writers, including Flannery O'Connor, Edward Lee, and Pulitzer Prize winner Robert Olin Butler.

Next, in the fourth section, we dedicated the entire section to cartoons and comics that utilized our themes. We identified cartoons or comics about hell created by the Walt Disney Studios, Warner Brothers, Jeff Larson, DC Comics, Peter Kuper, and Lev Grossman, among many other studios and individual artists.

Finally, in the fifth and final section of Appendix E on the motifs of hell in popular culture, we have identified and discussed several examples of the employment of our themes in the world of games and gaming. Indeed, in that section, we supplied examples and discussions of role-playing games, as well as video games. And not surprisingly, many of the examples we have chosen employed many of the techniques and the content of much of what we have seen throughout this study on hell.

Andrea Mantegna, *Christ's Descent into Limbo*, 1470–1475.
Tempera and gold on panel, 15.2 x 16.6 in.
Location unknown. Barbara Piasecka Johnson Collection.

Appendix F
Levels of Hell

An intelligent hell would be better than a stupid paradise.
—Victor Hugo

Introduction

Throughout this work on the history of the idea of hell, we have shown that from the time of the ancient Chinese and their idea of *Diyu*, many cultures in human history have chosen to divide hell into compartments or levels, often according to the sins that have been committed.

The purpose of this appendix is to explore the idea in history that hell has several levels or compartments in which humans may be punished and rehabilitated. This appendix will unfold in the following parts. First, we will examine the idea that hell has levels or compartments in the ancient world. More specifically, we will speak of ancient Egypt, Babylonia, and Persia in the ancient world.

Second, we will discuss the idea in the Islamic tradition that hell, or *Jahannam*, in classical Arabic, has seven different chambers of levels of hell that descend in order of the severity of the punishment or rehabilitation.

Next, we will explore the idea of levels of hell among the ancient Jews, particularly in the Hebrew Bible and apocalyptic works, like the Book of Enoch. Finally, we will explore the notion that hell has levels or compartments in subsequent examples in the Judeo-Christian tradition that includes the views of certain early church fathers as well as Dante's "Inferno," which includes nine separate levels or compartments of the idea of hell, all the way up to three thinkers in the twentieth century.

Finally, we will make some observations about the idea of hell having levels from the time of Dante to the twentieth century in the world of Western literature, including John Milton, Arthur Rimbaud's poetry and many other examples from the West.

Levels of Hell in the Ancient World

Among the ancient Egyptians, there was the belief that a god named Kherty who served as a ferryman across the River Styx. Kherty is attested in the early second dynasty. Kherty is important for our purposes because he takes the souls of the dead through what was called *Duat*, a land full of gods, demons, and monsters, many of which were out to kill the souls who came across the ferry with Kherty.[286]

These metaphysical creatures would prey upon the souls of the dead who had to fight them off with spells and weapons, so the ancient Egyptians were often buried with spells and amulets to help them to stay in the netherworlds.

For the souls to make their way through *Duat*, they had to pass through twelve separate gates lined with sharp spears and guarded by snakes who breathed venom and fire. The only way to pass through was to say the names of the guardians at each gate. Many of the Egyptian kings were buried with these names so they did not forget. Some kings were even buried with a map of hell, complete with the twelve realms of hell.

A second culture that held to the idea of hell having levels or compartments was the ancient Babylonians-Assyrians. Scholar Alfred Jeremias (1864–1935) completed a work in 1902 entitled *Assyro-Babylonian Religion: Future Life, Babylonia.* Professor Jeremias, on the evidence of texts that explore the realms of *Kur,* a dark and dreary cavern located deep beneath the Earth.

Another item that Dr. Jeremias established was that the entrance to hell was believed to be in the Zagros mountains in the Far East, and more importantly, the realm of Kur had seven different gates or levels through which a soul needed to pass. The god Neti was the gatekeeper. Erishkegal was his messenger and was related to the god Namtar.

Professor Jeremias also maintained that the seven gates corresponded to seven levels of punishment or rehabilitation, from least severe to apostasy, where the most severe were sent in ancient Babylonia.

A third ancient culture that has suggested several possible fates or levels of punishment in the afterlife is the ancient Persian religion Zoroastrianism. The principal text on the issue is the sacred *Gathas. The Gathas* are seventeen hymns traditionally believed to have been written by the prophet Zarathustra, also called Zoroaster.[287]

Some of the Gathas are directly addressed to Ahura Mazda, the good god in the ancient Persian scheme. In one of the earliest of the Gathas, the text maintains that upon death the human soul must go through a series of tests or stages by which it is determined how pure the soul is for salvation.[288]

The name for the Zoroastrian hell is *Duzakh*, in which happens the most minor and severe punishments for sins. According to the *Book of Arda Viraf*, Duzakh is a place of constant stench. Like in Egypt and Babylon, souls if Duzakh are organized into seven compartments or levels, according to the sins they committed on Earth.[289]

The most serious of these sins, and thus those in the lowest levels of the Zoroastrian hell, are adultery, slander, and murder, as well as abuse of spouse or children, neglecting animals, and just plain being lazy. When a person dies, his or her soul is judged by Ahura Mazda and sent to one of the seven compartments of hell, which are in descending severity.[290]

This brings us to the second section on the levels of hell in human history in which we will remind ourselves of what we have learned in an earlier chapter of this work on "hell" or *Jahannam* in the Islamic faith.

Hell and Jahannam in Islam

There are many traditions on the locations of Heaven and Hell in the Islamic faith, but not all of them appear to be compatible with each other. For example, some Muslim scholars describe hell as "the lowest regions of the Earth," while one Iranian scholar al-Majlisi (1037–1110), describes hell as "surrounding the Earth."

The best scholarship on hell in Islam in English is that of Einar Thomassen and his article "Islamic Hell," published in the journal *Numen*. [291] Dr. Thomassen suggests that the seven levels of *Jahannam* mentioned in Al-Qur'an are the same levels of hell mentioned in traditional hadith literature, both Sunni and Shiite.[292]

Those seven levels, as we have shown earlier in this study of the history of hell, are:

1. Jahannam. Reserved for Muslims who have committed grave sins.
2. Al-Laza. "The blaze."
3. Al-Hutama. "The consuming fire."
4. Al-Sa'ir. "Intense heat and flames."
5. Al-Saqar. "The scorching fire."
6. Al-Jahim. "The hot place."
7. Al-Hawaya. "The abyss for hypocrites."[293]

Various similar models have developed among scholars of Islam, such as Christian Lange and A. F. Klein, except in their view, *Al-Laza* and *Al-Saqqar* are switched. Another scheme of the layers of hell was suggested by eleventh-century scholar al-Thalabi, noted Sunni scholar of *Tafsir*.[294] Thomas Patrick Hughes describes Thalabi's seven levels of hell this way:

1. Adim, surface level (Humans and Jinn.)
2. Basit, plain level (The prison of winds.)
3. Thaqil, region of distress (The antechamber of hell, like Christian purgatory.)
4. Batih, place of swamps (The dwellers have no eyes and have wings in place of feet.)
5. Hayn, region of adversity (Serpents devour infidels.]
6. Sijjin, store or dungeon (Souls tormented by Scorpions.)
7. Al-Saqar, place of burning (A damp and great cold.)[295]

In addition to having these levels, al-Thalabi also had much to say about Judgment Day, or *Yawm al-Qiyamah*, in classical Arabic. Thalabi says that hell is a large pit over the Bridge of *As-Sarat*, over which all sinners must cross and from there each falls into one of the seven different compartments or levels of *Jahannam*.[296] Additionally, al-Thalabi suggests that along with the pit and the levels of hell, Jahannam also features mountains, rivers, valleys, and even oceans filled with "fire, blood, and pus."[297]

Two other important features of the idea of hell in Islam are, first, that one's stay in *Jahannam* is not eternal. Rather, it only lasts long enough for one's sins to be forgiven or justified by Allah. And secondly, since Allah is All Good, it is possible that any Muslim *nafs*, or "soul" can still attain expiation in the eyes of the Divine.

This brings us to the levels of hell or *Sheol*, among the ancient Jews, both in the Hebrew Bible, as well as in Apocalyptic literature such as the Book of Enoch, the subject matter of section three of this appendix.

Levels of Hell among the Ancient Jews

The writers of the Hebrew Bible mention *Sheol*, or the ancient Hebrew underworld, sixty-six times. As we have shown earlier in this study, most of these references were about who is there, what it is like, and what happens there.

By the time we get to the apocalyptic Book of Enoch, particularly Book One, we begin to see in ancient Judaism the idea that Sheol has compartments or levels. The book is ascribed to Enoch, the father of Methuselah and the grandfather of Noah. The book of Enoch contains unique material on the origins of demons and the *Nephilim* in early Judaism. The older portions of First Enoch are called "The Book of Watchers." And is estimated to be dated between 300 and 200 BCE.[298]

The First Book of Enoch is important for our purposes because Sheol is divided into four compartments or levels where everyone who goes to Sheol will be assigned to a particular section based on moral worthiness. According to the Book of Enoch, there are four such chambers or compartments of Sheol.[299]

One chamber Enoch tells us is a bright spring of water where the righteous happily await the Day of Judgment. In a second chamber of Sheol can be found the moderately moral who look forward to their eventual reward. In a third and deeper chamber of Sheol, the victims of murders wait for justice to be done in their cases.

In the fourth and deepest chamber of Sheol can be found the most wicked of human beings This idea was a prefigure of the later Jewish idea of Gehenna, a hell where people are tormented with fire.[300]

There is the tradition that there were seven Heavens, or *Shamayim,* in Classical Hebrew, as well as a corresponding seven chambers of Sheol, in the Second Temple period around 70 CE. In the *Pirkei Avot* 4:21, Rabbi Ya'akov suggests that the dead may suffer in a kind of antechamber of Sheol, like the idea of Purgatory in Roman Catholicism.

For the most part, the Talmud does not speak about levels of Sheol. At *tractate Eiruvin*, section 19a, the text teaches us that there are three "gates to hell." One is in the wilderness, one is in the sea, and one is in Jerusalem. This text does not imply, however, that these three gates lead to three separate compartments of Sheol.

The Babylonian Talmud uses the expression *Tzoah Rotachat*, which in English means "boiling excrement." This is a place in Gehinnom, and the Talmud tells us, "It is a place where Jews who committed certain sins will be consigned." Specifically, "where Jews committed serious sins, and they are sent there for punishment." The Talmud says nothing about whether there are other sections of hell where people are assigned according to their sins.

This brings us to the idea of levels of hell in traditional Christian history, the topic of the final section of this appendix on levels of hell in world history.

Levels of Hell in Early Christianity First to the Twentieth Century

The earliest Christian text that implies levels of punishment comes in the Gospel of Luke 12:46–48 (NIV). Verse 47 speaks of "those who did not follow their master's will, shall be beaten with many stripes." The text goes on to relate in verse 48:

> **But those who did not know, yet committed things deserving of stripes shall be beaten with fewer of them.**

Another New Testament text that implies different levels of punishment is the Gospel of Matthew 25:31–32 (NIV). This text tells us:

When the son of Man comes in his glory, and all the angels with him, he will sit on his glorious throne. All the nations will be gathered before him, and he will separate the people from one another as a shepherd separates the sheep from the goats. He will put the sheep on his right and the goats on his left.

Thus, the New Testament alludes to degrees of punishment in hell. The comparison in Luke 12 is of servants not being prepared, and punishment is given according to their knowledge of what they were supposed to do.

John Chrysostom (347–407 CE) pictured hell as being associated with various degrees of unquenchable fire and "Various kinds of torments and torrents of punishment."

The classic case of a Christian thinker sketching out levels of hell, as we have shown earlier in this history of hell, is the nine circles of hell to be found in Dante's "Inferno."[301]

In an earlier chapter of this study, we have maintained that Dante envisioned nine separate "circles" or *Bolgias* of hell. *Bolgia* is the Italian word for "ditch." These circles, in order of severity, are the following:

1. Limbo. Those who never knew Christ resided there, Dante gives Ovid, Homer, Socrates, Aristotle, Julius Caesar, and many others here.
2. Lust. Here Dante finds Achilles, Paris, Tristan, Cleopatra, and Dido, among many others.
3. Gluttony. Overindulging can be found here. Dante mostly cites characters from classical literature.
4. Greed. Here, Dante and his companion, Virgil, only mention Pluto, the mythological king of the underworld.
5. Anger. Dante and Virgil are threatened by the Furies when they try to enter through the walls of Dis, or Satan.
6. Heresy. Dante and Virgil find several military leaders known for their disbelief, such as Farinata degli Uberti, an Italian general and aristocrat.

7. The Self-Murderers, Harpies, and Suicides. Here the violent are punished alongside Harpies.
8. Fraud. Here, Dante introduced the Malebolge, or "Evil pockets" in Italian. Here Dante and Vigil find those who commit fraud, panderers, seducers, and perjurers. Dante and Virgil find the biblical Cain here, as well as Ptolemy and Antenor of Troy.
9. Treachery. This is the deepest circle of hell. It is the place where Satan resides. This is primarily where traitors to family reside.[302]

After making their way through the nine circles of the Inferno, Dante and Virgil travel to the center of hell, where they meet Satan himself. He is described as a three-headed beast. Each mouth is busy eating a specific person. The mouth on the left is chomping on Brutus, the right head is consuming Cassius, who betrayed and caused the murder of Julius Ceasar. The third is in the process of eating Judas Iscariot, who did the same to Jesus Christ.[303]

For Dante, these are the ultimate sinners in that they consciously committed acts of treachery against their Lords who were appointed by God. For Dante, you can be no worse morally than these three historical figures.[304]

In the twentieth century, many writers and scholars such as C. S. Lewis, J. P. Moreland, and Pope John Paul II, who, at The Vatican on July 28, 1999, suggested when "speaking of hell as a place the Bible uses a symbolic language, which must be correctly interpreted. Rather than a place, hell indicates a place for those who freely and definitively separate themselves from God."

Both C. S. Lewis (1898–1963) and J. P Moreland (1948–) have cast hell in terms of "eternal separation from God." They also both offer certain biblical passages that imply that although punishment in hell is eternal and irrevocable, it will, nevertheless, be proportional to the deeds committed by every soul. Both Lewis and Moreland give Matthew 10:15 and Luke 12:46–18 as proof texts for their judgments.[305] The passage from the Gospel of Matthew 10:15 (NIV) tells us this:

Truly, I will tell you, it will be more bearable for Sodom and Gomorrah on the Day of Judgment than for that town.

Levels of Hell in Western Literature

Earlier in this appendix and elsewhere in this study, we have spoken of Dante's nine levels or concentric rings of hell. John Milton's *Paradise Lost* from 1667, opens with the story of the fallen angels who are confined in hell at a level just above Satan himself.[306]

Arthur Rimbaud alludes to the idea of hell, as well as its having levels or separate compartments, in his 1873 publication *Season of Hell.* Rimbaud also says a great deal about his own suffering in a plaintiff fashion.[307]

In 1944, French philosopher Jean-Paul Sartre authored a play he called *No Exit*, to make the argument that "Hell is Other People."[308] Although he was not a religious man, Sarte was fascinated with his peculiar brand of hellish suffering.

A year later, in 1945, British writer C. S. Lewis, in his work *The Great Divorce*, borrows its title from William Blake's *The Marriage of Heaven and Hell* (1793) and its inspiration from the *Divine Comedy*. The narrator of Lewis' work is likewise guided through Hell and Heaven. Hell is portrayed by Lewis as an endless, desolate, always twilight city. The night in Lewis's account is actually the abode of the Devas. Various levels or compartments of hell are variously described in his vision of the underworld.[309]

In her 2007 book entitled *Hell in Contemporary Literature,* Rachel Falconer suggests that a wide range of literary texts should be included when discussing hell in contemporary life. Among her examples, she has included writings by Primo Levi, W. G. Sebald, Anne Michaels, Alasdair Gray, and Salman Rushdie.[310]

Ms. Falconer also includes a number of contemporary films in her analysis, including Francis Coppola's *Apocalypse Now* and the *Matrix Trilogy.* She also relies heavily on the theoretical philosophical works by Mikhail Bakgtin, Emanuel Levinas, Algerian philosopher Jacques Derrida, Judith Butler, David Harvey, and Paul Ricoeur.

This brings us to the major conclusions we have made in this final appendix of the study on the history of hell. This will conclude our study of the history of hell in the history of the world from the ancient Egyptians and Chinese to the late twentieth century.

Conclusions

We divided Appendix F into four main sections. In the first of these, we have described and discussed the idea of levels of hell in three ancient cultures, the Egyptians, the Babylonians, and the Persian Zoroastrians. We began the first section with a discussion of the god Kherty, who served as the ferryman across the River Styx. We also have shown that one job of Kherty was to navigate the dead through what was called *Duat*, the ancient Egyptian word for hell.

Next, in section one of this appendix, we explored the levels of hell or compartments of hell among the Babylonians-Assyrians, chiefly through the work of Alfred Jeremias, who sketched out perspectives on the realm of *Kur*, the Babylonian name for hell. As we have shown, Professor Jeremias also pointed out that Kur had seven gates that may have corresponded to seven compartments of hell.

Thirdly, still in section one of this appendix, we have sketched out the beliefs on levels of hell as expressed in the ancient *Gathas*, seventeen traditional hymns thought to have been written by Zoroaster himself.

In this portion, we have indicated that the Babylonian word for hell was *Duzakh* and that the Gathas divided Duzakh into compartments that went from sins that are least severe to those like murder, adultery, slander, and suicide. The Gathas also maintain that there are seven separate compartments where punishment takes place in Duzakh.

In the second section of this appendix on levels or compartments of hell, we have reiterated what we presented in an earlier chapter about the idea of levels of *Jahannam*, or hell, in the Islamic faith. As we have shown, in Islam there are seven separate levels or sections of hell in descending order from least severe to most severe.

We also have shown that there is some disagreement about the names of these compartments of *Jahannam*, as well as who is to be found at each of these levels. We also have pointed out that in Islam, one's time in *Jahannam* is not eternal and because Allah is all-Good there is always the chance that any soul may be forgiven or rehabilitated.

In the third section of this appendix on levels of hell, we concentrated our attention on the views of the ancient Jews and their perspectives on levels of hell. In this section, we have concentrated our efforts on views to be found in the book known as First Enoch. As we have shown, First Enoch relates that hell has four separate compartments.

Next, we have shown some sections of the Talmud that also appear to imply that hell, or Sheol, has different levels of punishment and that one of those views, in the *Pirkey Avot*, suggests that the dead sometimes suffer in an antechamber like Purgatory in the Roman Catholic faith.

In the third section of this appendix, we have sketched out some views on levels of hell to be found in the Christian tradition, from the Gospels to the church fathers to Dante, all the way up to three figures of the twentieth century—C. S. Lewis, J. P. Moreland, and Pope John Paul II. What we saw in all three of these twentieth-century thinkers is that they each put the emphasis on hell to be related to one's distance from God.

Finally, we provided a summary of many of the most important literary examples in the contemporary West where the idea of levels or compartments of hell is put on display. We also gave an analysis of Rachel Falconer's study on hell in contemporary literature, an analysis that included literary examples, films, and the theoretical philosophical works on which Ms. Falconer depends. This brings us to Appendix G on images of the idea of a hell mouth.

Lucas Cranach the Elder, *Danse Macabre*, woodcut. The mouth of hell straddled by Lucifer with the pope and Roman Catholic dignitaries inside.

Appendix G
The Motif of the Hell Mouth in Western History

The idea of depicting the mouth or entrance to hell, as the jaws of a great being, has been a part of Western history at least as early as the Anglo-Saxon period around the year 800 CE.
—Meyer Schapiro, *Romanesque Art*

Introduction

This appendix introduces and discusses the literary and artistic motifs known as the Hell Mouth and the Jaws of Hell. We mentioned the motif earlier in this history, and now we will devote an entire appendix to the phenomenon.

The most thorough scholarly work on the Hell Mouth motif is that of Meyer Schapiro (1903–1993), whose study entitled *Romanesque Art*[311] remains the standard work on the phenomenon in question. Professor Schapiro was a faculty member at Columbia University and spent his entire career teaching and researching. Although he was born in Ukraine, he considered himself an American scholar.

We will divide this appendix into the following parts. First, we will comment on the history of the Hell Mouth phenomenon from around 800 CE until the present. In the second section, we will look at several prominent examples of the Hell Mouth or Jaws of Hell in Western art. Finally, we will make some observations about how the motif of the Hell Mouth is employed in the contemporary world.

The Hell Mouth: The History of an Idea

According to Professor Schapiro, the first example of depicting the entrance to hell is the gaping mouth of a great beast was in Anglo-Saxon art around the year 800 CE. From there, the motif spread all over Europe, including England, France, Germany, and Belgium, among many other nations.

The oldest example known to Professor Schapiro is an ivory carving of the theme that is now owned by the Victoria and Albert Museum. He also points out that most examples before the twelfth century were English. Many of them are depictions of the Harrowing of Hell, the Christian belief that Jesus Christ went to hell between his Crucifixion and the Resurrection.[312]

Professor Schapiro speculates that the motif may have been borrowed from a pagan myth known as the "Crack of Doom," a synonym for the End of the World in the Greco-Roman times.[313] Middle English dramatic literature contains the fullest and most dramatic depictions of the phenomenon.[314] William Shakespeare uses the "Crack of Doom" motif in Act IV, scene one of *Macbeth*.

In the Anglo-Saxon *Vercelli Homilies,* at 4: 46–48, Satan is likened to a dragon swallowing the damned.[315] Many times in the history of Judaism and Christianity, the Leviathan of the Book of Job's 41:1 has often been shown depicted as the Jaws of Hell. The Old English poem from the *Exeter Book*, the Mouth of Hell is compared to the mouth of a great beast with brilliant eyes and large teeth.[316] Later in the Christian Middle Ages, the classical figure of Cerberus, the Hell Hound, also became associated with the Hell Mouth image. *The Hours of Catherine of Cleaves* includes another image of the Hell Mouth in which the hell-beast has large, almost electric, eyes.[317]

In the fifteenth century, the western portal of the Saint Lawrence Parish Church in Nuremberg, completed in the 1340s, also features the Jaws of Hell swallowing the damned. Another fifteenth-century version of the Hell Mouth motif can still be viewed at the St. George's Church in Alsace. It is usually dated in 1495.

El Greco, in his *Adoration of the Holy Name of Jesus*, completed between 1578 and 1580, owned by the National Gallery, also includes a depiction of the Jaws of Hell swallowing the damned. In the same century, reformer artist Lucas Cranach also completed a Hell Mouth that shows the monster swallowing Roman Catholic dignitaries and popes in the fifteenth to sixteenth centuries.

This brings us to the second section of this appendix on the motif of the Hell Mouth, or Jaws of Hell, in which we will describe other notable examples of the phenomenon, beginning with the Winchester Psalter, a twelfth-century manuscript owned by the British Library.

Other Notable Examples of the Hell Mouth Motif

The Winchester Psalter (Cotton MS, Nero C. iv.) is also known as the "Psalter of Henry of Blois" because he was the most likely benefactor of the manuscript. The text has 142 vellum leaves of 32 x 22.25 cm and is usually dated in the twelfth century. The most important of those for our purposes is an illustration of an archangel locking the gate of the Hell Mouth. The Jaws of Hell appear to belong to an aquatic monster with one bright eye, the left, showing. His mouth is filled with the souls of humans who have been consigned to the Underworld.

A second notable example of the motif of the Hell Mouth or the Jaws of Hell is a stained-glass window from the twelfth-century Bourges Cathedral. The piece is constructed with brilliant shades of red and blue. The owner of the Hell Mouth appears to be a great aquatic creature, perhaps the Book of Job's Leviathan from chapter forty-one. The souls of the dead within the giant jaws all have anguished looks on their faces.

A third notable example of a European Hell Mouth was completed by Pieter Bruegel in 1563. He called the oil on panel painting *Dulle Griet*, also known as *Mad Meg*. The painting in question shows a virago, Dulle Griet, who leads an army of women whose goal is to pillage hell. The painting includes an anthropomorphic mouth of hell, and a monster with bright eyes, wide nostrils and large horns protruding above the great mouth.[318]

An illustration of the Queen Mary Apocalypse from the British Library shows an angel holding a key while attempting to secure the souls in hell who are about to fall into the giant Jaws of Hell. The monster in question has two large teeth, one on the lower and one on the upper jaws. A large bird with a metal collar around its neck stands in the mouth of the beast.

Another noteworthy example of the Hell Mouth motif can be found in the manuscript known as the *Apocalypse of Michael* designated as MS1733. Folio 43r. It shows a three-headed Cerberus devouring souls of the damned. Some scholars maintain it is a depiction of the Book of Revelation 20:10:

> **And the Devil that deceived them was cast into the Lake of Fire and Brimstone, where the beast and the false prophet are located. And they shall be tormented day and night, for ever and ever.**

Another notable example of the Hell Mouth motif or Jaws of Hell phenomenon is contained in what is known as the fifteenth-century Bedford Book of Hours located at the British Library. Angels flanked by saints greet souls who have passed judgment. The damned souls below are forced into a fiery Hell Mouth, and roundels feature demons grinning as they beat the human souls with mallets.

Finally, in a text known as the "Harley Manuscript," designated at the British Library as MS3999, at folio 21r, we find details of a marginal drawing with a bat-like Hell Mouth, in which the souls of the damned are being devoured. The creature in question has bat-like, black wings and two foreboding eyes as it gathers up in its arms the souls of the dead.

This brings us to the third and final section of Appendix G on the motif of the Hell Mouth or the Jaws of Hell. In this section, we shall introduce and then discuss some of the employments of the motif in the contemporary world.

The Motif of the Hell Mouth in the Contemporary World

Finally, there are several ways in which we see the motif of the Hell Mouth or Jaws of Hell appear in contemporary culture. In this section, we will discuss:

1. Television series *Buffy the Vampire Slayer*
2. Comic
3. Book

4. Hell Mouth as an oven or fireplace
5. Strange phenomenon of Portal to Hell

The television episode in question called "Welcome to the Hellmouth" is an American supernatural drama that originally aired on March 10, 1997. The narrator follows Buffy Summers on the first day in a new school called Sunnydale High. The main dramatic tension in the series is that Buffy must take on the role of a Vampire Slayer to save the school and the town. The high school used for the external scenes is Torrance High School, the same school used for the series *Beverly Hills 90210*.

Hellmouth is a 2019–2020 comic book published by Boom! Studios. The event is a crossover between *Buffy the Vampire Slayer* and *Angel*, both responsible by the influence of director and writer Joss Whedon. As Hellmouth threatens Sunnydale to the brink of extinction, Buffy Summers must join forces with the Vampire Angel to save the high school and the city.

The book on our list is Ron Schwab's *Mouth of Hell*, published by Poor Coyote Press in 2016. Schwab is the author of a popular Western series called the *Wranglers*. In *Mouth of Hell*, Schwab employs many of the traditional features of the motif, as well as many new ones.

The Hellmouth as an oven or fireplace motif has been employed by various artists, mostly from California and Italy, where they turn their desk, fireplace, or other parts of the home into what amounts to a Hell Mouth. Two fine examples of this phenomenon are the "Hell Mouth Fireplace" designed by Joseph Pasco for the Villa Della Torre Allegrini in Fumane, Italy. The Los Angeles home that uses the Hell Mouth as a fireplace is owned by Bijan Pakzad, who built the house and the fireplace in the mid-1940s.

In the Pakzad home, the other example of Hell Mouth as a fireplace, can be seen in a mid-twentieth-century, mouth-shaped fireplace in modern America. The California living room also features trendy, mid-century modern chairs. There is a delightful contrast and harmony of colors and textures—rough stone, gleaming marble, smooth wood, shaggy rug, dark floor, and white cabinets. But the fireplace is the central image of the room.

There is also a second example of a Hell Mouth designed by Mr. Pakzad. This one serves as the mouth of a fountain in the artists's place of business on Rodeo Drive in Los Angeles. It is fashioned from clay, and the mouth of a creature serves as the entrance, or open-in, of the fountain in question.

Finally, what has been called a "bizarre, 72-foot-wide Hell Mouth," can be found in the Napa Valley region of California. It is a bizarre portal to hell that long has terrified locals and among them it is known as the "Glory Hole." The 72-foot wide spinning vortex was formed after water levels of Lake Berryessa and its dam got too high.

This brings us to the conclusions of Appendix G on Hell Mouths and Jaws of Hell.

Conclusions

The main purpose of this appendix is to describe and discuss the phenomenon known as the Hell Mouth or the Jaws of Hell. We divided the appendix into three main sections. In the first of these, we made some comments and discussed the history of the motif of the Hell Mouth, beginning with Professor Meyer Schapiro's example of the phenomenon from the Anglo-Saxon period around 800 CE and then several examples mostly from Europe in the fifteenth and sixteenth centuries.

In the second section, we introduced seven notable examples of the Hell Mouth or Jaws of Hell phenomenon. These included the Winchester Psalter, a twelfth-century stained-glass window at the Bourges Cathedral, Pieter Brugel's painting known as *Dulle Griet* or *Mad Meg*, the British Library's Queen Mary Apocalypse, the Apocalypse of Michael, the fifteenth-century Bedford Book of Hours, and the British Library's Harley Manuscript, where the monster of the Hell Mouth looks very much like a bat.

In the third and final section of Appendix G on the phenomenon of the Hell Mouth, we have introduced five examples of where the motif can be found in contemporary culture. These included:

1. One television show, *Buffy the Vampire Slayer*
2. One comic, *Buffy and Angel*
3. One book, Ron Schwab's *Mouth of Hell*
4. Two examples of a Hell Mouth as a fireplace. One from Italy and one from California.
5. And one strange phenomenon in the Napa Valley of California called by locals the "Glory Hole."

This brings us to Appendix H, the motif of the harrowing of hell.

Miniature from the *Hours of Catherine of Cleves*, circa 1440. Morgan Library & Museum.

Appendix H
The Motif of the Harrowing of Hell

Now that He ascended, what is it but he also
descended first into the lower parts of the underworld.
—Ephesians 4:9

Introduction

The purpose of the eighth appendix to this history of views about hell and the afterlife is to discuss the phenomenon that is known as the Harrowing of Hell. That is, that Jesus, between his death and Crucifixion and his resurrection, descended into hell. We will begin with some background information on the Harrowing of Hell.

In the second section of Appendix H, we will speak of the vocabulary that has been associated with the Harrowing of Hell. In the third and final section, we will speak more specifically about the idea of the Harrowing of Hell—mostly in the Christian tradition—from the New Testament to some of the early church fathers, and beyond.

Background Information on the Harrowing of Hell

The "Harrowing of Hell," or in Latin, *Descensus Christi ad Inferos*, or "The descent of Christ into Hell or *Hades*," is an Old English and Middle English term referring to the period between the Crucifixion of Jesus and his resurrection.

Jesus Christ's descent into the world of the dead is referenced in the Apostles' Creed, as well as the Athanasian Creed, where both prayers employ the Latin *Quicumque vult inferos*, or He "descended into hell."[319] In the New Testament 1 Peter 4:6 (KJV) that proclaims,

"The good tidings were proclaimed by Christ to the dead."

The Harrowing of Hell is commemorated in the liturgical calendar on Holy Saturday, according to the *Catholic Encyclopedia*, volume seven. In that anonymous article, the author suggests that the phenomenon of the Harrowing of Hell first appeared in the *Gospel of Nicodemus* in a section called "The Acts of Pilate." This text references the Harrowing of Hell in more than a dozen places.

The motif of the Harrowing of Hell and a discussion of it also appears in the homilies of Alfred of Eynsham, around the year 1000 CE. This is also the first use of the word "Harrowing" in the Christian tradition. A volume of Aelfric's homilies was edited by Benjamin Thorpe in London in 1844.[320] The fullest and deepest treatment of the Harrowing of Hell can be found in Middle-English dramatic literature. As a motif in Christian art, the Harrowing of Hell is also known as the *Anastasis*, a classical Greek word that means "Resurrection."

Many of the artistic depictions of the Harrowing of Hell are owned by the Metropolitan Museum of Art in New York City. For example, item 68.224 fol. 1r is an anonymous panel of the Harrowing of Hell dated in the thirteenth century. A second piece is entitled *Christ's Descent into Limbo* that came from the school of Andrea Mantegna in the fourteenth century. A third piece owned by the National Gallery of Art is a painting by Hansielich and dated ca.1550.

The MET also owns a fourth painting completed by an anonymous Russian artist called The *Resurrection of Christ and the Harrowing of Hell*, usually dated in the eighteenth century. And Hieronymus Bosch completed the painting *Christ Breaking Down the Gates of Hell* in the fifteenth century. Another painting by Bosch is entitled *Christ in Limbo*. It is dated 1575 and is owned by the Indianapolis Museum of Art in Indiana.

The Detroit Institute of Art owns a painting called *Christ in Limbo*. It is attributed to Hern met de Bles and is usually dated in the mid-fifteenth century. It is interesting how many names of pieces of art are associated with the Harrowing of Hell—*Christ in Limbo*, *Christ in Hell*, *The Harrowing of Hell*, etc.

Finally, one of the most recent depictions of the Harrowing of Hell is a painting by Joakim Skovgaard entitled *Christ in the Realm of the Dead*. It is dated between 1891 and 1894. It is owned by the State Museum of Kunst.

This brings us to the second section of Appendix H, in which we will discuss the terminology and vocabulary of the phenomenon of the Harrowing of Hell.

Terminology and Vocabulary of the Harrowing of Hell

The Greek wording of the Apostles' Creed regarding the Harrowing of Hell is *katelthonta*, and in Latin, it is *descendit ad inferos*. The Greek *ta katota*, or "the lowest," and the Latin *inferos*, or "those below," is the underworld, the netherworld or the abode of the dead.

The English word "harrowing" was originally the Old English term *hergian*, which meant "to hurry" or "to despoil." Hergian is seen in the Homilies of Aelfric around 1000 CE. Later on, the expression the Harrowing of Hell referred to the idea that Jesus descended into hell, as in the Apostles' Creed, as well as the idea developed later that Jesus triumphed over *Inferos*, or "those below," including the release of hell's captives, particularly for some reason the release of Adam and Eve.

In fact, there was a concerted effort to speak of the Old Testament worthies who knew nothing of the life and teachings of Jesus Christ, so some traditions designated different limbos for them, as well as unbaptized babies. The former was known in the church as the "Limbo of the Patriarchs," because they did not know Jesus, while the latter was known as the "Limbo of Infants," because they were not baptized.

At any rate, the English word limbo comes from the Latin *Limbus*, which means "on the edge" or "on a boundary." Meaning in relationship to hell. For many medieval Christian theologians and philosophes, then, there were three compartments to hell. Those were:

1. The Hell of the Damned
2. The Limbo of the Patriarchs.
3. The Limbo of Infants.[321]

This brings us to the third and final section of Appendix H, in which we will explore the history of the idea of the Harrowing of Hell from the New Testament times to its development in the early church fathers.

The Harrowing of Hell from the New Testament until the Homilies of Aelfric of Eynsham

Among the books of the New Testament, there are six different passages that scholars have pointed to to express the idea of the Harrowing of Hell. These may be summarized this way:

1. Matthew 12:40
2. Acts of the Apostles 2:24
3. Acts of the Apostles 2:31
4. Ephesians 4:9
5. Colossians 1:18
6. First Peter 3:18–19.

The first of these likens Christ's harrowing to Jonah being in the belly of the whale for three days. Acts 2:24 relates that "God raised him up being freed from death." Acts 2:31 speaks of King David as a resident of the Limbo of the Patriarchs. The passage from Ephesians tells us that "If he ascended, he must have descended too." And we discussed the other two passages from Paul from Ephesians and Colossians, as well as the passage from First Peter earlier in this appendix on the Harrowing of Hell."

Many of early church fathers from the second to the ninth centuries also made references to Christ's Harrowing of Hell. Among these early church fathers were:

1. St. Melito of Sardis (second century)
2. Tertullian in his treatise on the Sou (second to the third century)
3. John Chrysostom, Paschal Homilies (fourth and fifth centuries)
4. Hippolytus, Treatise on Christ and the Antichrist (second to the third century)
5. Ambrose of Milan (fourth century)
6. John of Damascus (sixth century)

These six Christian church fathers all contributed to the perspectives of the Homilies of Saint Aelfric of Eynsham who is considered the first great Christian thinker with an inclusive view of Jesus's Harrowing of Hell.

This brings us to the conclusions of Appendix H on the Harrowing of Hell and images of the Hell Mouth and the end of this history of hell from the Egyptians and ancient Chinese until the Christian medieval period.

Conclusions

We divided this eighth appendix into three parts. In the first of these, we gave some background information to more fully understand the theological and artistic motif. Indeed, at the end of that first section, we provided a catalogue of Western depictions of the Harrowing of Hell from medieval times until the nineteenth century.

In the second section, we spoke of the Greek and medieval Latin vocabulary that was employed in Western theology and philosophy. We also gave an account of the Latin term *Limbus*, from which we get the English limbo. We also described what many medieval thinkers thought about the three compartments or domains of hell—The Hell of the Damned, the Limbo of the Patriarchs, and the Limbo of infants.

In the third section, we explored the motif from the six references to it in the New Testament, followed by a number of the early church fathers who have written about the phenomenon. Among those early church fathers on the motif in question was Melito of Sardis, Tertullian, John Chrysostom, Hippolytus Ambrose, and sixth-century father, John of Damascus.

In the fourth and final section of Appendix H, we provided a history of images of the Hell Mouth in Western culture with an emphasis on well-known painters and artists in the West. We have introduced six paintings from the twelfth to the fifteenth century, as well as half a dozen more from the sixteenth to the twentieth century, ending in Edvard Munch's 1903 painting *Self-Portrait in Hell.*

This appendix completes this study of the idea of hell in the history of humankind.

Images of the Hell Mouth in Human History

1. Apostles' Creed is officially known by the Roman Church as *Symbolum Apostolorum*. It most likely originated in Gaul in the fifth century. The Athanasian Creed was most likely penned by Saint Athanasius in the early sixth century.
2. First Peter 4:6, King James Version.
3. Anonymous, *The Harrowing of Hell*, *Catholic Encyclopedia* 7.
4. Aelfric of Eynsham, *Homilies*, London: Early English Text Society, 1998.
5. *The Harrowing of Hell*, thirteenth century. Metropolitan Museum, item 68.224. folio r.
6. Anonymous, *The Descent into Limbo*, fourteenth century. Metropolitan Museum.
7. Hans Sielich."The Harrowing of Hell." National Gallery of Art. [ca.1550.]
8. Anonymous Russian painter, *The Resurrection of Christ and the Harrowing of Hell*, eighteenth century. Metropolitan Museum.
9. Hieronymus Bosch, *Christ Breaking Down the Gates*, fifteenth century. Metropolitan Museum.
10. Hieronymu Bosch, *Christ in Limbo*, ca. 1575. Indianapolis Museum of Art.
11. Met de Bles, *Christ in Limbo*, mid-fifteenth century. Detroit Institute of Art.
12. Joakim Skovgaard, *Christ in the Realm of the Dead*, sixteenth century. State Museum of Kunst, Dusseldorf, Germany.
13. Both Thomas Aquinas and Dante employed this three part compartment of hell, as we have indicated earlier in this study.
14. This same tripartite scheme was used throughout the Christian High Midde Ages from 1000 CE to 1500 CE.

Endnotes

1 For more on the notion of *Diyu*, see Donald Lopez, ed., *Buddhist Scriptures* (New York: Penguin Classics, 2004), 69–77.

2 Ibid., 69.

3 Ibid., 70–71.

4 Ibid., 72.

5 Ibid., 73–74.

6 Ibid., 75.

7 Ibid.

8 Ibid., 75–76.

9 For more on the god *Yama*, see Mark Cartwright, "Yama" in World History Encyclopedia, https://www.worldhistory.org/Yama; and Jaan Puhvel, *Comparative Mythology* (Baltimore: Johns Hopkins University Press, 1989), 285–286.

10 Puhvel, 285.

11 Ibid., 86.

12 Mark Cartwright, "Yama" in World History Encyclopedia, https://www.worldhistory.org/Yama

13 For more on the idea of *atman* in Hinduism, see Kamaleswar Bhattacharya, *The Atman-Brahma in Ancient Buddhism* (London: Canon Publications, 2015), 1–120.

14 Ibid., 1–17.

15 Ibid., 17–18.

16 Ibid., 20.

17 For more on the ideas of *Jiva* and *Ajiva*, see Jeffrey D. Long, *Jainism: An Introduction* (New York: I.B. Tauris, 2009), 90–107.

18 Ibid., 95–97.

19 Ibid., 97.

20 Ibid., 100–104.

21 For more on hell in African religions, see Akan Takruri, *100 African Religions before Slavery and Colonization* (London: Jamil White, 2017).

22 Ibid., 126–137.

23 Ibid., 136–137.

24 For more on the Tutsi god *Imana*, see Jennie E. Burnet, *To Save Heaven and Earth* (Ithaca: Cornell University Press, 2023).

25 According to recent statistics from the Pew Forum on Religion and Public Life, Gambia's Muslim population is 95 percent, while Senegal's is 97 percent. The study is called "The World's Muslims: Unity and Diversity."

26 For more on religion among the Yoruba, see Baba ifa Karade, *The*

Handbook of Yorba Religious Concepts (New York: Weiser Classics, 2020), especially 115–116.

27 For more on the Aztec religion and afterlife, see M. E. Smith, *The Aztecs* (Oxford: Blackwells, 2009).

28 For more on the Mayan religion, see Alexus McLeod, *Philosophy of the Ancient Maya: Lords of Time* (London: LEX, 2019).

29 For more on religion among the Pueblo Indians, see "Pueblo Indians," *Encyclopedia Britannica*, April 21, 2023, 1–10.

30 For more on the religion of the Cheyenne, consult: Mary Douglass, "Cheyenne Tribe: Facts, Religion and History," 2023, study.com, https://bit.ly/3RDkQoS.

31 Mika, "The Navajo Religion: A Complex System of Beliefs and Practices," October 6, 2022, indiancountryextensions.org, https://bit.ly/3RG4nA9.

32 Alice C. Fletcher, *The Omaha Tribe* (Lincoln: Bison Books, 1972), 43.

33 Smudging is a Native American ritual that links smoke with spirituality. See "Smudging: A Sacred Native American Ritual," November 1, 2023, powwows.com, https://bit.ly/3TzTcM2.

34 For more on the Seminole tribe, see "Seminole," May 23, 2018, encyclopedia.com, https://bit.ly/3NK2eCa.

35 For more on reincarnation among the Sioux people, see Antonia Mills and Richard Slobodin, *Amerindian Rebirth: Reincarnation Belief Among North American Indians and Inuit* (Toronto: University of Toronto Press, 2018).

36 For more on the god *Degei*, see A. M. Reed, *Myths and Legends of Fiji* (Honolulu: Literary Corporation of America, 1997).

37 Ibid., 94.

38 Ibid., 100.

39 For more on the Celtic underworld, see Peter B. Ellis, *The Mammoth Book of Celtic Myths and Legends* (Copenhagen: Mammoth Books, 2022).

40 Ibid., 17–59.

41 Ibid., 60–61.

42 For more on the Bahá'í faith, see William Garlington, *The Bahá'í Faith in India* (Los Angeles: Kalimat Press, 2023).

43 For more on the Seventh-day Adventists, see General Council of the Seventh-day Adventists, *What Seventh-day Adventists Believe* (Los Angeles: Pacific Press Publication Association, 2005).

44 For more on the Jehovah's Witnesses belief system, see Michael T. Floyd, *Jehovah's Witnesses: A detailed look at what they believe* (San Francisco: Northside Publications, 2018).

45 For more on the Latter-day Saints

belief system, see Russell Róbe, *Latter-Day Saint Beliefs* (Salt Lake City: Almus Publications, 2022).

46 For more on the Tamil faith, see "Tamil Culture and Life," May 2015, factanddetails.com, https://bit.ly/48zxE6t.

47 Ibid.

48 For the religion and text of ancient Egypt, see Peter Dorman, "Ancient Egyptian Religion," 2013, *Britannica*, https://bit.ly/48CCW0Y; Sir W. F. Flinders Petrie, *The Religion of Ancient Egypt* (Great Bend: Moran Press, 2015); M. A. Murray, *History and Religion in Ancient Egypt* (Museum Audiobooks, 2022); and Henri Frankfort, *Ancient Egyptian Religion* (New York: Dover Publications, 2011).

49 Dorman.

50 Petrie, 131.

51 Ibid., 133–135.

52 Frankfurt, 292–294.

53 Ibid., 294.

54 Petrie, 73.

55 Ibid., 91–97.

56 Ibid.

57 Ibid., 139–147.

58 For more on the Epic of Gilgamesh, see trans. N. K. Sandars, *The Epic of Gilgamesh* (New York: Penguin Classics, 1960).

59 Ibid., 100–111.

60 For more on the religion of the Sumerians, see E. A. Budge, *A Guide to Babylonian and Assyrian Antiquities* (London: The British Museum, 1922), 277–319.

61 Ibid., 277–279.

62 Ibid., 300–319.

63 Ibid., 380–383.

64 For more on the Canaanite religion, see Sebastian Berg, *Canaanite Mythology: Gods and Religion of Ancient Canaan* (Independently published, 2023).

65 Ibid., 14–16.

66 For more on the Zoroastrian religion, see Mary Boyce, *Zoroastrians: Their Religious Beliefs and Practices* (London: Routledge, 2000).

67 Ibid., 152–153.

68 Ibid., 163.

69 Ibid., 165–166.

70 Ibid., 167.

71 Ibid.

72 Ibid., 171–172.

73 Ibid., 172.

74 E. W. West, *Sacred Books of the East*, vol. 1 (London: Hansebooks, 2020), 391.

75 Ibid., 393.

76 For more on the idea and the god Hades, see Christine Ha, *Hades: Greek Gods and Goddesses* (San Francisco: North Star Editions, 2021).

77 For a detailed treatment of Theseus, see Mark Ruin, *The Gorgon & the Glass Slipper* (London: Gallimaufry Press, 2002).

78 Hesiod, trans. M. L. West, *Theogony and Works and Days* (Oxford: Oxford University Press Classics, 2009), 333.
79 Ha, Chapter 1.
80 Ibid., 53.
81 Ibid.
82 Ibid., 54–55.
83 Ibid., 56.
84 For more on Cerberus, see Francis Stevens, *The Heads of Cerberus* (New York: Intra Books, 2022).
85 Ha, 171.
86 Ibid.
87 D. H. Lawrence, *Sketches of Etruscan Places* (New York: Penguin Classics, 2008), 7–8.
88 Ibid.
89 Ibid.
90 Ibid.
91 Ibid.
92 Ibid.
93 Genesis 37:35, author's translation. All the Hebrew passages are translated by the author unless otherwise specified.
94 Author's research.
95 See NAB, RSV, NRSV, NIV, for example.
96 *Oxford English Dictionary* entry on "Hell" and Fofi G., *Old English Dictionary* (New York: Create Space, 2018).
97 Ibid.
98 Snorri Sturluson, *King Harald's Saga* (New York: Penguin Classics, 1976), 20.
99 Ibid.
100 Ibid.
101 Fofi, 181.
102 Ibid.
103 Author's research.
104 *Oxford English Dictionary*, entry on "Hell."
105 Ibid.
106 Ibid.
107 Ibid.
108 The Gaelic *ceilid* is also derived from the Sanskrit *kel*, Book of Revelation 9:11.
109 Hesiod, 29–30.
110 Homer, trans. Robert Fagles, *The Iliad* (New York: Penguin Classics, 1998).
111 Marcus Jastrow, "Targum Neofiti," *Dictionary of the Targumim* (New York: Judaic Press, 2004).
112 David J. Stewart, "Seventh-Day Adventist Heresy on Hell," August 2014, https://bit.ly/3vqYTBV.
113 The word *Hades* is employed eighty-six times in the New Testament.
114 The *a dein* origin seems the most likely.
115 See, for example, Luke 16:23.
116 Author's research.
117 Hesiod, 225; and Homer, 223.
118 *The Iliad*, book 6.
119 2 Maccabees 7:22–23.
120 Pirkei Avot 4:21.
121 The *Kaddish* is a hymn praising God recited in many Jewish prayer services, particularly in what is called the "Mourner's Kaddish" in English.

122 Bava Metzia 18a.

123 Most scholars date the Epistle of Barnabus sometime between 70 and 132 CE. The complete text is preserved in the *Codex Sinaiticus*, a fourth-century text owned by the British Museum, Ms. 43715.

124 Ignatius to the Ephesians is one of seven letters attributed to Ignatius. Tradition has it that Ignatius was martyred during the reign of Trajan, who was emperor from 98 to 117 CE.

125 Athenagoras, *Apology*, 5.4.

126 Clement of Alexandria, *Post Nicene Manuscripts*, 18:1–3.

127 Irenaeus, *Against Heresies*, Book 1, 10:1.

128 The Apocalypse of Peter is a second-century CE work purportedly written by the apostle Peter. This text was discovered in an archeological dig in 1866–1867 in Upper Egypt. It is dated sometime between 100 and 150 CE.

129 Oskar Skarsaune, *Jewish Believers in Jesus* (New York: Hendrickson, 2012), 366–368.

130 Peter, *Apocalypse of Peter*, Book 5.

131 Ibid., Book 7.

132 The *Acts of Thomas* is a description of Thomas' ministry to India, where he was tempted by a female demon and shown some scenes in Hell.

133 The *Apocalypse of Paul* is also known in Latin as the *Visio Pauli*, or "Vision of Paul." It is most likely a fourth-century CE text.

134 Saint Patrick in modern scholarship now suggests that his dates were 385–461.

135 Saint Patrick, eds. John Skinner and Philip Freeman, *The Confession* (Dublin: First Editions, 1998). St. Patrick, *Letter to the Soldiers of Coroticus* (Oxford: Oxford University Press, 2014).

136 *Soldiers*, 109.

137 Saint Jerome, *The Vulgate*. He made this comment speaking of Bathsheba in 2Samuel 11 and 12 and First Kings 1 and 2.

138 Saint Jerome, "Letter to Paula," *The Letters of Saint Jerome* (Dublin: Aeterna Press, 2016), letter 16.

139 Augustine of Hippo, *City of God* (New York: Penguin Classics, 2003). Augustine's Latin for this text is *Extra ecclesium nulla salus* or "Outside the Church, there is no salvation," Book 21, 12.

140 Ibid., Book 21, 14.

141 Ibid., Book 7, 3–4.

142 Augustine of Hippo, *Essential Sermons*, 178.3 (New York: New City Press, 2007).

143 Ibid., Sermon 21.

144 Hippo, *City of God*, Book 15, chapters 2 and 3.

145 Saadiah Gaon, *The Book of Beliefs and Opinions* (New Haven: Yale University Press, 1989).

146 The Hebrew word *Gaon* literally means "genius." In the Hebrew Bible it is used at Amos 6:8, where it refers to arrogance and haughty pride. The plural of this word is *Gionim*, which comes from the Hebrew verb *gaah*, meaning "to exalt."

147 See note 140.

148 Ibid., 100–124.

149 Ibid., 123–124.

150 Gaon, 125.

151 Ibid., 119–120.

152 Ibid., 120.

153 Ibid., 126–127.

154 Ibid., 127–128.

155 Ibid., 128.

156 Ibid.

157 Ibid., 129.

158 Ibid., 130.

159 Ibid.

160 Ibid., 131–132.

161 The full title of the *Kuzari* by Rabbi Helevi is, "The Book of Refutation and Proof on Behalf of the Despised Religion." It was completed in the Hebrew year 4900 or 1139.

162 Ibid., 7–10.

163 Ibid., 10.

164 Ibid., 7.

165 Ibid., 8.

166 Ibid., 121–129.

167 Ibid., 121–122.

168 Rabbi Helevi, "Ode to Zion," discussed in Nissan Mindel, *Rabbi Judah ben Levi* (Jerusalem: Kehot Publication Society, 2021).

169 Abraham Ibn Ezra wrote detailed commentaries on thirty books of the Hebrew Bible, including a stellar text on *Seffer Iyyov*, or the Book of Job.

170 Abraham Ibn Ezra, *The Judgments of the Zodiacal Signs* (Boston: Brill, 2017).

171 Ibid., 94.

172 Ibid.

173 Ibid., 95–96.

174 Abraham Ibn Ezra, *The Foundations of Reverence* (Jerusalem: Bar-Ilan University Press, 2020). This "Test View," as I have called it elsewhere, is a common response to evil and suffering in Judaism and Christianity.

175 Ibid. Ibn Ezra speaks of the Akedah in the third chapter of this text.

176 Moses Maimonides, *Guide for the Perplexed* (Chicago: University of Chicago Press, 1974), Chapter Six.

177 Moses Maimonides, *Mishnah Torah* (New York: Moznaim Publications, 2010).

178 Ibid. The orchard analogy is in Chapter Three.

179 Moses de Nahman, *Sefirot*. Published in English as *Law and Mysticism* (New Haven: Yale University Press, 2020).

180 Ibid., 17–23.

181 Ibid., 23–29.

182 Ibid., 30–37.

183 Ibid., 38–47.
184 Ibid., 48–53.
185 Rabbi Isaac Luria, *The Gates of Reincarnation* (New York: Independently Published, 2021).
186 Ibid., 216.
187 Ibid., 217–219.
188 Ibid., 219.
189 St. Brendan is believed by some to have reached the New World on his voyages. See Ann Carroll, *Journey into the Unknown: The Story of St. Brendan* (Dublin: In a Nutshell, 2015).
190 As Carroll has pointed out, although Brendan lived in the sixth century, his journal was not made available until the ninth century.
191 Carroll, 34–35.
192 Ibid., 35.
193 Ibid.
194 Gregory the Great, *Dialogues* (Jackson: Ex Fontibus Company, 2016).
195 Ibid., 200.
196 Venerable Bede, *Ecclesiastical History of the English People* (Oxford: Oxford University Classics, 2009).
197 Venerable Bede, *Commentary on Revelation*, ed. and trans. Faith Wallis (Liverpool: University of Liverpool Press, 2013).
198 Bede, "The Vision of Saint Fursa," in *History*, 219. Also see: Chris Wilson, *The Vision of Saint Fursa in the Thirteenth Century Didactic Literature* (Cambridge: Cambridge University Press, 2016).
199 Bede, *Commentary on Revelation*, 242.
200 Ibid.
201 Ibid., 242–243.
202 Ibid., 243.
203 John Scotus Eriugena, *Periphyseon: On the Divisions of Nature* (Eugene: Wipf and Stock, 2011).
204 Ibid., 39–41.
205 Peter Lombard, *Sentences* (Rome: PIMS, 2010).
206 Ibid., vol. 1:195.
207 Ibid., 196–199.
208 William Barclay Turnbull, *The Visions of Tundale* (Charleston: Legare Street Press, 2022).
209 Ibid., 29.
210 Ibid.
211 Thomas Aquinas, *Summa Theologica* (New York: Create Space, 2012).
212 Thomas Aquinas, *Summa Contra Gentiles* (London: Burns, Oates, and Washbourne, 1928), Question 69: 1–7.
213 Dante Alighieri, *The Inferno* (New York: Signet Classics, 2009).
214 All of the Arabic translations to English in this chapter are those of the author.
215 "Al-Farabi," Britannica, www.britannica.com/biography/al-Farabi.
216 Al-Ghazali, *On Disciplining the Soul* (London: Islamic Text

Society, 2017), 53.

217 Jalal as Din Muhammad Rumi. His poem on death and punishment is called "When I Die." See *Poem Analysis* (2021).

218 Ibn Tamiyyah, Hadith, Vol. I, no 286.

219 Chaim Pearl and Reuben Brookes, *A Guide to Jewish Knowledge* (New York: Hartmore House, 1976), 11.

220 Moses Hiyyam Luzzato, *The Ramchal* (New York: Targum Press, 2012), 441.

221 Ibid., 101.

222 Rabbi Yom Tov Lipman-Heller, *Midrash Samuel*, ed. R. Weisman (Jerusalem: Bnay Yakov, 1998), 217–218.

223 Moses Mendelsohn, *The Phaedo: Or Immortality of the Soul* (Oxford: Oxford World Classics, 2009), 278–279.

224 Martin Luther, *Table Talks* (New York: Beloved Publishing, 2014), 26.

225 John Calvin, *The Institutes of the Christian Religion* (Carol Stream: Hendrickson Publishing, 2008), 339.

226 Francis Turretin, *The Institute of Elenctic Thought* (London: P&R Publishing, 1997), 121–124.

227 Jonathan Edwards, *The Complete Sermons* (New York: Independently Published, 2019), 392–394.

228 Al-Suyuti, *Tafsir Al-Jalalayn* [Arabic text] (Damascus: Dar al-Taqwa, 2012), 279–281.

229 Al-Tamiyyah, *On the Oneness of God* (Damascus: Dar Al-Arqam, 2020), 17.

230 Ibn Rajab Hanbali, *Fleeing from the Fire* (Cairo: Al-Azhar, 2021), 268.

231 Yasir Qadhi, *The Sirah of the Prophet* (Karachi: Kube Publishing, 2023), 57–61.

232 John Bunyan, "Journey to Hell," in *Doctrinal Discourses* (London: Inys Whiteside, 1955), 42.

233 John Milton, *Paradise Lost* (New York: Hackett Books, 2001), 363–365.

234 Henry Giles, *Hello Janice: The Wartime Letters* (Lexington: The University Press of Kentucky, 1992), 119.

235 Frederick Denison Maurice, *On Eternal Life and Eternal Death* (London: Leopold Classics, 2015), 48.

236 John Stuart Mill, *Autobiography* (New York: Independently Published, 2019), 109.

237 J. W. Colenso, *Sermon Delivered October 17 and 18, 1882, at Durban* (Durbin: Generic Books, 2019), 31.

238 Fred Sanders, *F. W. Robertson's Life and Death* (London: *Scriptorium Daily*: August 15, 2010).

239 F. W. Farrar, *Eternal Hope* (London: Generic Books, 2022),

191–192.

240 Ibid.

241 Marquis de Sade, *Philosophy in the Bedroom* (London: Penguin Classics, 2006), 117.

242 Ibid., "Thoughts on Hell," 120–125.

243 Lord Byron, "Manfred" and "Cain," in *Lord Byron's Poems*, ed. Paul Muldoon (London: Farrar, Straus, and Giroux, 2016), 31–33 and 51–53.

244 Denis Diderot, *On Rousseau.* See Diane Thompson's syllabi for her course "World Literature II: England," 1.

245 John Keats, "The Fall of Hyperion." A revised edition with a long prologue was left unfinished and was published after his death in 1856.

246 Ibid.

247 John Keats, *Selected Letters*, ed. John Barnard (London: Penguin Classics, 2015), 217–219. and 464–466.

248 Lord Byron's marriage and honeymoon were in 1815. His only daughter was born in 1816.

249 Lord Byron, "A Vision of Judgment," see Robert Southey, *Lord Byron and His Times*, ed. James Kennedy (London: Hard Press, 2018).

250 Percy Shelly, *Prometheus Unbound* (London: Kessinger Books, 2010).

251 William Blake, *The Marriage of Heaven and Hell* (New York: Dover Books, 1994).

252 John Furniss, *The Sight of Hell* (London: Curious Publications, 2020).

253 Austin Holyoake, "Heaven and Hell," *The Reasoner*, May 27, 1856.

254 Charles Robert Maturin, *Melmouth the Wanderer* (New York: Penguin Books, 2001).

255 Christine Rosetti, *Goblin Market* (Oxford: Oxford University Press, 1875).

256 Vasily Grossman, "The Hell of Treblinka," *Znamya*, November, 1994.

257 Shmuel Marvil, "The Street," in *Poetry in Hell*, Stanza 34.

258 Akihiro Takahashi, "Ground Zero, 1945: A Schoolboy's Story," *The Asian-Pacific Journal*, September 3, 2007.

259 Wallace Stevens, "The Comedian as the Letter C," in *Harmonium* (New York: Dover Books, 1952).

260 "Two Portraits of One Lowdown Saloon in 1919 in Greenwich Village," Ephemeral New York, https://bit.ly/3QGUnXC.

261 Albert Camus, *The Plague* (New York: Knopf and Doubleday, 1991), 111.

262 Niko Kazantzakis, *The Last Temptation of Christ* (New York: Simon and Schuster, 1988), 53.

263 John F. Kennedy, "On Secret Societies," April 27, 1961.

264 Bertrand Russell, *Why I am not a Christian* (London: Touch Stone Books, 1967), 129.

265 E. M. Forster, *A Room with a View* (London: Warbler Classics, 2021), 91.

266 Dorothy Parker, *What Fresh Hell is This?* (New York: Generic Library, 1966), 33.

267 Pew Research Center, "Views on Religion," 1999–2014.

268 Andrew Mark Miller, "U.S. Religious Leaders Explain why Faith in God Hit Lowest Level Ever," Fox News, July 3, 2022.

269 Thomas Wittemore, *The Punishment of Hell Eternal* (Boston: James Dow, 1833), 12–13.

270 David Powys, *A Hard Look at a Hard Question* (London: Paternoster Books, 2007).

271 David Bateman, "The Eighth Circle of Hell in the 21st Century," *The Rocky Mountain Advisory*, February 19, 2019.

272 "Mouth of Hell as Monster," *Exeter Book*, Oxford University Library.

273 York Book of Hours with Hellmouth (1440), Morgan Library and Museum.

274 For more on the Ten Kings of Hell in Asia, see Yoshitoshi Tsukioka, *Hell in Japanese Art* (Tokyo: International Bi-lingual Editions, 2017).

275 *A Chinese Traveler in Medieval Korea*, ed. Sem Vermeersch (Honolulu: University of Hawaii Press, 2016).

276 Tsulioka, 17–21.

277 "Samsura," *The Concise Oxford Dictionary of World Religion*, ed. John Bowker.

278 For more information, see Jerome Taylor, "Chapmans Rebuilt Emin's Tent," *The Independent*, July 19, 2020.

279 J. S. Bach, "Toccata and Fugue in D minor," ca. 1708. The piece opens with a toccata section followed by a fugue.

280 For example, see *Dr Jekyll and Mr. Hyde*, 1931; *The Black Cat*, 1934; *Fantasia*, 1940; and *Phantom of the Opera*, 1962.

281 Hector Berlioz, "Dream of a Witches Sabbath," Paris Conservatory, 1830.

282 Franz Liszt, "Dante Symphony," Dresden, November 15, 1857.

283 Modest Mussorgsky, "A Night on Bear Mountain," June 23, 1857.

284 Wendy Heller, *Music in the Baroque Period* (Princeton, 2013).

285 Ibid., 11–13.

286 For more on the Egyptian god Kherty, see J. Hill, "Kherty," 2010, https://ancientegyptonline.co.uk/kherty/.

287 For more on the *Gathas*, see *The Gathas: The Sublime Book of Zarathustra* (New York: Create Space, 2007).

288 Ibid., 93.

289 Ibid.

290 Ibid., 94–95.

291 Einar Thomassen, "Islamic Hell," *Numen* 56, nos.1 and 2 (2009): 401–416.

292 Ibid., 404–405.

293 Ibid., 406–407.

294 Al-Thalabi, *Tafsir* 1:111–113.

295 Thomas Patrick Hughes, "Defining Muslims on the Afghan Frontier," *The Dictionary of Islam*, ed. Alan Guenther (Talor and Francis, 2017).

296 Ibid., 23.

297 Ibid., 24–25.

298 R. H. Charles, ed. and trans., *The First Book of Enoch* (New York: Independently Published, 2022).

299 Ibid., 131.

300 Ibid.

301 Dante Aleghieri, *The Inferno*, ed. John Ciardi (New York: Signet Classics, 2009).

302 Ibid., 7–116.

303 Ibid., 117–118.

304 Ibid.

305 Joe Rigney, "What C. S. Lewis Believed About Hell," *Crossways*, October 17, 2018.

306 John Milton, *Paradise Lost* (New York: Hackett Editions, 2005).

307 Arthur Rimbaud, *A Season in Hell* (Paris: Independently Published, 2016).

308 Jean-Paul Sartre, *No Exit* (New York: Samuel French, 1958).

309 C. S. Lewis, *The Great Divorce* (New York: Harpers, 2009).

310 Rachel Falconer, *Hell in Contemporary Literature* (Edinburgh: Edinburgh University Press, 2004).

311 Meyer Schapiro, *Romanesque Art* (George Braziller Inc., 1977), 19.

312 For more on the Harrowing of Hell, see J. S. Jackson, *The Harrowing of Hell* (New York: Independently Published, 2023); and the Book of Revelation 20:10 for the Biblical precedent for the Harrowing of Hell.

313 Schapiro, 23.

314 Anonymous, "The Harrowing of Hell," *Catholic Encyclopedia* 7.

315 D. G. Scragg, *Vercelli Homilies* (Oxford: Oxford University Press, 1992).

316 For more on Leviathan as Hell Mouth, see *Exeter Book's* depiction of Leviathan as a whale.

317 *The Hours of Catherine of Cleaves*, Morgan Library MS945, folio 107r.

318 Pieter Bruegel, *Dulles Griet*, 1563. Oil on panel, 115x161 cm. Mayer van der Bergh, Antwerp, Belgium.

319 The Apostles' Creed is officially known by the Roman Church as *Symbolum Apostolorum*. It most likely originated in Gaul in the fifth century. The Athanasian Creed was most likely penned by Saint Athanasius in the early sixth century.

320 Aelfric of Eynsham, *Homilies*, ed. and trans. Benjamin Thorpe

(London: Early English Text Society, 1998).

321 Both Thomas Aquinas and Dante employed this three-part compartment of hell, as we have indicated earlier in this study.

Index

D

E

H

I

J

K

L

M

N

Q

R

V

W

X

Y

Z

About the Author

Stephen J. Vicchio was born and raised in Baltimore, Maryland, in a working-class neighborhood. He was educated at the University of Maryland; Yale Divinity School; Hertford College, Oxford; and acquired a Ph.D. from St. Andrews University in Fife, Scotland. He has authored more than forty books, including essays, stories, plays, and books about the Bible, slavery, ethics, histories, and many other topics. His writing awards include the Frank Muir Prize for fiction, the A.D. Emmart Award for outstanding writing in the humanities, and the Thomas Grey Prize for Best Ph.D. Thesis in the British Universities for the year 1986.

www.ingramcontent.com/pod-product-compliance
Lightning Source LLC
LaVergne TN
LVHW050920080826
845145LV00001B/150

* 9 7 8 1 9 6 2 8 3 4 1 6 2 *